AUTHORITARIAN
RUSSIA

PITT SERIES IN RUSSIAN AND EAST EUROPEAN STUDIES
JONATHAN HARRIS, EDITOR

AUTHORITARIAN RUSSIA

ANALYZING POST-SOVIET REGIME CHANGES

VLADIMIR GEL'MAN

UNIVERSITY OF PITTSBURGH PRESS

Published by the University of Pittsburgh Press, Pittsburgh, Pa., 15260
Copyright © 2015, University of Pittsburgh Press
All rights reserved
Manufactured in the United States of America
Printed on acid-free paper
10 9 8 7 6 5 4 3 2 1

ISBN 10: 0-8229-6368-X
ISBN 13: 978-0-8229-6368-4

Cataloging-in-publication data is on file with the Library of Congress.

To Oxana and Eva

CONTENTS

ACKNOWLEDGMENTS

THIS BOOK HAS BEEN the result of numerous scholarly ventures over several years, and several institutions and many people have accompanied me in these ventures in various ways. First and foremost, I am indebted to my academic home, the European University at St. Petersburg, where I have been honored to teach and conduct research since 1996. The experience of an encouraging scholarly environment, support from the university leadership, and exchanges of ideas with colleagues in the Department of Political Science and Sociology and the Center for Modernization Studies have greatly enriched me and shaped my agenda to a major degree. I would like to thank, in particular, Grigorii Golosov, Boris Firsov, Oleg Kharkhordin, Boris Kolonitsky, Ella Paneyakh, Eduard Ponarin, Mikhail Sokolov, Anna Temkina, Dmitry Travin, Vadim Volkov, Andrei Zaostrovtsev, and Elena Zdravomyslova. A number of talented former students (some of whom went on to become scholars themselves) encouraged me to provide them with better examples of my own research—especially Elena Belokurova, Alexey Gilev, Kirill Kalinin, Egor Lazarev, Maria Nozhenko, Yevgeniya Popova, Andrey Scherbak, Anton Shirickov, Andrei Starodubtsev, Anna Tarasenko, and Margarita Zavadskaya (to name just a few).

I also owe a major debt to the Aleksanteri Institute at the University of Helsinki, where I have worked since 2012 as a Finland Distinguished Professor thanks to the support of the Academy of Finland. The Institute's director, Markku Kivinen, offered me a unique opportunity to be the servant of two masters and to work and live in two cities, St. Petersburg and Helsinki. My special thanks go to my Finland-based colleagues, especially Risto Alapuro, Sari Autio-Sarasmo, Jukka Gronow, Tuomas Forsberg, Markku Kangaspuro, Meri Kulmala, Jussi Lassila, Markku Lonkila, Arkady Moshes, Anna-Maria Salmi, Hanna Smith, and numerous others. We discussed various drafts of book chapters and some related pieces during many seminars and conferences, from Perm to Iowa City and from Uppsala to Vienna. Among many scholars with whom I found it useful to exchange ideas and share thoughts, I would like to thank Harley Balzer, Mark Beissinger, Irina Busygina, Samuel Greene, Henry Hale, Stephen Hanson, Stefan Hedlund, Tomila Lankina, Maria Lipman, Maria Matskevich, Marie Mendras, Petr Panov, Nikolay Petrov, William Reisinger, Thomas Remington, Kirill Rogov, Richard Rose, Cameron Ross, Peter Rutland, Richard Sakwa, Gulnaz Sharafutdinova, Regina Smyth, Konstantin Sonin, Daniel Treisman, Lucan Way, William Zimmerman, and Natalia Zubarevich. To this list can be added Alena Ledeneva, Mary McAuley, and Sergei Ryzhenkov, who supported me at various stages of the long research journey, both as scholars and as close friends; I greatly appreciate their professional and personal understanding and inspiration.

This book would never have appeared without support from several organizations. It represents part of the collective research program of the Center of Excellence "Choices of Russian Modernization," funded by the Academy of Finland. The Program on New Approaches to Research and Security in Eurasia (PONARS Eurasia) has served as a major forum for discussing many ideas contained in this book. I would like to thank the University of Pittsburgh Press and especially Jonathan Harris, who initially endorsed the book proposal, and Peter Kracht, who put it forward and turned it into a real project. Two anonymous reviewers provided a number of useful comments on the draft of the book manuscript. Finally, the friendly, detailed, and nuanced linguistic assistance provided by Alexei Stephenson, Frances Weightman, and Maria Roti was essential for making the manuscript readable.

The earlier versions of some parts of this book previously appeared in the form of articles: elements of chapter 4 are based upon "Party Politics in Russia: From Competition to Hierarchy" (*Europe-Asia Studies*, 60, no. 6 [2008] © Taylor & Francis); chapter 5 is based upon "Cracks in the Wall: Challenges to Electoral Authoritarianism in Russia" (*Problems of Post-Communism*, 60, no. 2 [2013] © M. E. Sharpe); and elements of chapter 6 are based upon "Regime Changes in Russia: Trajectories of Political Evolution," (*Russia 2025: Scenarios for the Russian Future*, eds. Maria Lipman and Nikolay Petrov [Palgrave Macmillan, 2013]). Needless to say, none of the above persons and organizations is responsible for any errors. All arguments in the book solely reflect my own viewpoints, which may not coincide with their opinions.

Last but not least, all roads lead to home. My family is the main and outstanding source of support in everything I do in my professional life. I could never have completed this work without love, patience, and encouragement from Oxana and Eva, to whom I dedicate this book.

PREFACE

IT WAS A VERY lovely and sunny day in the summer of 1990 when I sat at the reception hall in the Mariinsky Palace in (then) Leningrad. I was a twenty-four-year-old activist for the anti-Communist prodemocratic movement, which had gained a majority of seats during the recent city council elections. After this victory, I had received two rather different job offers from two groups of my acquaintances. One was from a team of sociologists, who conducted research on political and social changes in the city and in the country as a whole. They invited me to join their ranks and argued that my insider knowledge of emerging social movements would be a great advantage in launching a professional career in the study of politics. The other group included newly elected deputies, who were busy arranging a new system of city government; they believed that my experience of electoral campaigns and my reputation as an activist would be a key asset for improving a rather chaotic decision-making process. I had to choose between a junior research fellowship at the Institute of Sociology of the Academy of Sciences, and a somewhat mid-range position in the newly formed apparatus of the city council. The latter option initially sounded tempting, and I came for a job interview with the chair of the city council, Anatoly Sobchak. A professor of law who had been elected to the Soviet parliament during the first semicompetitive elections in 1989, he had gained great popularity as a vocal and outspoken critic of the Soviet system; the following year, Leningrad deputies invited Sobchak to serve as chair of the city council upon winning a seat in the by-elections. As usual, he took a long time to arrive, and while waiting for him, I chatted with a receptionist named Dima, a smiling, talkative guy the same age as myself.

Finally, Sobchak arrived, and we went to his extraordinarily large office, with its excellent view of St. Isaac's Cathedral. Without asking me anything or even taking my presence into account, my potential boss began a long and passionate speech, as if he were giving a talk before hundreds of people, even though nobody else was in the room (I think he used this opportunity as a testing ground for one of his public appearances, which were bringing him countrywide fame at that time). Sobchak's speech was full of bright rhetoric but rather vague in substance—he blamed the previous system, complained about current turbulence, and promised that the city would flourish under his leadership. After a seemingly endless speech, he paused, and I was able to ask a question I considered essential for my future job: "Anatoly Aleksandrovich, how do you perceive the system of city government that you plan to build?"

Sobchak turned toward me at last, shifted his attention down to earth, and changed his tone to a more sincere and frank register. "Well . . . there are the city council deputies, who are numerous, noisy, and disorganized; they have to respond to the complaints of ordinary citizens and mostly work in their local constituencies instead of having long discussions. Then there is the city executive committee; it should deal with matters of everyday routine, such as bumpy roads and leaking pipes, but not go beyond such duties. And I myself [a broad glance around the office], with the aid of my apparatus [a close look at me], will conduct politics in the city." I was shocked to hear these rather cynical words from a person who had a public image as a democratic icon. "But this sounds almost the same as what we had before, under the Communists . . . and what about democracy?" Sobchak was probably surprised that someone who was supposed to become a member of his emerging team had posed such a naïve question. He responded firmly, as certain university professors often do when they pretend to tell the truth to freshmen: "You know, we are in power now—that is democracy" (literally, in Russian: "*my teper' u vlasti, eto i est' demokratiya*"). This was somewhat astonishing—my great expectations of democratic politics were ruined, and I was unable to turn myself into a minor cog in the newly emerging political machine. I turned my back on Sobchak and left his office, not even saying goodbye. Then I walked directly to the Institute of Sociology, and joined the world of scholarship, not the world of politics.

It was the turning point of my entire professional career. Unfortunately, I had no opportunity to receive a formal education in social and political sciences—but despite (or perhaps thanks to) this fact, I later became a professor of political science in two universities and in two countries. And the lessons I learned from Sobchak in his office many years ago were worth dozens of textbooks on normative political theory to me. I realized that the ultimate goal of politicians is the maximization of power—in other words, they aspire to stay in power by any means for as long as possible and to acquire as much power as possible, regardless of their democratic rhetoric and public image; this is the essence of politics. The point is that some politicians are able to achieve this goal, but others are not so successful. In the former category, we observe dictatorships of various types—ranging from Mobutu in Zaire to

Lukashenko in Belarus—while in the latter we may observe varieties of other political regimes (not necessarily democratic ones).

In fact, Sobchak also failed to achieve this goal and did not maximize his power in Leningrad and (after 1991) St. Petersburg. Six years later, in 1996, as a city mayor, he faced tough electoral competition from his deputy, Vladimir Yakovlev, and lost by a tiny margin. His other deputy, namely Vladimir Putin, learned certain lessons from Sobchak in his career as a politician—but these lessons were very different from those I'd learned, because of the difference between politics and political science. Putin, at least for the time being, was able to maximize his power as president and prime minister of Russia, although more recently he has been facing increasing challenges. And Dima, whom I had met on that memorable day, also learned some lessons: Dmitry Medvedev, too, has served as president and prime minister of Russia. He is still a very nice, frequently smiling, and talkative guy—but in a sense, he is still a receptionist.

This is a book about how and why Russia failed to become a democracy after the collapse of Communism, and about the causes and consequences of its trajectory of regime changes toward authoritarianism after 1991. It systematically examines various factors that have affected these changes and contributed to the country's authoritarian drift from a theoretical and comparative perspective. In this book, I focus on the role of agency and the interests and strategies of political actors in the process of authoritarian regime building, as well as the challenges and constraints they faced in Russia and beyond, and discuss possible trajectories of further regime changes in Russia against the background of global political trends. My argument is based upon the assumption that some countries are forced to establish democratic "rules of the game," either as a means of resolving major political and/or social conflicts, or because of international influence, or due to certain ideological motivations and preferences on the part of political leaders and the elite. However, post-Soviet Russia demonstrated none of these conditions. All political conflicts were resolved as zero-sum games; international influence had (and continues to have) a rather limited impact on domestic agendas; and whatever political ideas there were became subordinated to the interests of political actors. Due to this combination of circumstances, Russia's political actors were not presented with unavoidable constraints, and aimed to achieve their goals by establishing and enforcing the most favorable rules of the game for themselves, maintaining informal "winning coalitions" of cliques around rulers. In the 1990s, these tactics were only partially successful, given the weakness of the Russian state, a troubled economic transformation, the heterogeneity of segments of the ruling elite, and controversies surrounding the institution-building process. In the 2000s, Vladimir Putin corrected these errors and mistakes; thanks to economic growth and the revival of state capacity, he was able to successfully pursue the reshuffling of winning coalitions, and to impose conscious and consistent institutional changes. The Russian political regime seemingly achieved a stage of authoritarian consolidation on the basis of an inefficient low-level equilibrium, which could not be easily broken without significant losses for the country's elite and some segments of society. When, in the 2010s, given Russian society's rising dissatisfaction with the political regime and the system of governance, the preservation of the status quo regime became a daunting task for Russia's rulers. They responded to these new challenges with an aggressive anti-Western foreign policy as well as "tightening of the screws" on the domestic front, but faced increasing economic troubles. Despite these strategic moves by the Kremlin, the risk of further political disequilibrium is likely to increase over time, although this does not necessarily mean Russia's successful democratization in the foreseeable or more distant future.

This book bears the title *Authoritarian Russia*, which reflects the current state of the country's political regime. However, I by no means believe that this authoritarianism will dominate Russia forever and that the country is doomed to be a captive, unable to go beyond a vicious circle. The goal of the book is to explain the logic of regime changes in post-Soviet Russia. It demonstrates that the authoritarian regime emerged as a byproduct of the efforts of political actors who sought power maximization, distorted political competition, designed a biased set of institutions, and secured their rule using fear and lies as their major instruments. But this logic has also meant that the authoritarian regime in Russia can be dismantled if and when Russia's rulers are unable to maintain their dominance and Russia's citizens are able to resist their rule strongly enough. The path to freedom will not be easy, but I believe that one day a book titled *Democratizing Russia* will be welcomed by readers— although, for example, in Brazil's case the time lag between the appearances of two books with analogous titles spanned sixteen years.[1] Indeed, many previously authoritarian regimes across the globe have transformed into democracies, and I see no grounds to think that Russia should be an exception.

AUTHORITARIAN RUSSIA

CHAPTER 1

REGIME CHANGES IN RUSSIA

THE ROAD OF DISILLUSIONMENT

AUGUST 22, 1991, WAS a genuine holiday, when crowds of happy people occupied central squares in Moscow, Leningrad, and some other major Russian cities. Sometimes even those who were barely acquainted or had never met wholeheartedly congratulated each other. They celebrated the ultimate failure of the coup organized by certain conservative Communist leaders of the Soviet government and the victory of the new political actors led by the popularly elected president Boris Yeltsin and the Russian parliament, who had defended the ideals of freedom and democracy. At the time, this event was merely perceived as a successful completion of the democratization process launched in 1985 by Mikhail Gorbachev. Yet coup organizers were imprisoned, the authoritarian regime was broken down, the ruling Communist Party, which had monopolized political power over seven decades, was eliminated, many key figures of the past disappeared from the political scene—in other words, the previous political order completely faded away, seemingly paving the way toward political freedom.[1] Indeed, Francis Fukuyama's highly popular argument about "the end of history" and the coming worldwide triumph of democracy[2] could be vividly illustrated by the numerous images of festivities in Moscow streets.

However, more than two decades later, during the winter of 2011–2012, some of the passionate supporters of political freedoms who had sincerely celebrated the end of Communism in August 1991, as well as their children or even grandchildren, have been forced to attend new rallies in Moscow over and over again, bearing the banners of fair elections and raising their voices against arbitrary authoritarian rule by the Russian authorities. During these two decades, Russia not only failed to approach democratic standards, but moved away from the ideals that had seemed so attractive and had almost been achieved in August 1991. Without looking into a crystal ball, only a few

★

witnesses of the Communist collapse could predict this shift of trajectory in Russia's political development. After a series of rapid and turbulent changes in the 1990s, and some element of shallow stabilization in the 2000s, Russian politics in the early 2010s was far from both a Soviet-type political order and from democratic political solutions. Not only did the economic system completely change over two decades, and state and nation building diverge from that of the Soviet empire, but even the available freedoms exhibited a distinctive pattern: Russian citizens enjoyed a wide array of individual freedoms against the background of a somewhat limited (and, of late, shrinking) set of civic freedoms, while the degree of political freedoms was reduced to almost nothing (although they did not disappear completely, remaining merely on paper). The list of troubling features of Russian politics in the 2010s included unfair and fraudulent elections, the coexistence of weak and impotent political parties with a dominant "party of power" (which was also weak and impotent), heavily censored (and often self-censored) media, rubber-stamping legislatures at the national and subnational levels, politically subordinated and shamelessly biased courts, arbitrary use of state economic powers, and widespread corruption. These assessments resonate with numerous critical evaluations of Russia's politics and governance by domestic and international agencies and experts:[3] despite the huge variety of their analytical frameworks and the use of diverse methodologies, techniques, and approaches, almost everybody agrees that the political regime in present-day Russia is genuinely nondemocratic (although for various reasons some observers, until very recently, hesitated to label it "authoritarian"). Similar statements are even more loudly expressed in both the international and Russian media, as well as in public discussions in Russia, which became more active, open, and heated during the wave of mass protests in 2011–2012 but then grew quieter during the Russian annexation of Crimea and the rising confrontation with the West over Ukraine in 2014.

A simple comparison between public expectations in Moscow's streets in August 1991 and Russia's political development over the following two decades (which was far from meeting these expectations, to put it mildly) provides grounds for discussing several critical issues. The great expectations of the recent Russian past have changed to bitter disillusionment and doubts about its political present, as well as major fears and concerns about its political future. Nevertheless, one must go beyond this disillusionment and these considerations, and posit key items for the research agenda: what is the logic underlying Russia's political regime's dynamics? What went wrong with the great expectations of August 1991? Why and how have more than two decades of post-Soviet political transformations moved Russia further and further away from democracy? What are the causes of its political trajectory, and how has this country, which was able to put an end to its authoritarian Communist regime, turned to a great "flight from freedom"? What we can expect from the current trends of Russia's political evolution and what are the chances of the country overcoming authoritarianism and moving toward democracy and political freedoms—or, alternatively, is this developmental path closed to Russia for many years or even decades, if not forever?

I suspect that answering these questions is important not only for political observers of Russia, nor even only for Russia's citizens and politicians, who have to respond to numerous challenges in a rather gloomy but ever-changing political and social environment. It is also important for understanding patterns of political dynamics in various states and nations from theoretical and comparative perspectives. From this viewpoint, Russia's post-Soviet experience of transformation from a nondemocratic Communist regime to another form of authoritarianism, in a sense moving from the frying pan into the fire, is worth considering as a "crucial case"[4] of regime change, and its analysis might shed light on causes of the rise of a new nondemocracy despite the fall of Soviet authoritarianism. Yet as often happens in social and political science, these questions have no unidimensional and simple "correct" answer: the study of global politics presupposes the existence of different competing explanations for the same political phenomena, and I do not claim that my approach to these issues is the only possible way of explaining Russia's political regime changes after the Soviet Union. What is presented in this book is based upon a vision of politics (I call it "realist") that is less oriented around normative ideals and mostly related to positive analysis. I believe that for an understanding of the world of politics—in Russia and elsewhere—it is important to discuss less how things should (or even should not) go on, and more how they really are. This is the essence of the framework of analysis offered here. In this chapter, after highlighting major definitions, I outline key relevant arguments, and provide an overview of the book.

SETTING THE SCENE: CRITICAL JUNCTURES AND REGIME TRAJECTORIES

Before discussing the book's major topic—namely, regime changes in Russia—I have to set the scene: outline key terms, elaborate meanings, and clarify frameworks. Otherwise, the author is often at risk of facing misunderstandings from readers; the bitter statement that "two political scientists have three different opinions" is not always far from the truth.[5] Instead of offering new concepts, I try to adjust existing ones to serve as working definitions, more or less fine-tuned for purposes of this book (though other scholars might apply them in somewhat different settings and come to very different conclusions). This exercise will save time and effort and make clear what I mean.

First and foremost, my understanding of politics as a struggle between various agents to gain, wield, and retain power is probably universal—it can be equally applied to a given country or a university department. However, Robert Dahl's well-known concept of power (based upon his definition that "A has power over B to the extent that A can get B to do something that B would not otherwise do")[6] is important in this context: not only is power a complex set of relationships based upon various means of authority (which, in turn, correspond to certain models of legitimacy), but there is also a limited set of those who participate in the struggle to take and hold power, both actual and would-be political actors. Usually, these actors represent different segments of the elite, or those who, according to John Higley and Michael Burton, "are able to affect political outcomes regularly and substantially."[7] Whether members of the ruling groups or of the opposition (the counterelite), in this power game they use various resources and strategies, similarly to chess or tennis players. Actors can be both individuals and groups or organizations (e.g., political parties, companies, and even foreign governments), but they are the major (and sometimes even the only) participants in this power struggle, while the rest of society (i.e., the masses) are involved in this process on an occasional basis at best, when they are involved at all.

However, the essence of politics, the power struggle of political actors, relatively rarely looks like an endless bloody and deadly fight, or what Thomas Hobbes during the seventeenth-century English revolution famously labeled "the war of all against all" (*bellum omnium contra omnes*).[8] More often, similarly to competitive games, the conditions and (sometimes) outcomes of this struggle depend upon a set of formal and informal "rules of the game," namely political institutions.[9] In fact, formal rules (e.g., constitutions and laws) might be very different from informal institutional arrangements, and sometimes even less important than the latter, as in the Soviet Union, which claimed its system of government to be a parliamentary republic in the 1977 Constitution, whereas in reality the Politburo, the highest body of the Communist Party, was in charge of adopting major decisions. Nevertheless, the basic meaning of institutions (both formal and informal) is straightforward: they determine the major rules of the game and the sanctions for their violation.[10]

From this perspective, the very notion of "political regime" is worth reconsidering, given the dozens of definitions of political regimes. Different authors use them in various contexts—from the form of governance (e.g., presidential or parliamentary regimes)[11] to the particular type of politics (e.g., totalitarian or authoritarian regimes).[12] In this book, the term "political regime" is understood as the regular and substantive arrangement of actors and institutions in a given polity. Drawing parallels with competitive games, if we need to explain to someone a distinction between, say, chess and tennis, we have to make at least two major distinctions: between those who play the games and use their resources and strategies (actors), and the sets of rules of these games (institutions).[13] However, victory (or maximizing power) is the ultimate goal of players in all competitive games as well as of actors in all political regimes. Of course, some political regimes (just like games) change their sets of actors and rules over time. But the logic of these changes is rather different—they might be evolutionary, slowly and gradually evolving over decades or even centuries, or revolutionary, implying sudden and radical breaks over not only years or months, but even days.[14] Imagine a routine chess game, which consists of moving pieces on the chessboard; applying blows to the opponent's head with the chessboard instead would constitute a major change of the game's regime. A consolidated political regime is in equilibrium,[15] and the process of regime changes, which is based upon changes of the sets of actors, or of institutions, or (often) both, is disequilibrium by definition. In other words, the process of political regime changes is similar to a movement from one type of equilibrium to another.

Since Aristotle, typologies of political regimes have been numerous. For the purposes of this book, however, I will use the most simple (if not the most primitive) one, and divide political regimes into two categories—democracies and nondemocracies.[16] A democratic regime is defined here along the lines proposed by Joseph Schumpeter: "the democratic method is that institutional arrangement for arriving at political decisions in which individuals acquire the power to decide by means of a competitive struggle for the people's vote."[17] This definition of democracy, regarded as "minimalist," or "electoral," is sometimes criticized as a wild oversimplification of the real world. Indeed, most contemporary democracies include numerous essential elements, ranging from the rule of law to observation of rights of minorities. But despite intensive discussions on whether the minimalist approach is able to capture the essence of democracy,[18] one should take into account the red line of major distinction between democracies and nondemocracies: even if free and fair electoral competition might be perceived as an insufficient condition for democracy, no one denies that it is a necessary condition: there is no modern democracy without electoral contestation. This basic requirement is summarized in Przeworski's notion: "democracy is a system in which parties lose elections . . . there are periodic winners and losers."[19] These "periodic" shifts between winners and losers might take a long time (in Japan, the ruling party, the LDP, remained in power for thirty-eight years despite competitive elections). One might even argue that electoral competition serves as the cornerstone for maintaining political and civil freedoms as well as political accountability of rulers, not vice versa.[20]

Most of the modern political regimes that do not fit the criteria for electoral democracy in one way or another will be regarded in this book as nondemocratic or authoritarian (I use these two labels interchangeably). Although scholars sometimes refer to the term "dictatorship" as a logical opposition to "democracy,"[21] I will try to avoid its use in this respect. In everyday life, "dictatorship" is often associated with repressions and government-induced violence, but in fact many rulers in nondemocracies rely upon carrots rather than sticks as major tools of their dominance and control over fellow citizens, and post-Soviet Russia is one such case. As to the rules of the game, the world of nondemocracies is much more diverse than the world of democracies: to paraphrase Tolstoy's *Anna Karenina*, "democracies are all alike; every nondemocracy is undemocratic in its own way." Among authoritarian regimes, one might find traditional monarchies (such as Saudi Arabia), military dictatorships (such as Latin America in the 1960–1980s), and one-party regimes (such as the Soviet Union and present-day China).[22] However, there is a minimal common denominator: if democracies are based upon electoral competition, nondemocratic regimes tend to avoid or at least restrain it, although political competition might flourish in authoritarian regimes in nonelectoral forms (ranging from hidden struggles among ruling cliques to brutal and violent coups).

The maintenance of equilibrium in authoritarian regimes is an even more difficult task than in democratic ones. Authoritarian rulers have to avoid two kinds of threat simultaneously. One is the threat of disobedience by their fellow citizens, and the other is the threat of disobedience by members of the elite. In reality, both threats are critical, but their avoidance requires different skills. Dealing with citizens requires careful and well-judged use of the combination of carrot and stick vis-à-vis society at large and/or its major groups and segments. But dealing with the elite also requires building and maintaining their loyalty: it should be successfully coopted into informal "winning coalitions" among dominant actors (i.e., the core leaders of the ruling groups, or sometimes the autocrat alone) and at least some of the subordinated actors.[23] A balanced use of carrot and stick is essential for these actors too, and this task is daunting for many authoritarian rulers, who have to survive under both of these threats. No wonder that in many nondemocracies the distinction between "regimes" and "ruling groups" is unclear both factually and analytically, and this is why I shall sometimes treat these terms as interchangeable.

Furthermore, the instruments of achieving legitimacy in nondemocracies are quite diverse, and this is why the role of elections in these regimes is varied, from complete lack thereof to genuine participation by various parties and candidates. If one were to place post-Communist Russia onto the world map of authoritarian political regimes, it would fit into the global category of "electoral" or "competitive" authoritarianism (further in this book, I will use these labels interchangeably).[24] These regimes, although authoritarian, incorporate elections that are meaningful; they stand in contrast to various "classical" or "hegemonic" versions of authoritarianism, which are best known for their "elections without choice"[25] (among post-Soviet countries, Turkmenistan fits this regime type most vividly).[26] However, in electoral (or competitive) authoritarianism, and in contrast to electoral democracies, elections are marked by an uneven playing field, based on: formal and informal rules that construct prohibitively high barriers to participation; sharply unequal access of competitors to financial and media resources; abuses of power by the state apparatus for the sake of maximizing incumbent votes irrespective of voter preferences; and (often but not always) multiple instances of electoral fraud. The uneven playing field serves as a defining distinction between electoral authoritarianism and electoral democracy.[27] Although electoral authoritarian regimes existed in various countries for many years (Mexico under the PRI [Partido Revolucionario Institucional] might serve as a prime example),[28] it became a widespread, even ubiquitous phenomenon after the Cold War in many regions of the globe including the post-Soviet area, with Russia certainly no exception in this respect.[29]

The recent proliferation of electoral authoritarian regimes and their replacement of "classical" versions of authoritarianism result from the effects of two different, although not mutually exclusive forces. First, the regular holding of elections under tightly controlled and limited competition allows rulers of authoritarian regimes to effectively monitor their country's elite, the state apparatus, and the citizenry, thus averting the risk of the regime's sudden collapse due to domestic political conflicts.[30] Second, authoritarian rulers across the globe often hold elections due to their need of means to legitimize the status quo regimes in the eyes of both domestic and international actors.[31] However, the practices of authoritarian elections are risky: although many nondemocratic regimes resolve these tasks more or less successfully, elections in and of themselves, as well as protests following unfair elections, can often become challenges to a regime's survival, as the experience of the Arab Spring and of the color revolutions in some post-Communist states demonstrates. The variety of these outcomes raises an important question: why is it that in some countries, electoral authoritarian regimes persist for decades (as in Mexico under the PRI or in Egypt until the Arab Spring), while in other cases this proves either to be a temporary developmental stage in the wake of democratization (e.g., Serbia),[32] or to result in the replacement of one electoral authoritarian regime with another (as in Ukraine before the Orange Revolution and under the rule of Viktor Yanukovych)?[33] An analysis of regime changes in post-Soviet Russia may shed light on the sources of strength and/or weakness of electoral authoritarian regimes.

Finally, the term "regime changes" also requires some clarification. In recent decades, the study of democratization—the process of transition from nondemocratic regimes to democracies—has become very popular among scholars.[34] In a broader perspective, democratization is the major (although not the only) element of political modernization, which assumes that various countries in the world pursue the transfer, adoption, copying, or invention of Western-type political institutions.[35] However, this process is far from universal and straightforward: sometimes, the slogans of democratization in different parts of the world serve as smokescreens for the shift from one format of authoritarian regimes to other formats of nondemocracy: this applies to post-Soviet Russia as well.

Discussions on regime change began to shift from structure to agency in the 1980s, against the background of collapse of authoritarian regimes, and this fact greatly contributed to a "prodemocratic bias" in this research field.[36] Many scholars preferred to concentrate mostly on "success stories" of democratization and paid less attention to other varieties of postauthoritarian transformation, to the risks of the process of regime change that lead to nondemocratic outcomes. It is not surprising that in the 1990s, after the sudden collapse of many Communist regimes and the successful democratization of East European countries, actor-centered analyses of regime change to some extent resembled the paradigm of a Hollywood film. According to that paradigm, the "good guys" (prodemocratic actors) are confronted by the "bad guys" (antidemocratic actors) and the film invariably has a happy ending (the victory of the "good guys").[37] Later on, when the failure of democratization in post-Soviet countries in the 2000s became apparent, this Manichean vision of regime change shifted to another movie-based paradigm, one known as *film noir*. According to this vision, post-Soviet politics is dominated only by "bad guys," who represent the world of evil and tend to resist democracy for various reasons (mostly related to their personal preferences).[38] Thus, the "bad guys," who are often able to seize and/or usurp power, are responsible for their countries' descent into the hell of authoritarianism. But politicians in the real world are somewhat far from these movie characters, and this is why neither the paradigm of Hollywood film nor of *film noir* is always useful for explaining the process of regime change.

My understanding of the logic of political changes (including those of political regimes) is rather different from that of movies. To put it bluntly, it is useless to blame Yeltsin or Putin for being "bad guys" and ruining Russia's democratic hopes. In fact, their personalities are not much worse than those of many democratic politicians in various countries. But democracy does not emerge simply as a result of the good intentions of "good guys," as many people tend to believe. Rather, most politicians across the globe (including Yeltsin and Putin) are rational power maximizers and these labels are inappropriate. They are neither good nor bad guys—as we might say about most ordinary people. They simply pursue their own self-interest, which under certain conditions might be aligned with democracy or oppose it, depending upon their own perceptions, resources, and strategies in the struggle for power vis-à-vis other actors (who have similar intentions).[39] Undoubtedly, institutions play a major role in choosing a prodemocratic or antidemocratic side in making political choices in the process of regime change. Moreover, the same politicians can serve both prodemocratic and antidemocratic goals at different moments in this process, given the high level of uncertainty and the background of changes in the arrangement of actors and/or institutions.

In other words, during the process of regime change any major (or even minor) strategic choice made by political actors and by society at large can result in unintended consequences, and some of these might affect further directions of regime change—similarly to what often happens in chess or in arcade games. Which constitutional proposals should be chosen or rejected? To call or not to call for elections, and, if so, which electoral rules should be applied? Which candidates are worth voting for? Should one join protests against certain political and policy decisions by the authorities or abstain from these collective actions? These strategic choices, made at certain "critical junctures,"[40] can impose certain constraints on further trajectories of regime change in a path-dependent manner. And if once the choice leads to a dead end, then the return to a turning point becomes quite difficult, and the costs of this long and winding road can be prohibitively high. The analysis of the process of regime change in Russia offered in this book will focus on critical junctures, choices made at these turning points, and the trajectories and dead ends that resulted from them.

TOWARD POST-SOVIET AUTHORITARIANISM: THE ARGUMENT IN BRIEF

My explanation of the authoritarian trajectory of Russia's political regime after the Soviet collapse is based on the assumption that the country had no structural, cultural, or historical preconditions for becoming a nondemocracy in the late twentieth century. Even though the background, traditions, and recent experiences of Russia were not greatly conducive to democratization, they were less problematic than those of many successfully democratized states and nations. And even the complex nature of post-Communist transformations in Russia (which included not only regime change but also simultaneously market reforms and state and nation building)[41] was not much different from some other countries of Eastern Europe and the former Soviet Union. What was really different in Russia was that the struggle of political actors and their power maximization faced rather weak institutional and political constraints, and they were able to pursue their goals much more successfully than their counterparts in various parts of the globe.

Indeed, why is it that in 1993 Boris Yeltsin was able to fire on the opposition-dominated parliament with tanks, yet none of the presidents of the United States ever considered such a method of dealing with Congress during the periods of divided government? Why is it that in 2004 Vladimir Putin was able to eliminate more than three hundred hostages alongside the terrorists in the school in Beslan, North Ossetia, without serious criticism from Russia's political elite or the general population? The answer is very simple: both Yeltsin and Putin met negligible resistance to these actions, and their costs were much lower than the benefits they gained afterward. Unlike United States presidents, who would be at risk of impeachment or at least losing support among the elite and the masses if they proposed dissolving Congress, Russia's leaders were able either to ruin institutions (as happened with the Russian parliament in 1993) or rearrange them to serve their own interests[42] (as happened with the abolishment of popular elections of regional governors after the Beslan affair in 2004). In addition, the elite's resistance to the actions of dominant actors has been either damaged (as in the case of firing on the Russian parliament in 1993) or limited by efficient coopting (as in the case of the post-2004 gubernatorial appointments). And in both cases society at large remained largely indifferent and passive, playing virtually no role in these events. Thus, after firing on the parliament, Yeltsin was able to impose the constitution, which granted him a wide array of powers, and Putin was able to impose de facto presidential appointment of regional governors irrespective of popular vote, because neither other actors nor any institutions were able to prevent them from doing so. Given this lack of constraints, rational power maximizers were able to achieve their goals in "pure" forms without major concessions. Following the maxim of the historian Lord Acton ("power tends to corrupt, and absolute power corrupts absolutely"), one can assess the nondemocratic consequences of these choices—not only in terms of corruption as such, but also in terms of the trajectory of regime changes, which in both cases leaned further toward an authoritarian direction.

Contrary to these and other stories of unconstrained power maximization at critical junctures of regime change in Russia, almost all success stories of democratization result from the constraints imposed on would-be dominant actors (who are, in fact, rational power maximizers) by institutions, or by other actors, or sometimes even by themselves. I focus on four possible sources of these constraints: *the domestic elite conflict* as major competition for would-be dominant actors, *international influence, society at large,* and the *ideologies* of dominant actors. These sources in one way or another contribute to the limits of authoritarian drift of dominant actors during the process of regime change in various political and institutional settings. However, none of these sources played an important role in post-Communist Russia. All open political conflicts among the domestic elite (namely, the Communist coup of 1991, the presidential-parliamentary clash of 1993, and the "war of Yeltsin's succession" of 1999–2000) were resolved as zero-sum games, and the winners of these conflicts had no incentives to limit maximization of their powers. International influence on Russia in terms of both linkages and leverages (identified by Steven Levitsky and Lucan Way)[43] was and still is relatively insignificant. The role of society at large in Russian post-Communist politics has been secondary at best, at least until very recently. And, finally, irrespective of the contents of any specific ideas, ideology as such has probably been the least meaningful factor in Russian politics since the Soviet collapse.[44]

One might compare the process of regime change in Russia with inefficient market building in two major respects. First, the demand side of politics, or the political preferences of the general population, was more or less latent during the two post-Soviet decades, and the elite, who did not face any serious challenges from this angle, did not have their hands tied to any meaningful extent. Popular opposition to the status quo was limited to words rather than deeds.[45] Even in the 1990s, when mass surveys demonstrated low public support for the existing political regime and its leaders, any alternatives to the status quo (such as tough dictatorship, return to the Soviet political order, or full-fledged democratization) were either unattractive or unrealistic to the eyes of Russian citizens. This "resigned acceptance" of the status quo regime by the masses was a kind of suboptimal equilibrium.[46] In the 2000s, the rapid economic growth, which contributed to a rise in the well-being of many Russian citizens, as well as the disappearance of some alternatives to the status quo, played a major role in the increase of public support for the regime.[47] Yet in the early 2010s the rise of public demand for change, which occurred simultaneously with the generation shift (as the first post-Soviet generation became adolescent), resulted in the turbulent although rather shallow wave of mass protests in 2011–2012, the decrease of public support for the status quo regime, and the search for new alternatives.[48] More recent developments, after Russia's annexation of Crimea and the beginning of the major ultimate conflict with the West over Ukraine in 2014, reversed this tide of public mood and suppressed dissent at least for a while. However, the demand for change might become the decisive factor in Russian politics in coming years, thus affecting the further trajectory of regime change.

On the political supply side, the building of monopolies by Russia's rulers became the essence of regime change.[49] When the dominant political actors in Russia faced weak constraints to power maximization, they opted to guide further regime changes along the road of disillusionment toward the rise of authoritarianism. At the same time, they could not completely abandon certain democratic institutions (first and foremost, elections) not only because of the legacy of late-Soviet democratization (when these institutions emerged) but also because of the need for legitimation of their powers. Instead, they attempted to adjust these institutions to their own interests and purposes—very much in spite of Sobchak's above-mentioned understating of democracy. Boris Yeltsin was highly imperfect at carrying out this adjustment in the 1990s, against the background of the deep and protracted transformation recession of the Russian economy, the weak coercive capacity of the Russian state, the heterogeneity of informal winning coalitions, and inconsistent and controversial institution-building efforts. But his successor, Vladimir Putin, corrected a number of Yeltsin's errors in the 2000s, when impressive economic growth and the restoration of state capacity allowed him to implement successful reshuffling and strengthening of the winning coalition, and conduct major institutional changes. He effectively used elections, political parties, and the parliament as instruments of his dominance. By the end of Putin's second term in office, the political regime, which he built so carefully, consistently, coherently, and consciously, seemed to achieve a state of equilibrium. After the preservation of the status quo authoritarian regime became the major strategic goal of the ruling groups, some observers expected no further disequilibrium, and considered Putin to likely deserve as much as an A+ grade in the global college for dictators. But electoral authoritarian regimes are often vulnerable to disequilibrium from within, and this is what happened in Russia during the wave of protests in 2011–2012, when the monopolist political supply met the rise of demand for political changes. Such regimes are even more vulnerable to disequilibrium from the top, and this is what might be the case for Russia after 2014, when the leadership of the country launched a major confrontation with the West, "tightened the screws" in domestic politics, targeting public dissent and brainwashing their fellow citizens by using lies and exploiting fears, and conducted an increasingly irresponsible economic policy. This controversy drives the current political agenda in Russia and will probably define the possibilities and conditions of the further trajectories of regime change.

AN ANALYSIS OF CRITICAL JUNCTURES

To summarize, over two decades of regime changes in post-Soviet Russia, when at certain critical junctures Russia's political actors faced the choice between moving in an authoritarian or a democratic direction, they opted for the former option almost every time. Democracy was not eliminated completely from their political agenda but served as a smokescreen for the project of authoritarian regime building: rather, democratic elements were deliberately and successfully utilized for antidemocratic purposes. As a result, almost every further step in the process of regime changes in Russia since 1991 became a movement away from democracy, if not a total "flight from freedom." The logical chain of these steps became a path-dependent consequence of the previous choices made by political actors, and this regime's evolutionary trajectory over time turned into a road of disillusionment in a more straightforward and consistent way. Among these critical junctures, I focus on the following:

> **1991**—the rejection of adoption of the new Constitution of Russia and of new "founding" elections; partial preservation of previous institutional arrangements in Russian politics, inherited from the Soviet period;
>
> **1993**—a sharp conflict between the Russian president Boris Yeltsin and the Russian parliament, which resulted in violent dissolution of the parliament; the zero-sum game of the resolution of this conflict contributed to the adoption of the new Russian constitution, which granted broad unchecked powers to the president of the country and accumulated a significant authoritarian potential;
>
> **1996**—the crucial Russian presidential elections; the incumbent Boris Yeltsin was reelected after an unfair campaign accompanied by a number of abuses; however, Yeltsin refused to implement initial plans to cancel the elections, which included the dissolution of parliament and banning some opposition parties;
>
> **1999–2000**—the struggle of various segments of the Russian elite for political leadership on the eve of presidential turnover; Yeltsin's chosen successor, Vladimir Putin, defeated his rivals in this struggle, won the elections to become the new president of Russia, and was finally able to maximize his own power by compelling the loyalty of all significant

political, economic, and societal actors (the mechanism of "imposed consensus");

2003–2005—the elimination of real and even hypothetical obstacles to monopolist dominance of the ruling group; major institutional changes, aimed at securing this political monopoly (the abolishment of elections of regional governors, changes in laws on political parties and elections, and the like);

2007–2008—due to the expiration of the two terms of his presidential powers, Putin picked a loyal successor, Dmitry Medvedev, to take the presidential post in the absence of serious political competition, while Putin held the post of prime minister; Medvedev then implemented constitutional amendments on extension of the terms of both the president and the parliament of Russia;

2011–2012—Putin initiated a "second substitution," a job swap between himself and Medvedev, and returned to the presidency after a cycle of unfair parliamentary and presidential elections; accusations of large-scale electoral fraud provoked a wave of protests in Moscow and other Russian cities; these protests contributed to the rebirth of the prodemocratic political opposition in Russia and to the rise of mass demands for political changes;

2014—against the background of the ousting of Ukrainian president Viktor Yanukovych, Russia annexed Crimea and initiated a bloody conflict in the southeast regions of Ukraine, claiming that it was fundamentally opposing the rise of Western influence in post-Soviet Eurasia, if not the West as the eternal and existential enemy of Russia. These major events fueled the Kremlin's attacks on the domestic front in terms of further perversion and demolition of democratic institutions, and imposition of more strict constraints on real or imagined public discontent, as well as increasingly arbitrary decisions in policy making and militarization of the country. The consequences of this shift are (and will continue to be) unquestionably devastating for the country, but the process of deterioration is far from complete as of yet.

Why and how were these political choices made, and what are their causes and consequences? What kind of steps can be made at the next critical junctures of Russian politics and might they affect further changes in the regime's trajectory? And, finally, to what extent will the road of disillusionment lead Russia to a dead end? Or will some alternative path of regime change toward democratization be chosen instead? These issues will be discussed in more detail in the following chapters of this book.

In my analysis of post-Communist regime changes in Russia vis-à-vis recent theoretical and comparative discussions in the field, I outline three major scholarly trends in chapter 2: "pessimists," who perceive Russian political developments through the lens of path-dependency because of its history and culture, in the manner of genetically inherited illnesses; "optimists," who consider Russia's authoritarian tendencies as a partial and temporary deviation from its pathway of political modernization, similar to growing pains; and "realists," who focus on regime changes as byproducts of power struggles, and tend to analyze authoritarian regime building as a result of political "poisoning" caused by special interests. My position is on the side of the "realists," based on a synthesis of rational choice and historical institutionalist theoretical frameworks. I point out the major reasons that Russia made nondemocratic choices at every critical juncture of its post-Soviet political development from 1991 to 2014, and the reasons for the preservation of the current status quo political regime in the country, as well as the risks of its disequilibrium.

Major crises and choices in Russian politics during critical junctures in 1991–1999 include the avoidance of major constitutional and political reforms for the sake of economic transition in 1991 (the "triple transition" issue, also known as "the dilemma of simultaneity"), the presidential-parliamentary conflict of 1993 and its aftermath, the attempt to postpone or abolish the presidential elections of 1996, and the "war of Yeltsin's succession" of 1999. Chapter 3 explores the interests, resources, and strategies of major political actors, the political and institutional constraints they faced during this period, and the outcomes of Yeltsin's reign in terms of regime changes in Russia.

The political consequences of authoritarian regime building under Putin are discussed in chapter 4, with attention drawn to changes in the rules of the game regarding the separation of power, center-regional relations, and electoral and party systems. The chapter examines the major incentives and strategies of the political actors, as well as the factors that contributed to the successful consolidation of electoral authoritarianism in Russia and the maintenance of its persistent yet inefficient equilibrium (known as the "institutional trap"), which was reached in the 2000s. Vladimir Putin and his entourage's successes and failures in terms of authoritarian regime building, and what lessons students of the global college for dictators and of the global college for democratizers might learn from Russia's experience of the 2000s, will also be considered.

The challenges of disequilibrium in Russia's authoritarian political regime emerged after the wave of protests in 2011–2012 and have become more acute since 2014, when the aggressive turn both in foreign policy and in domestic affairs resulted in the regime's increased vulnerability, under the influence of numerous factors ranging from the impact of the international environment to economic troubles. Chapter 5 focuses on strategies of regime survival at any cost, and on the regime's attempts to use fear and lies as major political instruments. In such a climate, discussion of the possible paths of Russia's future political development is difficult.

The tentative conclusions and major lessons of Russia's political evolution after the Soviet collapse are explored in chapter 6. What are the differences between electoral authoritarianism in Russia and in many other countries in the post-Soviet arena and beyond, and what are its strengths and weaknesses? Why are the incentives for major political reforms still relatively weak despite rising discontent with the status quo among Russia's elite and society at large? What factors influence the possible continuity and change of current trends? What can we learn from the Russian experience to help understand political developments across the globe? To what extent are these lessons country-specific and context-bound and to what extent do they reflect a more general logic of regime change? Given the rising demand for political changes in Russia and the continuous supply of the status quo, how can the current trends toward deterioration be overcome? Finally, opportunities for the emergence of democracy, good governance, and the rule of law in Russia, and possible mechanisms of transition in this direction, are also discussed.

CHAPTER 2

RUSSIA'S FLIGHT FROM FREEDOM

WHY?

IN SEPTEMBER 2009, Vladimir Milov, the former deputy minister for energy of the Russian government and at that time one of the leaders of the oppositional Solidarity movement, announced his candidacy for the Moscow city legislative elections as an independent candidate. In accordance with electoral law, Milov collected 4,550 signatures from voters in electoral district No. 13, as necessary for official registration of his candidacy, and submitted them to the district electoral commission. But the electoral commission denied Milov's registration, and labeled all voter signatures (including Milov's own) legally invalid. Despite numerous appeals by Milov for revision of this verdict at the Central Electoral Commission and the court, it remained unchanged: neither Milov nor other Solidarity activists were allowed to run for election. Only six parties gained access to the elections, which were held on October 11, 2009. The lion's share of votes and seats were designated in advance for the progovernmental party of power, United Russia. At the polling station where the leader of the Yabloko oppositional party, Sergei Mitrokhin, and his family had voted, United Russia received 904 out of 1,020 votes, and Yabloko received 0. Only after a noisy media scandal and Mitrokhin's legal claim to recount the votes did the local electoral commission announce revised results of the voting: while all Yabloko votes were initially mistakenly transferred to another oppositional entity, the Communist Party of Russia, the number of United Russia votes was recounted as the same; thus, official voting results remained unchallenged despite multiple accusations of fraud.[1] Although both episodes were widely covered by Internet media outlets, the Russian public remained largely uninterested in these cases, as well as many similar developments in electoral politics. Moreover, according to certain research, which includes data from both mass surveys and focus groups, the majority of Russian citizens considered (for example) the 2007 parliamentary elections and the 2008 presidential elections as "free and fair,"[2] even though most experts evaluated them as unfree, unfair, nontransparent, and fraudulent.[3]

Both these stories are fairly vivid examples of not only electoral misconduct practices in Russia, but also the Russian political regime in general. Both the electoral law (in the former case) and its implementation (in the latter case) served not as mechanisms of democratic political struggle, but rather as mere political tools oriented toward biased and unfair imitation of electoral competition. In other words, elections (a cornerstone of democracy) serve merely as a façade for authoritarianism, while de facto "rules-in-use" provide only formal legal arrangements.[4] Similar rules of the game, which undermine and pervert the very foundations of democracy, the rule of law, and good governance, are routine in many other areas of Russian politics and economics. Although Russia is hardly unique in this respect, and similar structures can be found in different countries and regions across the world,[5] it is vital to understand the genesis and logic of the evolution of the Russian regime.

The major question for those trying to analyze the trajectory of the Russian political regime sounds very simple: "why?" In other words, why did the fall of the Communist regime in Russia in 1991 not lead to the emergence of new democracy (as happened in Eastern Europe), despite not resulting in the rise of new repressive dictatorships, as happened in Central Asian countries? The answer to this seemingly basic question is not so obvious, in terms of both Russia and other countries and regions. Scholars widely discuss the causes of democracy and nondemocracy, why some countries become democracies and others do not, and the experience of present-day Russia can serve as an argument in this debate. This chapter is devoted to a critical reassessment of the various explanations for the nondemocratic political trajectory of post-Soviet Russia, as well as to elaboration of a framework for analysis of regime changes and its application to contemporary Russian experience.

In the 1970s–1980s, Soviet citizens sometimes joked that optimists were learning the English language (due to their expectations of a war with the United States), pessimists were learning the Chinese language (likewise, preparing to go to war with China), and realists were learning to use the Kalashnikov rifle so as to be ready to fight with anyone. In a sense, this joke has not lost its relevance. But it could be paraphrased in terms of scholarly approaches to the study of patterns of post-Soviet politics in Russia. To put it bluntly, in search of answers to these questions some scholars are leaning toward the "pessimist" camp, which is concerned about the legacies of Russian history and culture; others are heading into the "optimist" group, which places its hopes mainly on Russia's economic development and international engagement; and there are also "realists," who emphasize the impact of the interests and strategies of political and economic actors in their struggle for power.

In this chapter, I discuss the arguments for each of these viewpoints, then provide a brief overview of the international experience of building democracies and dictatorships in the modern world in order to understand which of the arguments sound convincing and which do not. In light of this analysis, I will focus on the logic of regime changes in post-Soviet Russia. The resulting explanatory framework of the process of political transformation in Russia will be analyzed in further detail in three subsequent chapters.

PESSIMISM, OPTIMISM, AND REALISM IN ANALYSES OF RUSSIAN POLITICS

Political forensics is similar to medical diagnosis. Scholars have to discover the pathology of political systems just as doctors, who, having observed the pathology of the human body, try to identify the causes of a disease to determine whether it can be healed, and propose appropriate methods of treatment. In reality, not all diseases develop in the same way. Some illnesses are inherited, while others emerge from contagion effects; some dangerous illnesses cannot be cured, some cause only difficult growing pains, and others can result in death. The emergence and continuation of authoritarian regimes in the contemporary world is widely regarded by political experts as a political pathology, especially when it comes to countries where some forms of nondemocracy are replaced by others. What are the causes of these serious diseases? What is their etiology and pathogenesis? The arguments of political scientists who are trying to find the answer to these questions—both in Russia and elsewhere—differ from those of medical doctors, because political diagnostics sometimes apply overly diverse analytical tools. No wonder political scientists sometimes come to rather different conclusions, and their forecasts are quite often poorly grounded (the author of this book is no exception). In their defense, one should take into account that although they offer wrong diagnoses more often than medical doctors, their errors rarely cause lethal consequences.

Following this analogy, one might argue that "pessimists" are looking at Russia's nondemocratic trajectory as a logical outcome of chronic inherited diseases, which are so deeply embedded in Russian history and culture that they cannot be reversed, at least in the short term. Conversely, "optimists" consider contemporary nondemocratic trends in Russia to be byproducts of its protracted growing pains, or of the post-traumatic stress disorder that emerged in the wake of the collapse of the Soviet system and its complex transformation. They focus on economic development and state building in Russia, and hope that the positive influence of international linkages and globalization processes will be the force that brings the gradual erosion and subsequent demise of an authoritarian regime. Finally, "realists" analyze the impact of the opportunism of major actors and their special interests on the processes and evolution of regime change and institution building. They believe that authoritarianism is the result of intentional actions by these actors, who pursue a power monopoly, just as disease can be the result of deliberate poisoning of the human body. Regardless of who exactly is the suspect in this poisoning and which poisons are considered most dangerous, one must be skeptical of the prospects of overcoming authoritarianism, since the search for an effective antidote that can overcome the effects of poisoning is a difficult task in politics as well as in medicine. These three approaches should be treated merely as ideal types: they are not juxtaposed to each other but, rather, are complementary. In reality, the opinions of the same scholars might include elements of various explanations of authoritarian politics in post-Soviet Russia. Their arguments are worth analyzing further.

Pessimists tend to point out that democracy in Russia lacks a strong background—neither in the Soviet period nor earlier in history did this country ever have a serious democratic experience. And since nondemocratic regimes are to a large degree related to those customs, traditions, and cultural constraints that are genetically inherited from history, authoritarianism is a byproduct of the "legacy of the past." This legacy is embedded in culture and contributes to the path-dependency that imposes major limits on institutional change.[6] This viewpoint is deeply pessimistic: societies that historically lacked immunity from these authoritarian viruses (such as the "right" culture and traditions) could become their victims in the long term, if not forever. Attempts to overcome these innate and genetic pathologies are very difficult, if not doomed, and the exceptional cases of successful therapy through sociocultural evolution are relatively rare.[7]

Explanations of the dominance of subversive institutions in Russia and other post-Soviet states rely upon cultural determinism and are based upon various interpretations of the role of the historical "legacy." The impact of "legacy" is often associated with the previous Communist regimes, which degenerated over time into "neo-traditionalism."[8] Some scholars have even considered centuries of Russian history to constitute a tradition of patrimonial rule and antimodernism,[9] looked on its early post-Communist period in the 1990s as its degradation into an "antimodern" society,[10] or even interpreted Russia's entire past experience as a case of peculiar Orthodox civilization,[11] or as a so-called "Russian system" that is completely incompatible with a Western-type democracy.[12] Irrespective of the point of departure, this patrimonial legacy contributed to the formation of a "Homo Sovieticus" as a distinctive and immortal social character, a highly adaptable conformist who is oriented toward the following of norms and rules of authoritarianism, prefers a "good tsar" over democracy, and thus cannot reject nondemocratic institutional arrangements despite Russia's numerous attempts at political modernization.[13] In other words, the deeply embedded arbitrary rule and repressive practices of the Russian state "from above" were combatted by defensive reactions "from below" in the manner of "weapons of the weak," as analyzed by James Scott in Southeast Asia.[14] Post-Soviet developments have not changed this situation significantly. Although the social organism, deeply affected by these genetically transmitted viruses, has often produced its own antidotes in order to adapt to these difficult conditions, it has also resisted the political changes that could reverse or at least weaken them. Thus, one may say that the legacy of the past has been unavoidable and that nondemocratic trends are likely to continue in Russia, while attempts to impose democratization are doomed in the short term, if not indefinitely.

This argument is consistent with numerous surveys analyzing Russian values and attitudes. Sometimes the average Russian citizen looks like a genuine supporter of the "iron fist," indifferent to civic and political rights, highly intolerant of minorities, very suspicious of property rights and seeking to revise privatization in an egalitarian manner,[15] and ready to abolish collective freedoms for the sake of individual well-being and the preservation of conventional order.[16] Following this logic, one might even conclude that in terms of political developments Russians got what they wanted and what they deserved, namely an arbitrary nondemocratic regime and the "unrule" of law. Thus, historical and cultural determinism becomes an excuse for the preservation of status quo authoritarianism in Russia.

But to what extent are the views of pessimists justified? Empirical evidence on the antidemocratic inclinations of Russians is at least mixed, both empirically and methodologically. A number of cross-national mass surveys demonstrate that the attitudes of Russian citizens toward democracy were not so different from those of citizens of East European countries (which are rather different from Russia in terms of democratization).[17] Moreover, several scholars challenge the view on Russian antidemocratic stances and focus on their strong adherence to at least some basic democratic institutions, such as free elections and media freedom.[18] Also, if one looks at recent experiences of successful democratization in various parts of the globe (ranging from Mongolia to Benin), where democratic values are even less rooted than in Russia, the very statement that the disease of antidemocratic past experience and present attitudes cannot be cured seems dubious.

The major methodological deficiency of historical and cultural determinism in analysis of the persistence of authoritarianism in Russia is its low discriminating power. Cultural and historical legacy as an argument cannot explain the pendulumlike trajectory of regime change, as well as its dynamics. If history and culture had an absolute impact, such changes would never be observed, at least within a short period of time. If the legacy of the past, once established, is an eternal construct, lazy scholars might repeat the same banal interpretations (without considering progression beyond such a legacy as a part of an academic and policy agenda). In sum, the cultural and historical explanations of the persistence of authoritarianism in Russia and elsewhere fall into the trap of a "residual category."[19] That is, while Russia cannot overcome authoritarianism because of its "wrong" culture, there is little chance of the "right" culture emerging because of the impact of authoritarianism.[20] Either way, the argument that cultural factors are the *causes* of authoritarianism is questionable: quite the opposite, one might regard the state of mass values and attitudes as its *consequences*. Finally, historical and cultural determinism in analysis of post-Soviet authoritarianism is politically vulnerable. Interpretations of this kind are not only heavily colored by ideological biases of the Cold War period,[21] but have also led to far-reaching policy recommendations. If in any given country the authoritarian trajectory is a product of "wrong" history and culture that cannot be ameliorated, one might say that it is best eliminated, similarly to the fate of the Soviet Union, or governed externally—by international actors, who are more capable and efficient in terms of democracy, good governance, and the rule of law. Without completely denying either of these two perspectives, one should nevertheless recognize that the practical implementation of such recommendations for Russia is hardly desirable for either domestic or international actors.

Unlike the pessimistic view of historical and cultural determinism, which considers Russia an eternal victim of the inherited disease of authoritarianism, optimists perceive recent nondemocratic trends through different lenses of scholarly optics. They observe that Russia is a "normal country" with a midrange level of socioeconomic development, and so one should not expect too much in terms of its dubious democratic credentials, and should not blame its rulers for authoritarian regime building.[22] From this perspective, Russia is viewed on the global scale as average, a mediocrity. Drawing parallels with the distribution of pupils in a school class, Russia is neither an "A" student of world politics (like Finland) nor a complete "F" student *à la* Zimbabwe, but rather something of a "C" student, not much different, from, say, Argentina (one of the fast-growing economies and emerging democracies of the early twentieth century, which recently lost even regional leadership to a more dynamic Brazil after some decades of turbulent regime changes). Like some "C" students, Russia is more or less coping with current troubles, but cannot radically improve (or worsen) its grades. Countries of this kind are more vulnerable to exogenous domestic and international shocks, which might contribute to deep traumas, thus causing protracted weakening of the social organism. According to this approach, in the case of Russia, the authoritarian trend is a result of the post-traumatic stress of the revolutionary transformation after the collapse of the Soviet Union.[23] The post-Communist revolution in Russia and its radical break with the legacy of the past caused discontinuous institutional changes—a newly established polity was not embedded within the existing political and institutional environment and lacked self-enforcement.[24] Against the background of the revolution, Russia was faced with the decline of state capacity and with the "unrule" of law, and authoritarianism merely filled the vacuum and minimized transaction costs.[25] In other words, in Russia the nondemocratic regime served as a buffer that minimized the consequences of the major shocks, or was similar to stitches or a plaster cast, which allow the healing of torn skin or broken bones, while the traumatized social organism could increase its capability for developing a new regime against the background of postrevolutionary stabilization. One may further consider this process as the equivalent of temporary growing pains, which can become protracted, but may be healable under intense treatment.

This line of reasoning is based upon analysis of the developmental trajectories of the Russian state. The gradual decline of Soviet institutions and their decay had commenced by the late-Soviet period, due to the technical incapacity of centralized economic planning[26] and a dramatic increase of agency costs, leading to the collapse of accountability by the low-level bureaucracy.[27] The breakdown of the Communist regime and the subsequent collapse of the Soviet Union fueled these processes to a large degree; the crisis of state capacity became an unintended consequence of democratization,[28] which, in its turn, contributed to arbitrary rule. The evidence of the fragmentation of the Russian state against the background of the transformation recession in the 1990s in both vertical and horizontal dimensions is clear to see. It includes various phenomena, such as the "state capture" by economic interest groups,[29] spontaneous state devolution from the federal center to regional fiefdoms,[30] the substitution of monetary policy by barter surrogates,[31] the criminal business of private protection,[32] and the like. In the 2000s, however, the Russian economy attained an unprecedented growth rate, and the Russian state partially restored its capacity. Soon after, agents of state capture became peripheral or were integrated into the new institutional environment. "Oligarchs" lost their control over the political agenda and were placed into subordinate positions within the state-led corporatism;[33] regional bosses lost their leverages of power and became dependent upon the federal center and large nationwide companies;[34] criminal "violent entrepreneurs" were either legalized or marginalized;[35] and so forth. In the words of Theda Skocpol, the state was being brought back in,[36] while nondemocratic trends, although apparent, had not turned Russia into a repressive dictatorship. Following this logic, one might expect that conservative postrevolutionary stabilization of the 2000s will not only extend the time horizon of major actors, but will also open up room for a new gradual drift toward democracy, while economic growth, globalization, and the international integration of Russia will lead to a decline of authoritarianism over time.[37]

At first glance, the expectations of gradual step-by-step democratization of Russia, driven by its economic growth, were convincing.[38] But in fact, in the 2000s Russia's ruling groups effectively used the strengthening of the state and economic growth to pursue their opportunistic interests. The strong state could become a tool for resolving the principal-agent problem within the hierarchy of the "power vertical,"[39] or a weapon against political opponents, as in the above-mentioned cases of Milov and Mitrokhin. Speaking more broadly and methodologically, one might argue that the restoration of state capacity and economic growth does not by default lead to the decline of authoritarianism and the emergence of democracy. This is especially true when these factors contribute to the rise of the predatory state, something that can negatively affect economic, political, and social development in the long run, as many historical analyses[40] and studies of contemporary politics in developing countries suggest.[41] To summarize, one should note that even though post-Soviet authoritarianism could be considered a byproduct of revolutionary transformation and might be even perceived as an unavoidable growing pain of the transitional period, time is not always a great healer. The Russian experience of the 2000s demonstrated that the conservative medicine against authoritarianism could be even worse than the illness itself; the post-traumatic stress resulting from this wait-and-see method of healing can easily turn into a chronic disease.

And finally, realists are confident that politics is nothing but a tough power struggle of somewhat cynical and opportunistic politicians, who wish to seize as much power as possible and to hold it for as long as possible. Realists[42] perceive the power struggle in politics, in business, and at war as a zero-sum game, and from this viewpoint the ultimate (if not always feasible) goal of any political actor is to impose his own dictatorship in a given polity.[43] This does not necessarily mean that all politicians are genuine supporters of authoritarian regimes: indeed, many politicians might be strong critics of dictatorships if they are not members of the ruling coalition themselves. In a similar vein, some politicians might be vocal supporters of democracy only as long as they themselves are among the winners of the political contest. Sobchak's above-mentioned notion "we are in power: that is democracy" could easily be shared by quite a few politicians across the globe. From this perspective, the very fact that "democracy is a system in which parties lose elections"[44] is the reason for risk-averse powerful politicians to eliminate or at least diminish the risk of power loss. Thus, they work hard to purposefully and intentionally establish a biased set of institutions, aimed at protecting their power monopoly and avoiding the risks of having power seized by their rivals. Given that "institutions . . . are created to serve the interests of those with the bargaining power to devise new rules,"[45] the institution-building process in many instances can become a cornerstone of authoritarianism: institutions influence the making of the rules of the game, much like the poisoning of the social organism mentioned earlier. Yet societies with a more or less established previous legacy of democracy possess immunity to such poisonings, or are at least able to minimize their negative effects, despite the fact that sometimes rather dubious politicians are able to seize power (the case of former Italian prime minister Silvio Berlusconi probably illustrates this situation best). However, societies that have to build new political regimes from scratch (including post-Communist Russia) are faced with the need to search for an effective antidote—otherwise the disease of authoritarianism can become chronic if not terminal, and the vicious circle of protracted and entrenched authoritarian "poisoning" will decrease the possible antidotal effects of democratic institutions for Russian politics.

An analysis of post-Soviet regime changes in Russia offers plenty of examples of why and how self-interested political actors consciously and consistently "poisoned" political institutions for the sake of maximizing their own power and restraining (if not eliminating) their rivals. This experience will be discussed in more detail in the following three chapters. The most noteworthy case may be the adoption and implementation of election laws in Russia in the 1990s (and later on, in the 2000s and the 2010s) which were oriented toward giving one-sided preferences to incumbents who had little intention of losing their positions through electoral defeat.[46] In this area, fuzzy legality pervaded major media regulations, rules for financing political parties and electoral campaigns, and the resolution of disputes among electoral contenders. In addition, selective implementation of these laws served as an effective tool of these politics.[47] In particular, the legal rule of recognition of elections as invalid was formulated as follows: "the electoral commission shall recognize elections as null and void if violations during polling or identification of voting returns prevent any truthful identification of the free will of voters."[48]

During debates over the lawmaking proposals in 1994, when someone proposed an exhaustive list of possible violations of laws to serve as grounds for nullification of elections, the idea was ultimately rejected. As one of Yeltsin's supporters suggested, "We should have an opportunity to denounce future results of presidential elections if Zyuganov or Zhirinovsky is going to win."[49] Thus, it is not difficult to find a reason for invalidation of any given elections based on such vague norms, thereby granting broad discretion to electoral commissions. The most notorious case was the mayoral election in Nizhny Novgorod in March 1998. When outsider populist Andrei Klimentiev, an entrepreneur with a criminal background, won an unexpected victory, the election was deemed invalid because during the campaign he promised to raise pensions and wages; this was considered an act of "bribery."[50] However, in the case of claims by opposition politicians (like Mitrokhin) of manipulation in favor of progovernment parties, this norm has effectively become a dead-letter law, very much in spite of the logic of electoral authoritarianism in Russia.[51]

Realist views on politics as a zero-sum power struggle are strongly rooted in the particular history of political thought traced from Niccolò Machiavelli through Vladimir Lenin. The latter was not only a major realist scholar but probably also the most successful practitioner of seizing and holding power in Russia since 1917. As for contemporary scholarship, Bruce Bueno de Mesquita and Alastair Smith have offered *A Dictator's Handbook*, a well-written and readable source from which cynical and opportunistic politicians can borrow some tried and tested recipes of poisoning political institutions to preserve one's power, as they might use a good cookbook.[52] While we can easily accuse politicians of cynicism and opportunism, should we demonstrate the same degree of criticism toward, say, companies that often do the same in order to maximize their profits in markets, or toward predators like dolphins, which do the same in order to catch fish in the ocean?

In this book, I will extend the realist argument to analyze post-Soviet political developments in Russia, and will focus on the strategies of political actors in their dirty business of poisoning. However, I do not exclude the arguments of pessimists on the role of the legacy of history and culture or of optimists on the impact of economic development and state building on political regimes. Rather, I will consider these aspects as auxiliary factors of Russia's regime changes, but not as the major causes that affect its post-Soviet political trajectory, with all its numerous turning points, zigzags, and dead ends. Yet the realist perspective on Russian politics is not apologetic toward authoritarianism from a normative viewpoint, but is rather a tool for its positive analysis. Instead of excusing or supporting "poisoners," we have to understand their motivation and the logic of their behavior, and explain the widely varied ef-

★

RUSSIA'S FLIGHT FROM FREEDOM

fects of different instances of poisoning, the nature and mechanisms of the poisoning of political regimes in general and the case of Russia in particular, and determine whether there is any chance of an effective antidote, and, if so, how to use it to cure the pernicious consequences of post-Soviet authoritarianism. However, the search for answers places other puzzles on the research agenda.

DEMOCRATIZATION: WHY NOT IN RUSSIA?

At first glance, if the logic of the realist approach to politics is correct, then all political regimes in the world should be nondemocracies of various colors—ranging from very bloody dictatorships to rather "vegetarian" nonrepressive authoritarianisms.[53] Should rational power maximizers achieve their goals, then authoritarian rulers will monopolize power, manipulate and pervert the institutional arrangements, bribe the elite and society at large, and hold on to their dominance until death. But in fact, even though the political history of the world is by and large the history of dictatorships, the current global political map looks rather different. Since the nineteenth century, at least, the gradual (although inconsistent) spread of democracies has gained momentum, and by the end of the twentieth century electoral (i.e., "minimalist") democracy became the most widely disseminated regime type in the world.[54] Yet well-established democratic institutions (first and foremost, free and fair elections) impose major constraints on power maximizers, forcing them to follow democratic institutions as a lesser evil in comparison with being severely punished for attempts to overthrow democracy. At the same time, within the settings of newly emerged political regimes, these constraints are either weak or do not exist at all. The question, then, is why—against the very logic of power maximization—some political regimes have democratized more or less successfully, and why democratization has not yet occurred in post-Soviet Russia.

Ongoing discussions aimed at answering this question have not brought a definite conclusion. At best, scholars can be more or less accurate in predicting the chances of some countries becoming democracies in the most general sense, but they cannot predict whether these countries are capable of turning into democracies "here and now," let alone offer scenarios and timelines for possible democratization. Most analysts failed to predict both the "Autumn of Nations" of 1989 and the Arab Spring of 2011. And even the end of authoritarianism does not mean democratization by default, as the experience of many countries (including post-Soviet Russia) tells us. Thus, I will mostly concentrate not on the causes of democratization (in Russia and elsewhere) but rather on its mechanisms and factors, which are not mutually exclusive but rather complementary.

The baseline of the democratization process (at least, in the minimalist terms employed in this book) is to present obstacles to power maximizers, who have to restrain themselves in their power struggle or face heavy losses. If these obstacles at a certain point become impassable and unavoidable, then political actors have to agree to lose power by electoral means, with the provision that one day they might come back into power—again, by electoral means. This is what is known as the "puzzle of democracy," the consent of losers to lose elections in the hope of regaining power by electoral means in further rounds of the contest.[55] But what are the reasons for the making and unmaking of these "confining conditions";[56] why do they place impassable and unavoidable obstacles before politicians in some cases but not matter much in others?

To summarize numerous scholarly debates and findings over the last several decades, I will roughly divide the major factors of successful democratization into structure-induced and agency-driven. Among structure-induced factors, a relatively high level of economic development (usually measured by GDP per capita) and a relatively low degree of inequality (usually measured by the Gini coefficient) are widely considered to be the most important predictors of democracy.[57] Also, some experts argue that countries that are relatively homogenous in ethnic, religious, and linguistic terms, and less vulnerable to territorial conflicts, are more likely to become democracies, although there is no consensus on this.[58] And though sometimes even relatively poor countries with relatively high degrees of inequality and numerous instances of ethnic and religious conflicts can be stable democracies (India is a prime example in this respect), these cases are rather exceptional. While structure-induced factors serve mostly as predictors of the probability of democratization, actor-driven logic outlines the mechanisms that may—or may not—turn a nondemocratic regime into a democracy one way or another. In fact, these mechanisms can be classified into four broad categories: (1) class struggle, (2) intraelite conflicts, (3) international influence, and (4) ideology and information.

The first category, class struggle, played a major role in democratization in nineteenth-century Europe and twentieth-century Latin America due to mass pressure on the ruling classes (i.e., the elite) and their claim to political rights. Given the rise in mass well-being in the wake of industrialization, urbanization, and the spread of education, the masses desired more redistributive policies. The spread of universal suffrage was the result of activism by social movements (first and foremost, the labor movement) so that the barriers for political participation in Europe were lowered and finally eliminated,[59] while the size of the electorate increased over time.[60] This happened not because of the goodwill of the elite but because of their fear of mass uprisings, strikes, and revolutions.[61] In short, in its early stages, democratization in a number of countries often arose as the byproduct of class conflicts that were resolved through forced political compromises due to the rise of mass political activism. More recently, mass social and political movements became driving forces for democratization in Latin America and in some East European countries during the process of elimination of Communist regimes (Poland between 1980 and 1989 is a prime example in this respect). Many scholars analyzed the impact of interclass alliances on the success or failure of these movements—such as the crucial role of the bourgeoisie[62] or the middle class[63] in democratization. Yet these alliances were not caused by but mostly resulted from the (usually large-scale and relatively long-run) involvement of society at large in contentious politics in various forms. Even though the ideas, slogans, tactics, organizational structures, and social bases of mass movements varied greatly in different countries and time periods, by and large mass social and political activism served as a major mechanism of democratization, though it did not necessarily guarantee its success.

In terms of the second category (intraelite conflicts), despite mass activism, various segments of the elite play a major role in any given polity, and the parameters of political regimes largely depend upon their arrangements and relationships with each other and with the wider society. Authoritarian rulers are not always able to successfully coopt all meaningful segments of the elite into informal "winning coalitions"[64] and/or coerce them. Intraelite conflicts can thus become inevitable, and in certain circumstances lead to protracted violent clashes, and even to revolutions and civil wars. But under certain circumstances the elite realizes that its chances to win in a zero-sum game are low, and, given risk-aversive incentives, comes to compromise on new rules of the game that open up opportunities for open competition by electoral means—that is, democracy. Of course, these compromises do not always work well—all parties in the conflicts face major temptations to transgress against the new rules and to deceive their partners, and this is why the mechanisms of "pacts" or "elite settlements" often prove to be unstable and short-lived. In addition, some of these agreements can easily turn into "cartel-like deals" over the sharing of the political market among major players, instead of creating a level playing field for all actors. To put it bluntly, democratization is just one of the possible outcomes of elite settlements, but other outcomes are not precluded: John Higley and Michael Burton counted only a few dozen cases of successful democratization via this mechanism in the entirety of modern history; often, such outcomes were reached only after a series of bitter experiences of endless battles and deadlocks, as the least harmful solution.[65]

Perhaps the best-known paradigmatic case of successful elite settlements was the 1688–89 Glorious Revolution in England, which was analyzed in detail by Douglass North and Barry Weingast. They considered the monarchy before the mid-seventeenth century as a predatory rule of the crown, which robbed landowners and urban merchants via excessive taxation, but also used these actors as junior partners in ad hoc winning coalitions. But against the background of the fiscal crisis, the English state attempted to rob both key segments of the elite, causing the emergence of a "negative consensus" coalition between these two groups, the Tories and the Whigs. This coalition rebelled against the king, destroyed the monarchy, and turned the country into what Hobbes labeled "the war of all against all" (*bellum omnium contra omnes*). The emergence of a dictatorship and attempts at the restoration of the monarchy did not resolve this conflict: members of the elite did not wish a return to the previous political regime and did not trust each other. It was only almost fifty years later that they came to a major institutional compromise, which placed major constraints on the fiscal powers of the king and established a representative government by holding competitive elections. This was the starting point of the democratization (as well as the economic growth) of the country.[66] A similar logic lies behind the famous Moncloa Pact of 1977 in Spain, when after the death of Franco the former supporters and former rivals of the previous authoritarian regime came to a compromise over new democratic institutional arrangements, despite the bitter memory of the civil war of the 1930s. After this agreement, Spain relatively quickly and peacefully turned into a democracy.[67]

In the third category, foreign actors might play a key role in the democratization of some countries. International influence on domestic political processes can be imposed by force—as in the cases of the democratization of West Germany and Japan after the Second World War by the United States and its allies. But this is not always possible if the domestic factors of democratization are weak: the experience of Iraq in this regard after the United States invasion and overthrow of Saddam Hussein in 2003 looks very contradictory, to say the least, if one assesses this country's democratic record. Thus, international influence might be complementary rather than substitutive for domestic factors of democratization. Also, one should take into account that foreign actors can promote not only democratization but also authoritarianism; in many instances, Russia as well as China attempted to play this dubious role vis-à-vis some nondemocratic regimes, especially in the post-Soviet area. However, even authoritarian regimes in the post–Cold War era were faced with the need to build democratic façades, for international as well as domestic reasons given their demands for foreign capital and investments: these factors, to some extent, contribute to the spread of "competitive," or "electoral" versions of authoritarianism.[68]

The major argument for international influence on democratization is the attractiveness of many Western democracies as normative role models. Authoritarian regimes cannot offer viable alternatives in juxtaposition to each other, ones attractive both for the elite and for society at large. This is why well-developed economic, trade, informational, migration, and educational linkages among countries with authoritarian regimes, on the one hand, and the United States and the European Union, on the other, decrease the chances of autocratic survival in the medium term. In turn, the United States and the European Union effectively use leverage for democratization in the form of aid, technical, and development assistance programs, and so forth.[69] The "success stories" of East European democratization, to a certain degree, have been determined by international (mainly West European) influence. The combination of the attractiveness of becoming part of a "Greater Europe" for the East European elite and wider society, the rapid and intensive increase of scope of linkages between Western and Eastern Europe, and the impact of European Union conditions for entering the club have pushed East Europeans toward democratization and the building of the rule of law. Alongside major domestic changes, this influence contributed to the collapse of an emerging authoritarian regime in Slovakia, the reversal of authoritarian trends in Croatia, and the revolutionary breakthrough toward democratization in Serbia, which finally brought its former dictator Milošević to the international court in the Hague and accepted the European institutional arrangements.

Finally, in the fourth category, ideology and information, authoritarian rulers themselves can launch a democratization process, although this outcome is usually unintended and undesired, and can become fatal. If an authoritarian ruler is guided by his ideas—a set of values, beliefs, and faiths—or relies upon ultimately wrong information, then he might behave not as a well-informed power maximizer but rather as an explorer traveling with an inaccurate or outdated map. For example, Chilean dictator Augusto Pinochet built a strong reputation as a hawkish enemy of democracy who coerced the opposition, and could have governed his country in the same manner until his death. But once he initiated the 1988 referendum on the continuity of his rule (expecting to win), he conducted the procedure without blatant fraud, and surprisingly lost. He decided to accept this expression of the popular will and launched political reforms, which restored democracy in Chile. But if Pinochet had had a crystal ball and could have correctly predicted the results of the referendum he proposed, this turnaround would probably not have occurred. The experience of Mikhail Gorbachev was even more telling. When he became the leader of the Communist Party of the Soviet Union in 1985, he had a wide array of choices for reforming the Soviet political system. He opted for a gradual and inconsistent liberalization of the Communist regime because of his desire to reformat it into what has been called "human democratic socialism" or "socialism with a human face." In practical terms, his initial reforms included the complete reshuffling (and weakening) of the ruling winning coalition, the weakening and subsequent abolition of censorship in media, and reliance on mass support as a tool of self-promotion. But the very first semicompetitive elections were fatal for the Communist regime: instead of gradual reform, the "stunning" elections of 1989 demonstrated the public desire for its total elimination,[70] and the ruling groups soon lost their control over the political process. Soon after that, the process of democratization went further, while Gorbachev himself ended up on the sidelines of political change. The "last true believer" in the idea of reforming Communism, Gorbachev was faced with the total loss of power and of the whole country that he governed,[71] not only due to his ideological commitments but also due to lack of information, considered the Achilles heel of numerous authoritarian regimes throughout the world.[72] In other words, ideology and information can matter for democratization as sources of wrong signals to authoritarian rulers.

Projecting all these structure-induced factors and agency-driven mechanisms of democratization onto the political map of post-Soviet Russia, one arrives at rather controversial observations. On the one hand, all structure-induced factors of successful democratization in Russia are already in place— moreover, the country looks to be in a better position than several established democracies.[73] By international standards, Russia's GDP per capita (adjusted for purchasing power parity) exceeds the "threshold" level of democratic stability outlined by Adam Przeworski and his coauthors[74] more than a decade ago. The same picture might be observed in terms of other socioeconomic indicators (such as the human development index),[75] and even though the level of inequality in Russia has increased to a great degree since Soviet times, it is comparable with that in the United States and much lower than in some Latin American democracies.[76] Finally, Russia is a rather homogenous country: its ethnic and religious diversity is relatively low (compared to many democracies across the globe), and if one leaves aside the special cases of the conflict-ridden ethnic regions of the North Caucasus, there is no evidence of mass violence or major threats of state collapse. All these factors would favor optimist arguments about the inevitability of democracy in Russia. On the other hand, none of the agency-driven mechanisms of democratization have ever worked in post-Soviet Russia (at least so far) and the developmental trajectory of regime change has headed in the opposite direction. In terms of the four categories outlined above:

(1) Mass participation and public involvement played, and continue to play, a negligible role in Russian politics after the Soviet collapse (the wave of mass protests in 2011–2012 was a rather minor rebellion, which did not alter this trend). Although the period between 1989 and 1991 was a time of extraordinary large-scale antiregime mobilization (which reached its apex at the moment of the breakdown of the Communist coup in 1991),[77] later on this wave was exhausted and its traces disappeared: after 1993, manifestations of contentious politics became almost invisible. Even the protracted transformation recession in Russia during the 1990s caused no major mass mobilization against the government. Socioeconomic protests were limited to ad hoc spontaneous and localized "rebellions," such as the collective action of pensioners against the reform of social benefits in early 2005.[78] Moreover, Graeme Robertson, in his comparative analysis of strikes in Russian regions in the 1990s (which was based upon the internal statistics of the Ministry of the Interior), came to the unorthodox conclusion that the most decisive factor contributing to the scope and scale of strikes was the conflict between federal government and the regional chief executives.[79] In fact, many strikes were inspired and provoked by the regional authorities, who effectively used this instrument to get federal funding from Moscow (as during this period, wage arrears were common in Russia, especially in the public sector). Therefore, mass participation served as a tool of intergovernmental conflict, and mass actions were cynically and effectively used by the elite to pass on blame.[80] Against such a background, it is no wonder that authorities were able to effectively contain and coopt manifestations of contention of different kinds (ranging from environmental activists to deceived investors); potential protests were localized and depoliticized, avoiding risk of the spread and politicization of a nationwide protest movement.[81] Indeed, the political (not policy-related) agenda of contentious politics after 1993 remained the priority of a very narrow milieu of professional activists, who were pushed into a hopeless "ghetto" and had almost zero effect on Russian politics. Although the rise of the new wave of protest mobilization after the December 2011 parliamentary elections in Russia was rather unexpected, the Kremlin was able to effectively contain it.[82]

(2) No elite settlements à la the Spanish Moncloa Pact or the Polish round-table talks of 1989 ever occurred in Russia after the late-Soviet period. The

Soviet and post-Soviet elite in Russia was not divided along ideological, ethnic, territorial, class, or any other lines of principle; some of the actors during the period of elite conflict just happened to find themselves in one of the competing camps, and sometimes effectively switched between different sides of the barricades. There was no history of previous deadlocks like that of Spain or Poland, and past experience of zero-sum resolution of several intraelite conflicts during the Soviet period had no meaningful impact in terms of incentives for the post-Soviet elite. Thus, arguments for elite settlement as a tool of resolution of intraelite conflicts were very premature, despite some ideas for roundtable talks proposed by certain activists of the prodemocratic movement to Gorbachev and his allies in 1990 after the wave of anti-Communist revolutions of 1989 in Eastern Europe.[83] And after the Soviet collapse, the new Russian leaders had no reason to make such compromises, as the next chapter will show. Even during the major clash between President Yeltsin and the Russian parliament in 1992–1993, none of the participants sought an "institutional compromise" in making the new democratic rules of the game,[84] and Yeltsin ultimately coerced his rivals in October 1993. After that, not only did elite settlements become impossible as a mode of democratization, but formal and informal compromises among the elite ended up as more or less tacit agreements about sharing political rent. They served as cartel-like deals around the inclusion and/or exclusion of some auxiliary subordinated actors within the framework of winning coalitions. Although these agreements played an important role in maintaining the equilibrium of the Russian political regime, they did not contribute to democratization, and to a certain extent hindered it.

(3) For good or for ill, international influence on Russian politics after the Soviet collapse was and still is rather insignificant. One should not be surprised that the largest area of the globe, with its relatively big population, visible and relatively well-developed economy, and huge military potential, is somewhat insulated from outside pressure in terms of domestic politics. Moreover, even in the 1990s, when Russia was heavily dependent on the financial aid of foreign nations and international organizations (such as the IMF), their assistance was rather limited, inconsistent, and contradictory.[85] But this is not the problem. In normative terms (i.e., as a role model) the West remained attractive for a significant part of the Russian elite and the wider society as a symbol of a high level of socioeconomic development. However, soon after the Soviet collapse it became clear that the multiple gaps that existed between Russia and its Western counterparts (ranging from mass values and attitudes to

legal order and living standards) would not be bridged in the foreseeable future. These lost illusions contributed to the rise of anti-Western and especially anti-American sentiments among the Russian elite, especially among the age cohort born in the 1960s (whereas younger people are less critical toward the West).[86] Yet while this disillusionment has greatly influenced the vicious and aggressive attacks in Russia on Western ideas and institutions (including democracy), these attacks look like a symbolic rebellion at best: despite recent isolationist trends, even the harshest anti-Westernists prefer to drive a Mercedes or a Toyota and use an iPhone or a Samsung, and want their children and grandchildren to graduate from Oxford or Harvard.[87] As for political institution building, this process, especially in the 2000s, took the form of imitating Western rules of the game: a façade of democratic camouflage merely covered the authoritarian core of elections, parliament, political parties, federalism, and the like. This strategy effectively maintained an authoritarian equilibrium in Russia for a while, but it was faced with major troubles in the 2010s. While the linkages between Russia and the West remained rather weak despite their tremendous increase after the Cold War, Western leverage over Russia, which was not very important even in the 1990s, was reduced to nothing by the 2000s (in sharp contrast to East European countries, where the West used sticks and carrots to place major constraints on their domestic politics) and was at last completely pushed out of Russia's domestic agenda in the 2010s, against the background of a major confrontation with the West. To put it bluntly, domestic political developments in Russia were not much affected by American and European actors, and this is why the role of international factors will be not considered in detail for further analysis in this book.

(4) Finally, ideological factors, such as the values, beliefs, and attitudes of Russia's political actors, played a fairly negligible role in the wake of regime change after the Soviet collapse. As a surprise to those fans of Tolstoy and Dostoevsky who perceived the Russians as reasonably spiritual and intelligent thinkers, juxtaposing them with a pragmatic and utilitarian West, the reality was just the opposite: Russian political actors often behaved similarly to textbook examples of the *Homo economicus*, with effective calculations of their costs and benefits and risk-aversion under conditions of uncertainty. Stephen Hanson, in his comparative historical analysis of the role of ideology in the formation of party systems in the Republic of France, Weimar Germany, and post-Soviet Russia, underlined the lowest ideological affinity of politicians (and wider society) in the Russian case, and argued that this factor had

a strong negative impact on Russia's party system.[88] Henry Hale, who analyzed party politics in post-Soviet Russia, went even further and denied the importance of ideology as a resource in party building after the end of Communism.[89] One might consider the nonideological nature of post-Soviet politics as more than the byproduct of its late-Soviet legacy, when the official Communist ideology was heavily discredited. Furthermore, the legacy of ideologically driven perestroika, initiated by Mikhail Gorbachev, posed a kind of taboo on emphasizing ideology for his post-Soviet successors. Since the ideological project of reforming the Soviet system sent it into total collapse, the major lesson learned by political actors was "no believing in anything": affinity with ideas is dangerous to one's career, and they are cheap without the material resources to back them up. While any ideology, in many ways, extends the time horizons of its followers,[90] in post-Soviet Russia most actors pursued only short-term pragmatic goals, and more or less successfully achieved them. But only political outsiders, with no chance to gain power, were inclined to believe in democratization as an ideological project.

This overview demonstrates the gap between the impact of structure-induced and agency-driven factors of regime change in post-Soviet Russia: despite the seemingly positive chances of democratization because of the former group of factors, the country moved toward authoritarianism because of the latter. The low degree of mass involvement in politics, the lack of incentives toward democratic pacts among the elite, the insignificant role of international influence, and the nonideological nature of Russian politics diminished opportunities for democratization of post-Soviet Russia: they could not pose major barriers that would constrain political actors in their power aspirations. Yet one might argue that these barriers failed to emerge primarily due to the impact of structure-induced conditions, such as the multiple legacies of the Soviet past. Without delving deeply into the numerous discussions on these contentious issues,[91] I will focus on the fact that these conditions were quite favorable for those cynical and opportunistic politicians who aimed at power maximization and were able to poison Russian political institutions and design the rules of the game to serve their self-interest. Indeed, it would be foolish to miss such excellent chances to grab power. And while immediately after the end of the Communism and the Soviet collapse certain arrangements of actors and institutions initially emerged as if by default, in the 1990s and especially in the 2000s the politics of authoritarian regime building resulted from conscious, consistent, and repeated efforts by political leaders and the subordinated members of their winning coalitions. These efforts, as well as several constraints they faced, determined the trajectory of political regime change in Russia in the post-Soviet period.

THE RUSSIAN POLITICAL REGIME: OUT OF THE FRYING PAN, INTO THE FIRE

Building a successful authoritarian regime and maintaining its equilibrium is probably an even more difficult task than successfully building a democracy. Political leaders who would seize and hold a monopoly on power have to resolve three major issues simultaneously. First, they have to avoid the risk of challenges from their own fellow citizens, who might protest against the regime if it does not suit their wishes. Second, they have to avoid the risk of disloyalty from members of their own winning coalitions, who might betray them in several ways (ranging from siding with the antisystem opposition to organizing a palace or military coup). These issues might be resolved through the skillful use of carrots and sticks, through coercion or repression, and/or by coopting some potential rivals as auxiliary junior partners in their winning coalition in the manner of a cartel-like deal, and providing them with additional benefits in exchange for loyalty. Third, the sustainability of regimes (both democratic and nondemocratic) is closely linked with their performance, and this is why rulers have to rely upon major tools of authoritarian government, such as bureaucracy, the military (or security) apparatus, and/or the dominant party. Still, many nondemocratic regimes have been faced with the "dilemma of performance": they "lost legitimacy if they did not perform and also lost it if they did perform,"[92] albeit for different reasons. While poor performance caused discontent from both the masses and the elite in the short-term perspective, good performance contributed to the rise of their demands for political freedoms in the long run.

The post-Soviet authoritarian regime, which began to emerge in Russia in the 1990s and became institutionalized in the 2000s, exhibited several major features that were different from both the "classic" authoritarian regimes of the Cold War era and the autocracies in some of Russia's post-Soviet neighboring countries. First and foremost, this regime not only refused to eliminate the major democratic elements that appeared in the late 1980s and early 1990s (such as elections, political parties, and the parliament), but actually maintained a quasi-democratic façade while neutering their substance. This practice of building "Potemkin democracies" is typical for many electoral authoritarian regimes, due to the need for international mimicry and coopting real and/or would-be domestic opposition as well as society at large.[93] This is especially true for those countries where authoritarianism was built on the ruins of failed democratic projects (Russia is by no means an exception in this respect). Second, Russia's authoritarian regime exhibited a rather low degree of repressiveness compared to its numerous nondemocratic counterparts across the globe. Russia's rulers offered their fellow citizens a wide range of individual freedoms and did not severely restrain civic freedoms, although political freedoms were limited if not subverted, while political repressions were very selective and targeted some personalities rather than groups and organizations. This strategy was rather effective in terms of mimicry and cooptation, and minimized the risk of domestic political conflict, but it also increased the costs of a possible shift to coercion from cooptation by the regime.[94] However, the state bureaucracy was highly corrupt and inefficient, the law enforcement agencies were deeply involved in business operations, and the nonideological party of power, United Russia, was loyal to the regime but had no incentives to care about its performance. None of these could serve as tools for socioeconomic reforms, and preservation of the political status quo became a goal in itself for them. These interests and incentives greatly influenced institution building in the 1990s and especially in the 2000s on the political supply side. As to the political demand side, it remained latent and largely indifferent to the regime and the short-lived wave of mass protests in 2011–2012 did not change the picture. Thus, the dynamics of supply and demand on Russia's political market, alongside its electoral nature and low repressiveness, became the major features of Russian authoritarianism.

How did the post-Soviet authoritarian regime in Russia emerge and evolve over time? A detailed answer to this question will be presented in the next three chapters, but the foundation is the following.

The breakdown of the Communist regime and the subsequent collapse of the Soviet Union in 1991 brought elements of democracy to Russia almost by default. Although some nascent democratic institutions did emerge in the last years of the Gorbachev reforms (first and foremost, competitive elections), major institutions were largely inherited from the previous regime. The threats of state collapse, separatism, and violent ethnic conflicts were sufficiently strong, while the economic situation was perceived as nearly catastrophic. The winning coalition of Russia's leaders had seized power in 1991 largely through fortunate circumstances rather than electoral competition. As such, under these circumstances they had no incentives for the advancement of democratization, in terms of pursuit of electoral competition and building of democratic institutions (very much in contradiction to Sobchak's understanding of democracy). However, this winning coalition of 1991 soon divided into two camps, one grouped around President Boris Yeltsin and the other around the Supreme Soviet. Fierce conflict between these two segments of the Russian elite flared up in 1992–1993, against the background of a severe economic recession and high inflation following the Soviet Union's collapse. Aside from major economic policy differences, the core of the contention was their uncompromising aspirations to dominance. Distribution of resources between these two sides was clearly unequal. Yeltsin was much stronger than his opponents and had broader public support, and the costs to pay for the coercion of his rivals looked relatively small in comparison. In September 1993, Yeltsin declared the parliament dissolved, but the latter refused to bow down and attempted to impeach him. As a result, after two weeks of stalemate, tanks shelled the parliament building and the Supreme Soviet was finally forced to surrender. This victory in a zero-sum game was a turning point in terms of institutional choice: in December 1993, faced with little resistance, Yeltsin was able to have a draft constitution adopted in a referendum that guaranteed him broad powers and an almost complete lack of checks and balances—this was the first major step toward the poisoning of Russia's political institutions.

However, democracy by default had not turned into authoritarianism by default. In fact, Yeltsin never wielded unchecked arbitrary rule, most likely for two major reasons. First, the natural heterogeneity of Yeltsin's fragile winning coalition contributed to its splintering into several competing cliques. Second, against the background of a protracted economic recession and the weakness of the Russian state, Yeltsin had neither the strength nor the resources (including support from the elite and the general public) to "wipe out" his potential opponents in all areas, while none of the other actors had the incentive or the resources to organize stable cooperation among themselves on a negative consensus basis. Under these conditions, Yeltsin changed his strategy from coercion of the opposition to a "cheaper" cooperation with subordinated actors, including some of his former opponents, and initiated a series of tacit cartel-like deals with various elements of the elite. A number of regional leaders who were willing to agree to sell their loyalty to Yeltsin signed bilateral agreements with the federal authorities, giving them various tax breaks and control over key assets, while businesspeople achieved their desires in the wake of privatization, and opposition parties were coopted into the new regime's framework without threatening to undermine it. The 1996 presidential election played a key role in supporting the cartel-like deals and maintaining the status quo. The possibility that the election might be canceled or its results overturned if Yeltsin lost was a critical aspect of his campaign, and his team even attempted to dissolve the State Duma, but the cost of undermining the status quo and ensuring the ruling coalition's survival by coercing the opposition (and not holding the election) was too high. In the end, the president's team was forced to accept costly cooperation with subordinated actors as the lesser evil. The election was widely considered unfair, with evidence indicating fraud in Yeltsin's favor, but the various political actors, including the opposition, did not challenge the result.

Soon after the 1996 elections, the new winning coalition broke apart like its predecessor, and a new round of fierce conflicts between the elite flared up on the eve of the 1999–2000 parliamentary and presidential elections, forming the major episodes of "the war of Yeltsin's succession." A loose coalition of regional leaders and "oligarchs," or tycoons, was ready to seize the position of dominant actor, and sought victory in competitive elections. But this scenario was not implemented in the end, to some extent due to the major shift in the balance of power that took place during the conflict. Specifically, Vladimir Putin and his entourage managed to win the backing of regional and business leaders, who were playing a key role as "gatekeepers" during the election campaign. After his victory and accession to the presidential post in 2000, Putin invested tremendous effort into effective building of his monopoly on power via the neutralization of political rivals, restructuring the winning coalition, maintaining wide public support, and changing major rules of the game.

Informal cartel-like deals with the elite had collapsed during Yeltsin's time because of the institutional inefficiency that forced the subordinated actors to search for autonomy vis-à-vis the dominant actor, and also because of the Kremlin's inability to impose sanctions on violators of such deals. Under Putin, new cartel-like deals took the form of "an offer he can't refuse," to quote the infamous statement from *The Godfather*. Thanks to a successful military operation in Chechnya, Putin was able to successfully restore the coercive capacity of the Russian state. Thanks to high oil prices, Putin was able to successfully capitalize on overcoming the economic crisis of the 1990s and reap the great fruits of 6–8 percent annual economic growth. Thanks to electoral legitimacy, Putin's mandate was unquestionable, while he severely diminished the autonomy of subordinated actors. The Russian parliament supported almost all presidential legislative proposals, regardless of their content. The newly formed party of power, United Russia, which was established in 2001, held the majority of seats in parliament from the very beginning of its formation. The regional leaders who previously used to wield full power in their "fiefdoms" now found their resources highly limited. In addition, they were replaced in the Federation Council—the upper house of parliament—by appointed full-time officials. Simultaneously, Putin launched an offensive against the independent media, with most media outlets forced to resort to self-censorship and/or coming under the direct or indirect control of the state and its allied business groups. Putin also openly clamped down on cronyism in state-business relationships, in exchange for renunciation of interference by major oligarchs in key political decisions. In short, after 2000, Putin restructured the winning coalition and launched institutional changes that weakened all actors but his own.

Some years later, Putin as a dominant actor was able to concentrate such a large amount of major resources in his hands that the costs of coercing rivals were drastically lowered for him. In 2003, Putin initiated legal prosecution of Mikhail Khodorkovsky, the major shareholder of the biggest private oil company, Yukos; Khodorkovsky received a long prison sentence for tax evasion and other serious crimes, and his business was taken over by the state-owned company Rosneft. After a series of manipulations during parliamentary elections, United Russia received more than two-thirds of the seats in the State Duma, while all other parties lost influence. In 2004 Putin initiated the abolishment of popular elections of regional chief executives, who became de facto appointed by the president. Changes to the electoral system, including an increase of the parliamentary election threshold to 7 percent, exacerbated the problematic status of the opposition and prevented disloyalty of political actors toward Putin. By 2007 United Russia had absorbed the absolute majority of regional chief executives and many powerful representatives of business, and the main strategist of the Kremlin asserted that the party of power would dominate Russia's political scene for the next ten to fifteen years.[95]

In the end, the institutional changes of the 2000s strengthened the "imposed consensus" within the wining coalition in Russia, eliminating all possible alternatives to the status quo regime and/or raising their costs to prohibitive levels for all actors. Putin, as the dominant actor of Russian politics, was able to consolidate his monopolist control over the Russian elite, and had relatively little trouble passing the office into the hands of a puppetlike loyal successor, Dmitry Medvedev, in 2008, while maintaining control over key levers of power as the prime minister. Although critical observers hoped that the presidential turnover would bring a new wave of institutional changes oriented toward political liberalization, this was not the case. Medvedev had neither the incentives nor the resources for reforms in this direction. Medvedev's most significant innovations were amendments to the 1993 Russian constitution extending the presidential term in office from four to six years (starting from 2012) and the State Duma's term in office from four to five years (starting from 2011). This move clearly pursued the goal of maintaining the status quo of the political regime under the new presidency of Vladimir Putin from 2012 on. Many observers perceived these changes as manifestations of the consolidation of the authoritarian regime in Russia. From the perspective of poisoning and distortion of political institutions, they were considered signs of the Russian political regime developing a chronic disease, given that Medvedev's presidency was not marked by any major signs of active disloyalty from the elite or the masses, and that public support of the political status quo remained high despite the deep (although not very protracted) economic crisis of 2008–2009.

However, this institutional equilibrium in Russian politics has been challenged in the 2010s. The first challenge emerged in the wake of the 2011–2012 national elections and postelection protests. When the return of Putin to the presidential post after Medvedev's interregnum was announced, United Russia failed to win a majority of votes in State Duma elections despite numerous instances of blatant fraud, and this became a trigger event for mass antiregime rallies in Moscow and some other Russian cities. Nevertheless, the regime was able to cope with these troubles and minimize the challenges by combining minor liberalization of electoral and party rules with the politics of fear. This episode was a relatively small crack in the wall, but alongside the regime change in neighboring Ukraine in 2014, it contributed to perceptions of major threats to the Kremlin because of democratizing pressure. The counterattack, launched by the Kremlin on the international arena, resulted in the annexation of Crimea, de facto war with Ukraine, and a major confrontation with the West. Domestically, it led to further "tightening of the screws," rapid deterioration of many formal (as well as informal) political institutions, aggravation of the (already severe) decline of political and civic freedoms, and numerous other problems.

A demand for political change in Russia will increase, especially among the younger generation. Some lessons from Russia's post-Soviet experience, as well as factors and chances for the future evolution of Russia's political regime, will be outlined in the last chapter of this book, while the next three chapters will be devoted to an analysis of how and why Russian politics after the Soviet collapse went down the long and winding road from the Soviet regime to the rise and decline of post-Soviet authoritarianism, much like moving out of the frying pan and into the fire, and what lessons for the future we can learn from this experience.

CHAPTER 3

THE ROARING 1990s

CONFLICTS AND COMPROMISES

ON THE EVENING OF December 25, 1991, the Soviet red flag was lowered from the Kremlin and the new Russian tricolor flag was raised in its place. The Soviet Union officially disappeared from the world political map, and new independent states (including Russia) emerged from its ruins. The Soviet collapse met little resistance in Russia by that time, and even emotional reactions were negligible: it was an event similar to the legal divorce of former spouses whose marriage was already de facto over. Post-Soviet countries were forced to choose their own pathways of political transformation and faced multiple problems of regime change, which to some extent were common but in other ways country-specific. After two decades, none of the post-Soviet countries (beyond the Baltic states) were able to establish full-fledged democracies. While in some of these countries (such as Uzbekistan) the issues of democratization never became part of the political agenda, in other cases (like Belarus) the failure of democratization contributed to the rise of authoritarianism, and countries like Georgia and Moldova were faced with irresolvable ethnic conflicts. And Russia, despite having the strongest economic and human potential in comparison with its post-Soviet neighbors, has also failed to achieve major progress in terms of democracy building: Ukraine and Armenia have become more free than Russia. Moreover, in the 1990s Russia's newly emerged democratic institutions, such as competitive elections, political parties, parliament, and media freedom, were heavily discredited; to a large degree, this experience played an important role in their systematic degradation and disempowerment in the 2000s. To follow a medical analogy, one might argue that the period of the 1990s was a time of numerous complex and protracted illnesses in Russia's nascent political regime: some were inherited from the Soviet past, some were typical (and probably inevitable) growing pains of the process of political regime change, but others resulted from inadequate diagnostics and inappropriate treatment. In other words, the cure was worse than the disease, and this medicine played a major role in turning the growing pains of the 1990s[1] into the chronic diseases of the 2000s.

The period of the 1990s, rightly or not, was given the dubious title of *likhie* in Russia's political slang (this could be loosely translated into English as "roaring").[2] For some experts as well as for many Russian citizens, this period was identified with the deep and prolonged economic recession. Others pointed out major ethnic conflicts in the North Caucasus, the rise of criminal violence, the notorious inefficiency of governance, and political instability, including major conflicts among key political actors. Under these conditions, Russian democracy was unable to overcome its birth trauma, which resulted from the painful experience of the Soviet collapse, but at the same time it was consciously sacrificed by those politicians who had little interest in fair (and risky) electoral competition and wanted to postpone their loss of power into an indefinite future. But the seeds of authoritarianism, which had been sown in Russian soil in the 1990s at the beginning of the thaw after decades of Soviet deep freeze, brought poisonous shoots in the 2000s. How and why were these seeds sown and germinated in Russia? Why did the new Russian rulers, who came to power in 1991 under the banners of democracy and freedom, turn the country toward the opposite political direction? And was this nondemocratic turn inevitable for post-Soviet Russia, or was it a by-product of major strategic decisions taken by Russia's political actors at several critical junctures of the "roaring" 1990s? These and other issues will be analyzed further in this chapter.

THE "DILEMMA OF SIMULTANEITY": THE POST-COMMUNIST CHALLENGE AND THE RUSSIAN RESPONSE

In late 1991, just before the collapse of the Soviet Union, the German sociologist Claus Offe published an oft-cited essay about the complexity of post-Communist transformations. He rightly argued that the scope of major changes in post-Communist societies was unprecedented in world history due to the simultaneity of transitions along three major axes. Countries in Eastern Europe and (then) the Soviet Union were presented with the need for simultaneous transformation of: (1) imperial state models inherited from the Soviet (and often pre-Soviet) era into modern nation-states; (2) centralized planned economies into free market economies; and (3) one-party authoritarian regimes into competitive democracies. Offe noted that while most West European countries solved these three tasks (not always successfully) one by one over several decades and even centuries, post-Communist countries encountered an entirely new phenomenon, the issue of "triple transition," which implied difficult and painful reforms in all these areas "here and now." Thus, the temptation of step-by-step gradual changes over time (e.g., first building the nation-state, then market economic reforms, with democratization coming only after these steps), as well as the risk of rejection of any reforms, was very strong. However, as Offe argued, the "dilemma of simultaneity" had a somewhat paradoxical solution: despite all the apparent challenges and risks, only the simultaneous pursuit of democratization, economic reforms, and state and nation building could bring post-Communist countries relatively quick success, while step-by-step protracted change could only deepen problems and crises.[3]

Assessing the experience of post-Communist countries more than two decades after the publication of Offe's essay, one might agree that the dilemma of simultaneity was resolved more or less successfully in several East European countries, which in the 1990s built both market economies and competitive democracies, and in the 2000s joined the European Union.[4] The trajectories of the countries of the former Yugoslavia were much more painful and tragic. The collapse of the state was followed by a series of bloody ethnic conflicts instead of democratization and market reforms, so the process of triple transition was more difficult and protracted; in the end, the tasks of reform were solved in this region, but at greater cost and less effectively. As for Russia and its post-Soviet neighbors, their trajectory of change was radically different. Even though Russia avoided the risk of complete collapse of the state and underwent almost no conflicts similar to those that emerged in the wake of transformation in the former Yugoslavia (Chechnya serving as a unique exception), construction of the nation-state was rather inefficient in both the 1990s and the 2000s, albeit for different reasons. Market reforms faced excessively high inflation and a deep and protracted transformation recession, which turned into economic growth only after the major crisis of 1998. And even though the market economy in Russia demonstrated impressive growth in the 2000s (until the 2008–2009 global economic crisis),[5] it is far from being free in terms of the business climate due to a lack of the rule of law.[6] Finally, democratization, which was launched with the first competitive elections and the emergence of new political parties in the late-Soviet years,[7] was stopped, diminished, and nullified in the 1990s, and almost completely eliminated in the 2000s. But what about the causes of these developmental trends, at least in terms of regime change? Why did Russia resolve the dilemma of simultaneity in such a perverse way? And why did Russia's alternative solution to the problem of triple transition result in partial and inconsistent outcomes in two of the three major areas of transformation (economic reforms and nation and state building), and have a negative impact on political regime change?

Answering these questions requires reconsideration of the major strategic choices of Russia's political actors, which were made at certain critical junctures in Russian politics in the 1990s and 2000s. These choices formed a corridor for their further motion until they reached a dead end in the 2010s. In my view, neither determinist nor voluntarist perspectives of analysis are very useful for understanding the logic of these choices: Russia's political regime trajectory was not doomed from the very beginning irrespective of the decisions of major actors, but at the same time one should not blame the actors for their good or bad will in making their decisions. This way of thinking is simplistic, incomplete, and often wrong. My approach is based upon the assumption that although structural constraints inevitably pose major limits on their choices, political actors in post-Soviet Russia (and elsewhere) define their strategic priorities based on the combination of their resources, perceptions, and previous strategies, aiming for the goal of power maximization under these conditions. Sometimes these choices are quite successful in terms of benefiting the actors themselves but impose major societal costs, although there are cases where the opposite is true. Russia's experience in the 1990s is important in this respect, given the extraordinarily high uncertainty caused by the collapse of the Soviet state and deep economic troubles, which heavily affected the making and implementation of major decisions. In fact, in 1991 most of the previous rules of the game became irrelevant with the end of the Communist regime and the Soviet state, as actors' opportunities for the use of coercion toward each other and society at large became limited, and the time horizon for planning shortened to months if not weeks. No wonder that many of their decisions resulted in unintended consequences for the political actors themselves and for the country as a whole.

The first and probably the most important critical juncture in post-Soviet Russian politics actually occurred even before the end of the Soviet Union, in October 1991. The collapse of the Soviet state had already become inevitable by that time, and Russia's political leaders, who had suddenly and rather unexpectedly found themselves rulers of a country faced with the urgent need for radical changes, found on their agenda the choice between alternative pathways for Russia's political and economic reform. The governability of the fading Soviet Union was extraordinarily poor, and there was high uncertainty about the possible consequences of strategic decisions.[8] The economy was on the brink of complete collapse, ethnic conflicts in various regions were turning into open violence, while nationalist and separatist movements raised banners of full-fledged independence, and Russia's president, parliament, and government, initially established as subnational governing bodies, had to deal with an overwhelming burden of nationwide issues. However, even with the risk of political and economic turmoil, Russian rulers based their authority on a high level of mass support (which was partly reflected in Yeltsin's strong resistance to the coup of August 1991), and the public expectations for a turn to the positive on the political and economic fronts in Russia were not hopeless. To summarize, in October 1991 Russia's political leaders had a narrow and short-term "window of opportunity" for strategic choices for the country's political development.

Following Offe's line of reasoning, one might consider a hypothetical solution to the Russian version of the dilemma of simultaneity in October 1991. From this viewpoint, the Russian parliament could have launched the process of adopting a new national constitution, thus establishing a new institutional framework for post-Soviet Russian statehood without the Soviet Union. It could then call for "founding elections" of Russian authorities under new institutional arrangements, strengthen statehood, and establish a new transitional government that could be based upon public support and could conduct urgently needed market reforms. To some extent, this was the logic of changes in several countries in Eastern Europe and among the Baltic states. But in Russia as well as in other post-Soviet countries this solution was not only unrealistic, but was never considered seriously as a possible developmental pathway by power-holders. Yet there is no way to experience alternate history, and we can never know what might have happened if simultaneous political and economic reforms (and/or any other sequence of the major transformations) had been adopted in Russia—discussing the probability for success or failure of these scenarios is highly speculative almost by definition. The Russian dilemma of simultaneity was resolved in a different way: (1) democratization was first postponed, then revised, and finally neutralized; (2) market economic reforms were conducted under the deep and protracted transformation recession until the 1998 economic crisis; (3) the problems of state and nation building were solved only partially, the territorial status quo was preserved almost by default, and central state capacity was greatly diminished.

The principal choice was made in October and November 1991. The Russian parliament, the Congress of People's Deputies, refused to discuss the draft of the new constitution, which had been proposed by the special Constitutional Commission. Instead, it agreed with the proposal made by the Russian president, Boris Yeltsin, which implied several institutional changes: (1) elections of subnational authorities were abolished in most Russian regions (except ethnic republics); (2) Yeltsin came to hold two combined posts simultaneously—those of the president and the prime minister; (3) the Congress granted Yeltsin extraordinary powers to release presidential decrees (which had legal force similar to laws adopted by the legislature), to appoint and dismiss members of the government without parliamentary approval, and to appoint and dismiss subnational chief executives in most regions and in the capital cities of these regions (again, except ethnic republics), all until December 1992.[9] As a result, Russia "froze" all the previous political institutions that existed in the country at the moment of this decision (this moment almost coincided with the Soviet collapse two months later) as well as the very model of its complex ethnofederal structure, which was inherited from previous decades but remained untouchable. Market economic reform became the top priority of the Russian elite (and of wider society). Soon after this decision, Yeltsin appointed his government, effectively led by the deputy prime minister Yegor Gaidar. The blueprint for economic reform, also known as the "Washington consensus," included a major package of price liberalization, financial stabilization, and large-scale privatization of enterprises.[10] The government launched these reforms in January 1992, but failed to achieve financial stabilization for a number of reasons, including the fact that all countries of the former Soviet Union (except the Baltic states) still used the same Soviet currency but were unable to implement a common monetary policy. Without discussing the many details of the thorny and complicated pathways of Russia's market transition, I will summarize their impact on political developments in the 1990s as the following: economic reforms in Russia were rather painful and protracted; the "valley of tears" of inevitable transformation recession[11] became much deeper and longer than in many East European countries, and only the default and large-scale devaluation of Russia's national currency in August 1998 marked the end of this process.[12] As for state and nation building, Russia avoided territorial breakdown and major violent conflicts related to separatism and secession (with the major exception of Chechnya), but these risks were averted at the expense of further decline of both the coercive and the distributive capacity of the Russian state, which was already dramatically weakened after the collapse of the Soviet Union and beset by protracted economic troubles. In short, while the very agenda of political reform in October 1991 was sacrificed for the goals of market transition, the relative costs and benefits of this choice turned out to be dubious at best. Its political consequences for regime change in Russia were important and irreversible.

First and foremost, the freezing of Russia's political institutions, which had been established in the late-Soviet period and designed under very different conditions and for very different purposes, led to their overloading. They were unfit for governing the country (rather than large subnational units, as had been the case with the Russian Federation before the Soviet collapse), the equivalent of a child's tricycle at the Tour de France. In particular, the two-tier Russian parliament (the Congress of People's Deputies and its permanent body, the Supreme Soviet), which was established after competitive elections in spring 1990, was initially designed as a sort of playground of Big Politics, but was not able to serve as an efficient arena for decision making.[13] No wonder that the Russian parliament (as well as regional and local councils) soon turned into easy targets for bombardment and outrageous criticism, and finally became victims of intraelite conflict. The moratorium on new elections also destroyed a number of new political parties that had emerged in 1990–1991. More importantly, the rejection of the very idea of establishing and accepting democratic rules of the game was driven by the Russian rulers' wish to have free rein in the wake of economic reforms. The problem, however, is that free rein meant precisely a lack of constraints for those in power, who had few incentives to establish democracy, given the risk of losing power.[14]

Why was the Russian dilemma of simultaneity resolved in a way that implied the rejection of political reforms and further democratization? The existing literature presents two major reasons for this strategic choice. One is based upon the critical assessment of economic conditions of the Soviet Union in 1991, which was close to complete collapse and chaos, and implies that the possible side effect of Russia's democratization could have been a rising demand for macroeconomic populism, which could actually worsen the economic crisis. Some experts have referred to the dubious Latin American experience and suggested "insulation" of the Russian government from public pressure as a condition for economic remedies (this idea was popular among some of Russia's economic reformers, who praised Chile under Pinochet as a role model and advocated similar approaches for Russia, although unsuccessfully).[15] While these threats and risks initially sounded reasonable, they were greatly exaggerated: East European countries were able to conduct simultaneous political and economic reforms without major failures on either of these fronts, and stabilization policy did not become a victim of populist public demands.[16] The other argument is based on the threat posed to Russia's nascent statehood by the many separatist and nationalist movements that mushroomed in a number of ethnic republics and in some other regions of the country against the background of the Soviet collapse.[17] It was unrealistic to expect that in late 1991 the Russian authorities could reach any agreement about the future of the post-Soviet federal structure of the new state, while calling new elections could increase the threat of disintegration and the risk of a territorial breakdown of Russia. This thinking lay behind the proposal for a moratorium on subnational elections and for the establishment of a hierarchical chain of executive subordination (which, however, did not include the ethnic republics of Russia at that time). However, I would argue that despite these issues, the very logic of strategic choice in October 1991 was driven by other considerations and expectations from Russia's rulers.

After the failure of the Communist coup in August 1991, the Russian president and the parliament were the ultimate winners—they were able to concentrate major levers of power in their hands. But they had not won by pure chance, in the manner of a lottery. Rather, their victory resulted from a coincidence of circumstances. The Soviet political regime fell apart, and previously forbidden fruit became easily available to those who shook the tree hard enough. Russia's new rulers, however, were not centered on ideological and/or organizational unity: the newly emerged winning coalition around Boris Yeltsin in 1990–1991 was largely ad hoc and based upon a negative consensus against the previous status quo and the Soviet rulers led by Gorbachev. It involved market-oriented liberals, anti-Communists who often called themselves "democrats" but also shared Sobchak's notions ("we are in power; that is democracy"), rent-seekers from various interest groups, and some officials who shifted their preferences toward the new winners at the right time. While the goal of power maximization was already achieved after August 1991 simply because of the end of Communist power, they then had little interest in power loss by electoral means.[18] From this perspective, the promotion of open political competition was not a desirable goal. For instance, the major reason for the moratorium on popular elections of regional chief executives imposed in October 1991 was the expectations of the political analysts of Yeltsin's administration, who predicted that Yeltsin's supporters were capable of winning in only ten of twelve regions and would lose in other areas.[19] If, in the words of Adam Przeworski and others, democracy is "a system in which incumbents lose elections and leave office when the rules so dictate,"[20] then the winning coalition around Yeltsin in October 1991 had no incentives for building a democracy—not because of their personal stances but because of the lack of rational motivation to risk voluntarily losing power. No other incentives were provided to build new democratic institutions instead of dividing the spoils and rents after the Soviet collapse, and the idea of establishing new institutional arrangements was ultimately rejected by the new rulers themselves. Russia's democratization was postponed as the default option, and then disappeared from the agenda of Russian politics, at least for the time being.

YELTSIN vs. PARLIAMENT: FIRST BLOOD

To a certain extent, the plan for advancement of radical economic reforms and the freezing of Russia's previous political institutions had its reasons: some of Yeltsin's supporters sincerely expected that upon overcoming the economic crisis, the democratization agenda would return to the list of priorities of

★

Russia's rulers.[21] We will never know whether these expectations were naive and deluded; the reality was very different. Quite the opposite: the deep and protracted economic recession posed new challenges for Russia's political institutions and for the rulers. First, the new winning coalition was too large and could not easily divide its gains without disadvantaging some of its participants. Second, Yeltsin was not only a pivotal actor in this coalition—his authority and (then) mass public support exceeded those of all his allies put together: thus he was able to restructure the winning coalition in an arbitrary way and made effective use of this tool during the entire period of his presidency. Third, in the wake of the troubles of economic reforms and the decline of mass public support for the rulers, the newly formed winning coalition soon broke down, and the allies (if not friends) of August 1991 turned into mortal enemies as early as 1992. When the parliament delegated large extraordinary powers to Yeltsin but did not receive any payoffs in terms of political and/or policy influence, a sizable part of its members naturally felt deceived. It is no surprise that some of Yeltsin's former supporters (including his own running mate, vice president Alexander Rutskoi) turned to harsher criticism of the government. Yeltsin, however, effectively used the increasing division within the political elite and the rise of political polarization to maximize his power: he was able to shift the blame for the hardship of economic reforms onto his political rivals.

The first collision began in April 1992: the new Congress of People's Deputies had to discuss the new (revised) draft of the Russian constitution, and also met to evaluate the government policy on economic reforms. By that time Yeltsin had lost the earlier support of the parliamentary majority, and some observers suggested that he make a deal with Congress: to agree with the parliament on adoption of the new constitution at the price of the resignation of Gaidar and other unpopular ministers. But such a compromise (which could diminish Yeltsin's powers, both de jure and de facto) was not particularly desirable to the president and his team. As a result, the idea of adopting a new constitution was postponed once again, and nearly buried, and government reshuffling did not change major economic policy directions; moreover, in June 1992 Yeltsin appointed Gaidar as acting prime minister. As early as April 1992, Yeltsin loudly announced that the Congress should be disbanded because it created major obstacles to economic reform in Russia. To a certain degree, these lamentations were reasonable: the parliament had voted for numerous populist proposals, whereas neither the president nor the government intended to implement these decisions (and had no resources for their implementation in any case), and Yeltsin's team greatly overestimated the negative effects of the populist rhetoric of parliamentarians on Russia's economic troubles (as even after the dissolution of the Congress these troubles barely diminished).

Political maneuvering during the following months of 1992 did not resolve the rising conflict between Yeltsin and the parliament, but rather exacerbated it. Although some politicians who represented sectoral and regional interest groups attempted to serve as mediators in this conflict, their efforts were largely in vain, not least because they merely revolved around maximizing their own rents and other benefits as side payments for demonstrative loyalty to both parties. Meanwhile, the Congress gradually lost patience with Yeltsin, who disregarded his rivals and paid almost no attention to their policy proposals. More and more parliamentarians, in turn, intended to take back the extraordinary powers delegated to Yeltsin in 1991, and diminish his ability to conduct unchecked rule. The problem was not only the asymmetry in the amount of resources held by Yeltsin and the parliament, but also the asymmetry in the nature of these resources. The Congress based its actions upon the principle of legality—according to the then acting constitution, it was empowered to adopt any legal decision through the voting procedure. However, by the end of 1992 mass support for the legislature fell drastically. The long sessions of Congress (which were broadcast on TV) were by and large perceived by the public as useless meetings of noisy (and sometimes even inadequate) freaks, and several harsh claims by parliamentarians met with little public approval; the parliament's legitimacy was dubious at best. As for Yeltsin, he was a popularly elected president, and although his mass support had decreased since 1991, he was still perceived as a legitimate leader despite the fact that his actions often violated the law. This fundamental contradiction between legitimacy and legality affected the outcome of the conflict between Yeltsin and his rivals to a certain degree.

By December 1992, the term of Yeltsin's extraordinary powers had expired, and he was forced to propose a candidate for prime minister for the approval of Congress members. Yeltsin quite predictably nominated Gaidar, who failed to get majority support (467 votes for, 486 against). This was not a hopeless result, especially given that the proposal for constitutional amendments, which demanded parliamentary approval for the appointment of key ministers, had also failed in Congress. But instead of arguing and bargaining with parliamentarians, Yeltsin chose an open confrontation. In a short and aggressive speech at Congress, he claimed that the conflict should be resolved through a national referendum on confidence in the president or the parliament, and urged his supporters to leave the plenary session, thus rendering it without quorum. However, this attack was poorly prepared: Yeltsin's supporters did not follow their leader, and power ministers responsible for military and security issues remained loyal to the constitution. After several rounds of behind-the-scenes talks Yeltsin agreed on a compromise solution: instead of the initial proposal, Congress agreed to organize a referendum on the basic principles of the new constitution, and Yeltsin had to propose a prime minister for approval by Congress. Unsurprisingly, Gaidar was proposed again, and lost by a large margin. In the end, Yeltsin nominated a new candidate, the former deputy prime minister for energy issues Viktor Chernomyrdin, who was enthusiastically approved by parliamentarians.

However, the conflict was not resolved. In fact, Chernomyrdin, despite loud criticism toward his predecessor Gaidar, did not significantly change the latter's policy directions, and parliament exerted only very minor influence on decision making. Yeltsin largely ignored the laws and decrees adopted by the legislature and had no intention of giving up his extraordinary powers. The parliament lacked any levers of control, save for its express disagreement with the actions of the president and his government. The idea of a constitutional referendum was buried by both sides, as were other ideas for resolving the conflict, including plans for simultaneous early presidential and parliamentary elections. After dramatic debates and an unsuccessful attempt to impeach Yeltsin, Congress scheduled the referendum for April 1993, with the following issues: (1) confidence in the president of Russia; (2) support for the economic and social policy offered by the government of Russia; (3) support for early Russian presidential elections; (4) support for the early election of Congress deputies.

The referendum campaign was marked by the unprecedented domination of the pro-Yeltsin side in the media. They harshly attacked Congress, which, in turn, asserted corruption in the government. The turnout at the referendum was 64 percent. The president received 58.7 percent of eligible votes, and his government's policy gained 53 percent; 49.5 percent of the active electorate voted for early presidential elections, and 67.2 percent for early parliamentary elections. However, the results of the referendum had no legal force; they simply demonstrated public attitudes toward both sides of the conflict. A plebiscitarian mechanism, in contrast to elections, cannot resolve conflict in and of itself. As a replacement for elections, the referendum failed to create a framework for a representative government based on the principle of the rule of law. Instead, Yeltsin felt encouraged to establish his plebiscitary domination based on the principle of arbitrary rule due to his relative popularity (or, rather, the unpopularity of his rivals). As for the parliament, it was now doomed to lose the battle.[22]

After the referendum, constitution making returned to the political agenda: the adoption of a new framework for political institutions, as well as calls for new founding elections, became inevitable. The major disagreements between Yeltsin and parliament lay at the heart of power, and concerned legal constraints on presidential rule in terms of appointment and dismissal of the government, and of possibilities of cohabitation with the oppositional legislature. While Yeltsin's proposed draft of the constitution involved a presidential–parliamentary form of government, the parliament offered a premier–presidential republic. The drafts were incompatible, and no compromise could be achieved. Under these circumstances, Yeltsin launched a coup: on September 21, 1993, he dissolved parliament, and announced the new parliamentary elections to be held on December 12, 1993. After this, parliament voted to impeach Yeltsin, and appointed Rutskoi as acting president. Thus, Russia ended up with a kind of diarchy. Some politicians and parties, as well as regional leaders, proposed a return to the previous status quo, and simultaneous early presidential and parliamentary elections. But on October 3, during a rally in Moscow, supporters of the parliament launched riots and tried to attack a major television station. Yeltsin's reaction was quick and bloody: the next day army troops shelled the parliament residence using tanks; according to official data, 146 people were killed during this storm of violence. Several leaders of the parliament and some opposition figures, including Rutskoi, were arrested, and some opposition parties prohibited. This was a zero-sum solution to the intraelite conflict: Yeltsin and his team effectively eliminated their rivals, who had lacked public support; the very idea of executive accountability before the legislature was buried, as was that of checks and balances. Yeltsin's camp won, and used the outcomes of the conflict to maximize power through the unconstrained creation of new rules of the game.[23]

Initially, upon disbanding the Congress, Yeltsin proposed that the new Russian constitution would be adopted by the new parliament: its lower chamber, the State Duma, was to be elected by popular vote, and the upper chamber, the Federation Council, would be formed ex officio by representatives of regional authorities. However, after the complete elimination of the Congress, Yeltsin received free rein in the arena of institution building. In October 1993, his team quickly redesigned the proposed draft of the constitution. It was offered for a referendum held simultaneously with elections to the State Duma on December 12, 1993 (the first convocation of the Federation Council being elected the same day). These elections were held according to the formal and informal rules imposed on the losers by the winners of the October 1993 clash. For these reasons, left-wing and nationalist opposition parties were deliberately excluded from electoral competition, and the radical left opposition boycotted the elections. The moderate left opposition, the Communist Party of the Russian Federation (KPRF), succeeded in having

Yeltsin's prohibition of their activity canceled, but fear of having it restored led to a sluggish and colorless campaign. Furthermore, the elections were rather unfair in terms of access of parties and candidates to campaigning tools. State-owned media provided minimal opportunities for free campaigning, while paid advertising was unlimited. Television news was full of indirect advertising for progovernmental parties (mostly Russia's Choice, led by Gaidar); they explicitly used state resources for campaigning, and the regional leaders nominated for the Federation Council also widely used their powers for election purposes. Finally, electoral commissions on all levels were appointed by the executive authorities, which used them as a tool for various manipulations throughout the campaign.[24]

The simultaneous holding of the 1993 elections and the constitutional referendum was the campaign's main feature. In fact, the new constitution was oriented toward legally securing the results of Yeltsin's victory over the parliament: presidential powers were maximized, while parliamentary checks and balances were fairly limited; the State Duma had no rights to form the government or affect its policy, while the president could disband the State Duma at virtually any moment in case of its disloyalty. And even though the constitution included a long list of declarations of human rights and individual freedoms, which were borrowed from many international sources, these declarations were more or less an empty shell, since the document did not grant working mechanisms of implementation of these rights and freedoms. In fact, only the president, who was claimed to be the legal guarantor of the constitution, could implement these rights and freedoms on the principle of benevolence. The constitutional doctrine was based upon the major assumption that the president has the right to do anything that is not directly prohibited by law, and one of the constitutional clauses (article 80) directly mentioned that "the president defines the major direction of domestic and foreign policy of Russia."[25] Yeltsin himself, arguing for adoption of the constitution before the referendum, openly compared the proposed model of government with that under the Russian monarchy in 1907–1917,[26] and soon after the referendum he stated his understanding of the system of government in Russia even more concisely: "To put it bluntly, somebody had to be the boss in the country; that's all there was to it."[27] The only legal constraint on presidential power, according to the constitution, was the limit on holding the presidency for more than two consecutive four-year terms.

From this perspective, the parliamentary elections had secondary importance next to the constitutional referendum. No wonder that the distribution of State Duma seats was not one of Yeltsin's primary goals, and that he did not express explicit support even to loyal parties (mostly Russia's Choice), instead focusing his efforts on the adoption of the constitution. While opposition parties criticized the draft of the constitution, Yeltsin demanded "don't touch the Constitution!" and the first deputy prime minister (one of the leaders of Russia's Choice) even proposed excluding these parties from electoral contestation. Yet the polls and the referendum brought rather contradictory results.[28] The official turnout was 54 percent, and in two ethnic republics (Tatarstan and Chechnya) regional authorities effectively boycotted voting. According to official data, only 58 percent of voters approved the constitutional proposal (roughly the same share of voters supported Yeltsin during the April 1993 referendum). But the full results of the referendum and the elections, with a detailed breakdown of data on the level of polling stations, were never published. Moreover, when the media published some critical analyses that posed major doubts about the validity of these results and accused the authorities of large-scale fraud some months after the polls, the Central Electoral Commission ordered the destruction of all ballot papers in the country.[29] Thus, true identification of the public will during voting became impossible, and we will never know how Russians really voted in December 1993; nevertheless, the constitution was considered to have been adopted by the people.

The 1993 intraelite conflict and its political consequences became a major critical juncture in post-Soviet regime change. The outcome of this conflict was based on the principle of "winner takes all":[30] it greatly contributed to the maximization of Yeltsin's power and to the imposition of his preferred rules of the game on Russia's political actors and society at large. The new constitution shaped the framework of Russia's political institutions, but it also included major authoritarian potential. As Adam Przeworski rightly noted (not with respect to Russia), "since any order is better than any disorder, any order is established."[31] The political order established in Russia in October–December 1993 to a large degree determined the further trajectory of Russian political development.

ALLIES AND RIVALS: BORIS YELTSIN AND OTHERS

One might expect that the new institutional arrangements that Yeltsin imposed on the Russian polity after the zero-sum resolution of the 1993 conflict on the "winner takes all" principle would inevitably lead to unconstrained, arbitrary presidential rule and to the ultimate coercion of political rivals (similarly to the behavior of Yeltsin's counterpart in neighboring Belarus, Alexander Lukashenko, who in 1996 also disbanded the legislature and imposed his own constitution on the country).[32] But the realities of Russian politics after 1993 were completely different. Until the end of his presidency, Yeltsin was far from being an unchecked dominant actor, and barely resembled "the boss in the country." Although new institutions should have allowed Yeltsin to govern Russia in a very dictatorial manner, he was forced to bargain with numerous subordinated actors, establish ad hoc informal alliances and coalitions, and at certain points demonstrated the art of muddling through at the brink of political survival. The twists and turns of Russian politics were rather sharp and unexpected. Why was a power monopoly not established at this time?

Although the 1993 constitution gave Yeltsin free rein in many ways, it was not the only source of presidential power. Maurice Duverger, in his analysis of French presidentialism, argued that apart from the constitution, two other sources play an important role in determining the scope of presidential power. The first is the origin of the presidency, and the second is the degree of presidential support in parliament and among the elite.[33] I would extend his argument and add to this list presidential popularity among the general public. These factors contributed to political rather than institutional constraints on Yeltsin: he obtained his preferred rules of the game, but could not play according to these rules in whatever game he wished. Yeltsin's choice of political strategies was constrained and even forced by the fairly limited amount of resources under his control. On the one hand, presidential power itself emerged in Russia in 1991 as a byproduct of late-Soviet democratization, and Yeltsin himself became president after a victory in competitive elections over five other candidates with 57 percent of the vote. He could not easily abandon elections or eliminate them, because the electoral nature of the Russian political regime was (and still is) the main source of presidential legitimacy. On the other hand, Yeltsin had to maintain his informal winning coalition against the background of severe economic recession, which led to a major decline in presidential popularity. After 1993, Yeltsin could not argue that the parliament (or any other actor) was an obstacle to effective policy making. Moreover, he was more and more perceived by the elite and wider society as an inefficient political leader, and often as an inadequate person (some of his escapades, like his drunken conducting of a military orchestra in Germany in 1994, only fueled these perceptions). The further weakening of the coercive capacity of the Russian state, and the lack of control of the central government (hereafter "the center") over ethnic republics and nonethnic regions, which claimed sovereignty and attempted to grab as much as possible by way of resource rents and financial flows, added more complexity to this picture.[34] Law enforcement agencies were in decay and heavily commercialized, so the functions of maintaining public order and resolving business disputes were often performed by criminal gangs rather than by the police and the courts.[35] Under these conditions, many Kremlin decisions remained merely on paper. Finally, the winning coalition that Yeltsin reformed around himself in the wake of the 1993 conflict was too heterogeneous and shapeless: it included various interest groups of rent-seekers, some segments of officialdom within the power vertical, and some ideologically driven market liberals, whose influence gradually declined after 1993—but neither the dominant party nor the state apparatus served as tools of coordination and control over these actors. In fact, the winning coalition had broken down into competing cliques.

Given these circumstances, Yeltsin could not coerce his real and potential rivals any longer, and his political (if not physical) survival remained his primary task for the rest of his presidency. Yet while Yeltsin was faced with a shortage of resources and unable to coerce his rivals unilaterally, no other actors were able to dominate Russia's political arenas: after 1993, there was no way to build a negative consensus coalition against the emerging status quo regime. Although during the 1993 parliamentary elections opposition parties of different colors won about half the seats in the State Duma, the presidential administration avoided the risk of a new polarization and open confrontation that would have resembled the 1992–1993 period. Despite attempts at no confidence votes against the government (in October 1994 and in June 1995), no unified oppositional majority was established in the State Duma, and most decisions (including major laws) were approved on the basis of ad hoc coalitions.[36] The fluidity and instability of parliamentary parties, the high degree of fragmentation, and weak incentives for coalition building among Yeltsin's rivals in parliament and beyond were advantageous for the ruling group, and the partial and inefficient equilibrium of the status quo regime emerged virtually by default.

Under these conditions, Yeltsin changed his strategy from coercion to a "cheaper" cooperation with subordinated actors, including some of his former rivals. Beginning in 1994, Yeltsin's camp initiated a series of tacit cartel-like deals with various segments of the elite, sharing powers and rents in exchange for political loyalty. A number of subnational leaders in ethnic republics and nonethnic regions were willing to sell their loyalty to Yeltsin, and signed bilateral agreements with the federal government, which offered them tax breaks and control over key assets[37] (Chechnya, which experienced two major wars in 1994–1996 and in 1999–2001, was the only outlier case in this trend).[38] Opposition parties and politicians were coopted into the new regime's framework without threatening to undermine it, and even when the Communists had the majority of seats in the new convocation of the State Duma (in 1996–1999), they also preferred political maneuvering and tacit compromises with the Kremlin to open confrontation with the ruling group.[39] Some businesspeople became major beneficiaries of the (in)famous loans-for-shares deals:[40]

the government arbitrarily designated key assets in oil industry and metallurgy to a tiny group of bankers, who channeled cash flows to Kremlin pockets, bypassing budgetary regulations and procedures; while the government had free use of this money before the 1996 presidential election campaign, businessmen, in turn, guaranteed their political support to the Kremlin. These moves were a great help to Yeltsin in maintaining the political status quo despite rising public discontent.[41] Loyal regional leaders not only delivered votes to incumbents[42] but also managed protests in their fiefdoms;[43] loyal opposition parties avoided challenging the regime and agreed to their subordinated status;[44] and loyal businessmen received incentives to invest in their newly obtained enterprises,[45] thus shifting from behaving like "roving bandits" to the pattern of "stationary bandits" (in the terms of Mancur Olson).[46]

The new parliamentary elections in December 1995 were triumphant for the KPRF: the party and its allies won nearly half of the seats in the State Duma, while the major progovernment electoral bloc Our Home Is Russia, led by Chernomyrdin, barely received 10 percent of the vote. In sharp contrast with the extraordinary 1993 races, the campaign of 1995 was reasonably fair: although progovernmental blocs and candidates used a wide range of administrative resources for campaign purposes, their impact was limited because of high party fragmentation and open contestation, so the voting results largely reflected voters' true preferences.[47] But parliamentary elections had a "second-order" nature due to the subordinated status of the State Duma: the legislature (i.e., its lower chamber) could not form the government or impose its policy decisions onto the executive, and its bills could be effectively blocked by the Kremlin.[48] The political effect of these elections was related to the very fact that they were held just six months before the presidential race and served as the equivalent of "primaries" among the elite, clearly showing the potential of prospective candidates. Judging by the 1995 electoral results alone, one might expect that the major oppositional candidate, the Communist leader Gennady Zyuganov, would be elected president, and the composition and policies of the government would be changed to a great degree. But, surprisingly for many observers, in June–July 1996 Yeltsin was reelected for a new term in office.

Before the start of the presidential campaign, in early 1996, Yeltsin's approval rating was about 5 percent, and given the gloomy economic conditions as well as the continuing war in Chechnya, a number of Yeltsin's allies were very skeptical of his electoral prospects.[49] Meanwhile, the risk of electoral loss was enormously high in terms of political survival for members of the winning coalition, who had no incentive to turn it into a coalition of losers. These risks in the Russian case serve as a vivid illustration of the well-known argument on the zero-sum nature of the presidential elections as one of the major "perils of presidentialism."[50] The possibility that the election might be canceled or its results overturned if Yeltsin lost was a critical aspect of the 1996 campaign.[51] In March 1996, Yeltsin's team attempted to dissolve the State Duma, the plan being to prohibit opposition parties (including the KPRF) and cancel presidential elections.[52] This was the critical challenge for Russia's rulers, who had to choose between the continuity of the electoral authoritarian regime (e.g., by holding unfair elections) and the possible shift of Russia's political regime to a "classical" version of hegemonic authoritarianism (e.g., with no elections or with "elections without choice"). The problem was that the costs of such a shift were too high. It would not only ruin the regime's legitimacy in the eyes of society at large, but also aggravate conflicts among the elite, possibly even more severely than in 1993. In the end, the president's team (initially bitterly divided over the issue of whether to launch a new coup d'état) was forced to accept the preservation of the status quo in terms of the rules of the game as the lesser evil. At this critical juncture of regime change, electoral authoritarianism survived in Russia, and the 1996 presidential elections, though unfair, were held.

Yeltsin's campaign staff effectively mobilized virtually all resources in the electoral bid. They used the administrative capacities of the state apparatus on national and subnational levels, controlled most of the media outlets, spent seemingly unlimited financial resources, including international credits and loans, and bought the loyalty of most of the interest groups, including payment of pensions and wage debts to military officers, workers of military industrial enterprises, coal miners, schoolteachers, and others.[53] On the eve of the elections, Yeltsin signed bilateral treaties with influential leaders from Russia's regions and granted them more powers, and the war in Chechnya was (temporarily) stopped. State propaganda intimidated voters with the horrors to come if the Communists returned to power. Some of Yeltsin's rivals were involved in his campaign (such as the popular retired general Aleksandr Lebed, who explicitly supported Yeltsin in the runoff); and others, such as the leader of the liberal Yabloko party Grigory Yavlinsky, were strongly pressured and limited in their access to the media. In contrast, Zyuganov was obstructed and discredited in the media.[54] Despite his huge proportion of core supporters, Zyuganov failed to gain more allies, was politically isolated, and was unable to attract a majority of voters to support him. After the first ballot he refused to continue to the final struggle for victory. Observers evaluated Zyuganov's campaign as rather inactive, boring, and old-fashioned, and even proposed some theories of behind-the-scenes deals between Yeltsin's team and the opposition.[55] Administrative pressure against voters played an important role in the electoral outcome in some regions; the dramatic increase in votes for

Yeltsin between the first and second ballots is clear evidence for this. Last but not least, electoral fraud in Yeltsin's favor was detected, although there is no evidence that it was crucially important. The KPRF did little to resist these vicious attacks, more or less accepted the election results, and announced a change of political strategy after the race, adopting the approach of "integration into power" and finally integrating into the status quo regime as a "semiopposition."[56]

As a result of his successful campaign, Yeltsin defeated Zyuganov in both the first (35 percent vs. 32 percent of votes) and the second (53 percent vs. 40 percent of votes) ballots.[57] However, Yeltsin's success was a Pyrrhic victory: the aging sixty-five-year-old, with a history of heart attacks and habit of hard drinking, was ultimately broken by his campaign. Between the first and second ballots, Yeltsin's life was threatened by a new heart attack and he did not fully recover.[58] After his reelection, the weakened Yeltsin was unable to effectively control his winning coalition, and his decision making was based on the division of spoils. Chief campaign manager Chubais was appointed as head of the presidential administration; Lebed took the post of secretary of the Security Council for three months, and then was fired; key positions in the government were used to reward certain entrepreneurs who had sponsored Yeltsin's campaign; and Chernomyrdin secured the job of prime minister. As for Yeltsin himself, in November 1996 he underwent heart surgery and was out of action for several months; he never returned to his previous state of health or his previous political influence. Still, the 1996 presidential election played a key role in maintaining the cartel-like deals among the elite, and the continuity of the status quo political regime. "Any order" was again better than "any disorder": even though the major actors (and the general public) were dissatisfied with the status quo, none of them were able (and willing) to change the existing institutional arrangements unilaterally. This inefficient and partial equilibrium, however, was soon challenged, with pernicious consequences.

THE WAR OF YELTSIN'S SUCCESSION

By 1997, the winning coalition around Yeltsin had become weak and shapeless. At the same time, Yeltsin was faced with two major challenges. On the one hand, the unwell lame-duck president desperately needed to pick a loyal successor, one who would be able to guarantee physical security and survival for him and his entourage. On the other hand, the deep public dissatisfaction with the state of affairs in the country urged him to change governmental policy in a more proactive way. In March 1997, Yeltsin finally used presidential power to launch a new attempt at economic reform. He reshuffled Chernomyrdin's government and appointed Chubais, and the former Nizhny Novgorod regional governor Boris Nemtsov, who had been considered a possible successor for the next presidency, to key positions. But such a solution hurt certain interest groups, which faced the risk of losing preferential access to rents and had no intention of supporting the Kremlin's desire to stop or at least diminish state capture by big business.[59] The resistance of the tycoons, or "oligarchs," was fierce: the former winning coalition was soon divided into competing cliques, who launched "the war of Yeltsin's succession." The political influence of Chubais and Nemtsov was undermined, and their reform agenda was effectively buried. The conflict with oligarchs over issues of privatization became an open one due to the actions of two major TV channels, controlled respectively by leading businessmen Boris Berezovsky and Vladimir Gusinsky. A noisy media campaign against Chubais and some of his cronies (who were implicated in receiving large honoraria for an as yet unpublished book about privatization in Russia) resulted in their resignation.[60] The notion of "oligarchy," widespread among observers of Russian politics,[61] was soon joined by the keyword "family," with the reference not only to immediate members of Yeltsin's family, but to the whole system of corrupt officialdom.

Meanwhile, on the eve of the new parliamentary and presidential elections scheduled in 1999 and 2000 respectively, everyone understood that Yeltsin had no chance of continuing his presidency after the end of his second term, not only because of the legal limit, but also due to his physical weakness and his low support among the elite and society at large. All the unresolved economic and social problems, the weakness of the state, legal disorder, and poor central control over regional fiefdoms remained in place, thus fueling the rise of public discontent. The issue of power transfer through electoral means became the top priority on the agenda of Russian politics, and this problem had no precedent solutions in Russian history—no Russian ruler had ever lost that post due to the outcome of elections. The list of potential claimants to the presidency included not only opposition politicians such as Zyuganov, Yavlinsky, and Lebed, but also previously loyal top executives such as Chernomyrdin, and Moscow's mayor Yuri Luzhkov. The lack of coordination among potential candidates increased uncertainty and risk; none of them was able to guarantee Yeltsin's survival and the continuity of the regime. In March 1998, Yeltsin quite unexpectedly fired Chernomyrdin's cabinet and appointed thirty-five-year-old Sergei Kirienko, who had been promoted to the post of minister of fuel and energy just a few months earlier.

The government resignation and Kirienko's appointment provoked a negative reaction from the Russian elite. The State Duma appointed Kirienko after three rounds of voting, and only when Yeltsin threatened to dissolve parliament. Since Kirienko had no links with any parties and/or interest groups, his opportunities for policy making depended purely on presidential support. Thus, Kirienko's reshuffled government was not a "political" but just a "technical" cabinet of professionals hired to conduct economic reforms. He tried to pursue Gaidar-like economic policy, but the lowest-ever oil prices on the world market, as well as increasing state debt and fiscal insolvency against the background of financial crisis on the emerging markets, made it impossible. The cabinet reacted with some delay, faced with resistance from various sides, and had limited political support.[62] In August 1998, the financial crisis came to a head: the state's default, the crash of the Russian national currency and its dramatic devaluation. When the government and the Central Bank announced these decisions, Yeltsin fired Kirienko's cabinet. It was then that the economic crisis in Russia developed into a political one.[63]

The August 1998 crisis had a decisive impact on Russian politics. The degree of uncertainty and risk jumped. Several oligarchs were faced with heavy economic losses and lost not only some of their assets but even their opportunities for state capture.[64] The regional elite had claimed more control over taxes and assets. Parties and parliamentary groups, irrespective of their ideological stances, blamed Yeltsin for the failure of the government. The president, however, appointed Chernomyrdin as acting prime minister and threatened to dissolve the State Duma if it disagreed. But such a scenario was unlikely; Chernomyrdin had limited chances of electoral success, and both the masses and the elite blamed him for poor government performance and for the policy that had caused the economic crisis. No one believed in his capacity to overcome the crisis and to reduce the degree of uncertainty. Also, the possible return of Chernomyrdin to the post of prime minister would make him Yeltsin's official successor and give him control over the state apparatus on the eve of new elections, thus causing problems for campaigns by other potential contenders. For these reasons, the State Duma twice voted against his reappointment as prime minister. Yeltsin was faced with a dilemma: he could insist on Chernomyrdin, dismiss the State Duma, and call new legislative elections, or compromise with the parliament. However, the possible outcomes of early elections, given the background of large-scale crisis, could be undesirable: only the Communists and their allies would benefit from this solution. For these reasons, Yeltsin changed his plans and proposed the sixty-nine-year-old foreign minister Yevgeniy Primakov as a new prime minister. In September 1998, Primakov, who had a strong reputation as an experienced spy and diplomat of the Soviet era, was not linked with any interest groups, and was not implicated in corruption, was unanimously accepted by an overwhelming majority of State Duma deputies.

Many observers perceived this compromise, and Primakov as a prime minister, to be a partial and temporary solution. According to the Russian constitution, the government was little more than a team of economic managers, hired and fired by the president. But contrary to some expectations, Primakov's government was able to acquire support from all factions of the State Duma and most segments of the elite; at last, the economic crisis was stopped, paving the way to postcrisis recovery. Primakov's political support soon grew, at the level of both popular attitudes and elite perception. He became conventionally considered as the most viable candidate for the post-Yeltsin presidency, one who would help various segments of the elite secure their positions after the new elections. He was acceptable to many parties and regional and sectoral interest groups. Elements of a new negative consensus among the elite, in the manner of a "cartel of anxiety,"[65] emerged around Primakov in early 1999. However, the constitutional division of power between the president and the prime minister doomed Primakov to be a hostage of the Kremlin. His independent approach directly contradicted the interests of the "family" and its business allies, and when Primakov proposed the idea of an informal pact between the president, the State Duma, and the government on the preservation of the political status quo before the elections, the Kremlin ultimately rejected his plan due to the risk of improving Primakov's preelectoral position and chances.

Simultaneously, Communists in the State Duma initiated the process to impeach Yeltsin, whose unpopularity had reached its highest point. In May 1999, 284 out of 450 State Duma members voted to launch impeachment proceedings, blaming Yeltsin for the Chechen War as a criminal act on his part. Since the Russian constitution required a two-thirds majority (i.e., 300 votes), this move had no legal consequences. These developments found Yeltsin and his "family" in similar circumstances to those faced by Gorbachev in late 1991, when the negative consensus among the masses and the elite had left him no room for political survival. However, unlike Gorbachev, Yeltsin still held administrative resources under his control, and responded to the threat. Just one day before the parliamentary vote on impeachment, Yeltsin fired Primakov, making him a major victim of the Communists' failed impeachment attempt, and appointed Sergei Stepashin, then minister of the interior and absolutely loyal to the president, as a new "technical" prime minister. But Stepashin had no political agenda of his own, attempted to maneuver between different cliques, and was faced with major resistance from the "family." In August 1999, Yeltsin fired him and appointed the former chief of the Federal Security Service, Vladimir Putin, as the fifth prime minister of Russia in seventeen months. The political crisis in Russia appeared to reach an apex just a few months before the new elections.

On the very day Yeltsin appointed Putin as a new prime minister, a campaign for new State Duma elections in December 1999 was officially launched. As mentioned earlier, due to the electoral timetable, parliamentary election gains were widely considered a kind of primary for the presidential race. The results of the Duma elections could be a major signal for the elite and the public alike against the background of high uncertainty. By that time, the former winning coalition had degraded into an open rivalry, while dissatisfaction with the Yeltsin-era status quo had become nearly universal: despite disagreements on every possible level, most of the elite and society at large expected Yeltsin's departure from the political arena—this was the essence of the negative consensus that had emerged in Russia before the elections. Furthermore, the formal and informal rules of the game, which had contributed to the 1998 economic crisis and default in Russia, were heavily criticized by virtually all observers (including those who had benefited from these rules after Yeltsin's reelection bid in 1996). During the 1999 electoral campaign, new ideas such as the rising demand for recentralization of the state and governance,[66] as well as empowering the legislature vis-à-vis presidential power, strengthening the party system, and the like, were presented in the policy programs of major political parties regardless of their policy positions on economic and social issues.[67] These critical stances reflected the rising demand for change on the eve of new elections.

Before the beginning of the 1999 campaign, a new coalition of regional leaders and oligarchs formed around Luzhkov with the intent of seizing the position of dominant actor. He was able to build bridges with some of his allies from other regions, but it was not enough to assure other segments of the elite, who preferred wait-and-see positions, of his chances. However, when Primakov, the most popular politician at that moment, joined forces with Luzhkov and headed the new electoral bloc Fatherland—All Russia (OVR), their coalition was perceived as a new, more effective, and predictable claimant for leadership. In theory, the success of the OVR in Duma elections could help Primakov's nomination for the presidential elections as the candidate of a broad elite coalition. With his impressive record of government service, Primakov seemed able to solve the "leadership dilemma" typical for post-Soviet states: the Russian elite badly needed a strong leader but were deeply afraid of the dangers of his personalist rule and his lack of accountability.[68] The consensus around Primakov even included the Communists, who were ready to support him in the presidential race, while Luzhkov was considered a prospective OVR candidate for the post of prime minister. Before the campaign, the OVR leaders distanced themselves from Yeltsin and harshly attacked his "family" and the Kremlin. Yeltsin, in his turn, reacted with a major delay. The pro-Kremlin electoral bloc Unity was only established in the process of the campaign, with Sergei Shoigu, minister of emergency situations, appointed as its leader, but its chances of passing the 5 percent threshold were then rather dubious.[69] However, the Russian electoral landscape soon changed due to unexpected events beyond the electoral contest.

In August 1999, Chechen guerilla troops suddenly invaded Dagestan and attacked the local police. Regular army and special police task forces repelled them into Chechnya. A short while later, a series of bomb explosions in apartment blocks in Moscow and other cities killed hundreds of Russian citizens. These events were shocking for the whole country; security threats turned from a rather abstract concept into a part of everyday life for many Russians. Soon after these explosions, sacks with explosive materials were found in one of the apartment blocks in the city of Ryazan. Subsequently, security services claimed that it was part of counterterrorist training, and that the sack was full of sugar instead of explosive materials. Some critics even guessed that the whole series of explosions was organized by the Russian security services, but were unable to provide evidence. Public opinion (strongly influenced by the media) blamed Chechen terrorists for these explosions. This was a major breakthrough in public mood toward Chechnya: during the war of 1994–1996 both the masses and the elite blamed the government for its bloody military operation, but after the Moscow explosions, calls for revenge became common. Putin, meanwhile, demonstrated a decisive and tough intention to punish terrorists.[70] In October 1999, Russian troops invaded Chechnya, launching the second Chechen war (which officially ended in 2001). The guerillas were pushed out into the mountains, and the Russian army seized most of the Chechen areas. The military campaign greatly strengthened Putin's political influence and authority, and altered not only public attitudes but also the perceptions of the elite on the eve of parliamentary elections.

The Moscow bomb explosions were also a serious blow for the OVR. The hope that the OVR was capable of protecting the country from major risks and uncertainty was buried; the contenders for national leadership were unable to demonstrate quick and decisive steps toward solving suddenly arising and extremely painful problems. The ousted Primakov had no power and no influence on the course of events; Luzhkov, whose popularity had been based on his strong performance as a mayor of Moscow, was widely criticized.[71] As Putin's popularity increased rapidly, the Kremlin successfully exploited this situation for its campaign against the OVR, while Unity was primarily associated with supporting Putin. Putin himself, although formally distanced from any party, openly announced Shoigu to be one of his best friends, and stated that he would vote for Unity. Soon after, electoral support for Unity skyrocketed.[72]

It was also a signal for major segments of the elite (including regional leaders), who shifted their loyalty from the OVR to the new potential winner, Unity. Even the OVR leaders, who were unable to leave their bloc during the course of the campaign, expressed their loyalty to Putin and Shoigu.[73]

As a major source of information about elections, television also served as a major campaigning weapon at the Kremlin's disposal. ORT and RTR, the largest national channels, strongly attacked the OVR by all possible means, including rumors that Luzhkov was guilty of organizing contract killings and the like. Simultaneously, Unity was shown in the most attractive light thanks to one-sided news coverage and indirect advertising: according to some analyses, these "information wars" definitely affected the choices of Russian voters and undermined the OVR support base.[74] But they may also have simply reflected the development of the intraelite conflict. Over the course of the campaign, the OVR first lost support among the elite and then among voters. Moreover, the disintegration of its electoral support was even faster than the growth of Unity's electoral popularity. A new liberal bloc, the Union of Right Forces (SPS), which included former government officials and politicians closely associated with Gaidar and Chubais, filled the deficit of supply on the electoral market to a certain extent; the Kremlin also backed its campaign. The electoral results clearly demonstrated a new arrangement of actors in Russian electoral and parliamentary politics. The KPRF received 24.3 percent of the vote, but only 130 Duma seats (including those of its allies), so the Communists were no longer able even to serve as "veto players" in parliament and beyond.[75] Conversely, Unity was the real winner of the elections with 23.3 percent of party list votes thanks to the defeat of the OVR (13.3 percent). The latter began to disintegrate soon after the parliamentary elections, and its leaders announced their open support of Putin and even claimed that the OVR was a preelectoral coalition only, without ambitious plans of party formation. Some deputies elected on OVR tickets in single-member districts even refused to join its parliamentary faction.

The unexpected outcome of the State Duma elections provided a new window of opportunity for Yeltsin. On December 31, 1999, he announced his resignation from the post of president of Russia on TV.[76] In accordance with the Russian constitution, the Federation Council called early presidential elections in March 2000, while Putin, as prime minister, was appointed acting president until the polling day. Putin's very first decree granted guarantees of immunity to Yeltsin and members of his family. In effect, Yeltsin transferred his presidential power to Putin as his heir. Yeltsin's early departure was mostly met with applause from the elite and society at large. In the first place, Yeltsin, who had lost all popularity and capacity to govern, had resigned at last. Second, the post had been passed to the major winner of the parliamentary elections. The elite and the masses were ready enough to recognize Putin as the new dominant actor. In this respect, the early presidential elections were little more than a tool for legitimation of an already-made decision. Thus, the Russian political regime survived the critical juncture of power transfer, avoiding the risks of open electoral contestation, which, for example, had caused major trouble for Ukrainian political leadership in 2004.[77] The conflict between the various segments of the elite who had claimed to be dominant actors after Yeltsin was resolved as a zero-sum game, although instead of the costly and risky use of coercion (the main form of conflict resolution in 1993), in 1999–2000 the winners effectively used cooptation.[78]

Against the background of his already high popularity, Putin had little chance of electoral defeat. Economic growth, which had become stronger and more visible by early 2000, also increased his public support. Other potential contenders were faced with a dilemma: either compete without great chances of success or refrain from campaigning. Primakov forcefully declined the idea of running for president, and soon retired from politics, while the OVR (as well as the SPS) proclaimed open support for Putin. After the dramatic clash over the Duma elections, the presidential campaign was rather listless. Putin merely used his incumbent position and popular support, which increased after his appointment as acting president. During the campaign, the open expressions of support for Putin among prominent public figures, political parties, and NGOs, not to mention regional and business elites, closely resembled the "good old days" of noncompetitive Soviet-style elections. Although neither political parties nor organized interest groups played a serious role in the presidential campaign, their positions symbolically represented the elite's consensus over a popular leader. Polling day, March 26, 2000, brought a convincing victory by Putin. He received 52.9 percent of the vote with a high voter turnout (68.7 percent). Although journalist investigation by the *Moscow Times* provided detailed and well-grounded evidence of fraud in the presidential elections,[79] the electoral results were never disputed by Russian politicians. Yet while the true numbers and figures might be different, the political outcome of the elections was clear beyond doubt. In the end, on May 7, 2000, Putin was inaugurated as the second Russian president.

THE ROARING 1990s: THE BALANCE SHEET OF REGIME CHANGE

The "roaring" 1990s were a time of harsh conflicts and temporary tacit compromises among Russia's political and economic actors. From the perspective of regime change and of overall political developments, they received mixed and contradictory assessments in scholarly literature as well as in Russians' perceptions.[80] The tasks of triple transition were solved only partially and in a very imperfect way. Although the protracted economic transformation after the 1998 default turned into impressive economic growth that lasted until 2008, the two other dimensions of the triple transition, namely democratization and state and nation building, demonstrated several major pathologies.

At the first glance, despite the bloody resolution of the 1993 conflict, Russia made some (incomplete and inconsistent) steps toward democratization. The new constitution (if rather imperfect in terms of separation of power) was adopted in the referendum, the new electoral system (again, rather imperfect) was adopted and implemented, three convocations of the new parliament were elected under fierce competition, and the new party system (also imperfect) began to develop. But these reforms were partial and superficial; they did not establish viable institutional guarantees of fair elections and of power turnover by electoral means. In other words, they did not imply the democratic accountability of the executive, which lies at the heart of electoral democracy. The 1996 presidential elections disillusioned those who wanted to believe in the democratic potential of Russia's nascent political regime. The struggle between various cliques and conflicts of regional and sectoral interest groups for rents and influence somewhat resembled a democratic competition, but it was based on other foundations. Due to the fragmentation and heterogeneity of winning coalitions, none of the actors in the 1990s was able to monopolize power: their resources were dispersed, and even the dominant actor had limited opportunities for takeover and redistribution under the conditions of a weak state. Due to the fact that the pluralism of cliques was maintained nearly by default, cartel-like deals among the Russian elite were temporary, fragile, and unstable.

These compromises deeply affected Russia's political institutions. They maintained some democratic elements, but from the perspective of the 2010s, one might consider that the turn toward full-fledged institutional decay in the 1990s was delayed and not denied. However, major troubles within Russian politics and governance became the price for maintaining this fragile status quo. For example, experts on electoral politics severely criticized Russia's nascent party system in the 1990s for its hyperfragmentation due to oversupply in all segments of the electoral market, which contributed to a very high level of electoral volatility. Nonparty politicians aligned with regional or sectoral interest groups, and they played a key role in national, and even more so in subnational electoral politics.[81] Center-regional relations in the 1990s demonstrated trends of spontaneous devolution of major leverages of power. They included broad regulatory powers, with many regional laws violating federal laws, while the regional authorities systematically failed to enforce federal laws.[82] This was also true for administrative resources, including the regions' capacity to influence appointments to federal agencies, even the security and law enforcement agencies such as the prosecutor's office and the police, as de facto control over them passed to regional political-financial groups, and even to criminal groups in a number of cases.[83] The regional authorities also possessed vast economic resources, including control over property rights and over budget flows, the subnational component of which, as a share of the total national budget, rose to almost 60 percent in 1998.[84] To a large extent, regional governments played the role of the veto actor in Russian economic policy.[85] In addition, the federal authorities lost influence over regional political regimes, and the regional elites soon transformed into veto actors in federal elections, thereby forcing the federal authorities to make new concessions with regard to further decentralization. State capture by rent-seeking oligarchs also inhibited effective policy making in various arenas. Finally, the experience of "divided government" in terms of executive-legislative relations led to the postponement or suspension of many important and much-needed laws, thus making it impossible to carry out reforms.[86] The inefficient institutional equilibrium in Russia ultimately contributed to the 1998 financial crisis.[87]

To summarize, one might argue that two of the major limits on Russian authoritarianism in the 1990s were imposed not by the array of political actors and institutions, but by two other exogenous constraints. The first was the weakness of the Russian state in the 1990s: it was faced with major decay in terms of its capacity. The second was that the fragmentation of the elite also prevented power maximization and led to constant reshuffling of winning coalitions. However, these tendencies were temporary and undesirable for many political actors. By the end of the 1990s, most of Russia's political, economic, and societal actors realized that the partial equilibrium of Russia's political regime, which had emerged by default after 1993, would be shaken and transformed. And even those actors who wanted major political changes had no clear agenda for possible directions of further reforms. In the 2000s, the demand for change was satisfied, but the remedy for the "growing pains" of the 1990s afflicted Russia's political regime with numerous chronic diseases.

CHAPTER 4

THE (IN)FAMOUS 2000s

IMPOSED CONSENSUS

ONE CAN IMAGINE THE reactions of an attentive and devoted observer of Russia's domestic politics who fell asleep, Rip van Winkle-like, in late August 1998 and awakened exactly ten years after, in late August 2008. It is quite likely that this observer would not recognize the country that had served as a focus of his/her interests, at least at first glance. He or she would be very surprised at the major ongoing changes. A deep and protracted transformation recession had been replaced by a decade of impressive economic growth and positive developmental trends of socioeconomic indicators (though these tendencies came into question once again after the global economic crisis of 2008–2009). Instead of major elite conflicts against a background of state weakness (both on nationwide and regional scales), the new hierarchical governance model known as the "power vertical" had been established, and the new dominant party, United Russia, had gained a majority of seats in the State Duma as well as in regional legislatures. The degree of mass support for Russia's political leaders and their policies had shifted from incredibly low to incredibly high numbers: the majority of Russian citizens sincerely supported the status quo regime.[1] Last but not least, over these ten years Russia twice changed its heads of state by electoral means: Vladimir Putin, who was first elected as president in 2000, left the post in March 2008, and forty-two-year-old Dmitry Medvedev, the former first deputy prime minister of the Russian government, became the third popularly elected president of the country.

After the initial shock, the observer would most likely agree with those experts who argued that Russia in the 2000s might serve as an example of a "normal" young democracy, one in the process of overcoming numerous painful pathologies and moving, if slowly and inconsistently, toward democracy and progress.[2] He or she would also agree with positive assessments of Russia among the group of countries (labeled BRIC at that time)[3] that were perceived as would-be new global leaders. It is possible that the observer could even agree with some positive views of Russia as a "success story" of post-Communist democratization, despite numerous troubles and shortcomings.[4] However, after a closer look and a more detailed analysis, the observer could not miss the fundamental deficiencies of Russia's political regime and of the rules of the game that lie at its heart. Despite the regime's legitimacy being electoral in nature, voting practices were unfree and unfair, not to mention marked by widespread electoral fraud. Similar observations would be relevant for other routines in Russian politics, such as the puppetlike parliament, which, according to the statement (mistakenly) attributed to its chair, had become "not the site for discussions";[5] powerless political parties, which played no role in government and policy formation;[6] loyal and subordinated nonstate actors, such as business agents,[7] major media outlets, and most of the NGOs;[8] arbitrary use of the economic power of the state; and a politically dependent and rubber-stamped judiciary. In addition, the ubiquitous corruption in Russia served not only as a byproduct of bad governance, but rather as a major substantive goal of ruling the country.[9] While the observer would have been familiar with many of these features since the period of the "roaring 1990s," their scope and scale dramatically increased in the 2000s. One might expect that the observer's initial optimistic impression would shift toward deep skepticism: he or she would come to the conclusion that behind the glamorous façade of fast-growing emerging power, which successfully overcame certain problems of the transition period, the fatal flaws of the political regime had become even more detrimental over the course of the decade.

What are the causes of these combinations of continuity and change in Russian politics during the 2000s, and how did they affect the evolutionary trajectory of regime change? Was this period, which some experts praised as "stability" and others condemned as "stasis," a departure from the turbulent stage of the "roaring 1990s," or rather its logical continuation? Why and how were Putin and his cronies able to monopolize political power in the country? What were the incentives and political strategies of the Russian leaders who successfully achieved their political goals? And why did Putin, who had invested tremendous efforts into authoritarian regime building in Russia, opt for a succession of leadership and transfer the presidential post to his nominee Dmitry Medvedev? The following chapter will seek answers to these and other questions.

SOURCES AND FOUNDATIONS OF IMPOSED CONSENSUS

In a sense, Putin's rise to power in 1999–2000 resulted from a chain of lucky circumstances. It so happened that Putin found himself to be the right man in the right place at the right time; unquestionably loyal to Boris Yeltsin, he was able to guarantee physical security for his patron, the latter's family members, and the country's ruling elite as a whole, and to maintain the foundations of the newly established political and economic order. Putin completed these tasks successfully. But his place in the political history of Russia went far beyond just the role of Yeltsin's successor; Putin's rule in 2000–2008 was a period of extraordinarily high economic growth on the one hand, and of tremendous monopolization of political power on the other. In this regard, Putin's first presidential terms were a sharp contrast to Yeltsin's rule, which involved a deep and protracted transformation recession and political fragmentation and major conflicts among Russia's elite.

From the perspective of formal rules of the game, the institutional legacy of Yeltsin's rule was quite favorable for his successor; it allowed Putin to monopolize political power through the effective use of the constitution, which placed vague and weak institutional constraints on presidential government and made him a dominant actor almost by default. However, these opportunities were rather limited because of three major political constraints, which Putin also inherited from his predecessor. First, due to the weakness of the Russian state, political leaders could not use just any tools to maintain their dominance; they had to be very selective in the application of both carrots and sticks to their subordinates, and only on a case-by-case basis. Second, due to the major fragmentation of Russia's elite, the winning coalition around the president was not a stable and efficient group of supporters and followers, but rather a loose conglomerate of competing cliques. Third, the degree of mass support for Russia's leaders and the regime as a whole in the 1990s was low: against the background of economic troubles, the political order was perceived as very inefficient. Thus, in 2000 there was only one way for Putin to become a dominant actor not only de jure but also de facto. He had to be more or less consistent with the ideal type of political leadership so aptly defined by Yeltsin soon after his victory in the 1993 conflict with the parliament: "somebody had to be the boss in the country; that's all there was to it."[10] But to be "the boss in the country" Putin had to accomplish three major interrelated tasks: (1) restoring and strengthening both the coercive and the redistributive capacity of the Russian state; (2) coercing various segments of the Russian elite to become subordinate to the Kremlin, and minimizing the risk of their disloyalty; and (3) achieving a stable high level of mass support for Russia's regime and its leadership. Tasks (1) and (3) first required major success on the part of the Kremlin in terms of economic development and the rearrangement of the Russian state,[11] while task (2) was first and foremost political in nature. Putin had to do more than just demonstrate who the boss in the country was through the use of coercion: after all, Yeltsin had also fired high-profile officials from time to time, and placed great pressure on his political rivals (as happened in October 1993 and almost happened in March 1996), yet he had achieved limited success at best. Putin had to establish a combination of positive and negative incentives for the Russian elite, who maintained their loyalty to the political leadership and to the political regime as a whole irrespective of the political circumstances at any given moment. In other words, Putin, as a dominant actor, had to offer his subordinates a combination of carrots and sticks that left them no choice of strategic behavior other than unconditional subordination to the Kremlin, either voluntary or involuntary. This mechanism of coordination among the elite might be considered "imposed consensus"[12] but its essence, its most vivid characteristics, were like those presented in the infamous statement from the movie *The Godfather*: "an offer he can't refuse."

Yet the crucial difference between the imposed consensus built in Russia under Vladimir Putin in the 2000s and the methods employed by the characters in *The Godfather* is important for understanding the logic of Russia's regime. While fictional Sicilian mafia characters mainly rely upon extensive and harsh use of violence (or the threat thereof), the Kremlin applied these tools vis-à-vis its rivals rather rarely and selectively (with some notable exceptions). Carrots, rather than sticks, served as the major instruments for achieving imposed consensus in Russia. The loyalty of various segments of Russia's elite to the regime, and to Putin personally, granted them access to tremendous rent-seeking opportunities in exchange for their support of the political status quo. This mechanism, based upon universal corruption, enriched the insiders of imposed consensus in terms of personal and/or corporate wealth, but it also allowed Russia's rulers to dismiss disloyal subordinated actors at any time by accusing them of abuse and/or malpractice (in most cases, this abuse and/or malpractice was very extreme). At first glance, maintaining imposed consensus by these methods was very costly and inefficient in terms of governing the country, but its benefits for the Kremlin exceeded any costs in terms of the regime's insulation from the risk of disloyalty by subordinated actors. As Bruce Bueno de Mesquita and Alastair Smith correctly note, paraphrasing Lord Acton, "if corruption empowers, then absolute corruption empowers absolutely."[13] Those subordinated actors whose status and wealth heavily depended upon their loyalty to the regime had no incentives for rebellion in any form. While Putin was able to establish and maintain imposed consensus due to his success in the recentralization of the Russian state and impressive economic growth, he also made effective use of this mechanism for his own empowerment through a biased set of systematic institutional changes. The authoritarian regime in Russia under Putin was institutionalized with the reformation of major institutions such as the separation of powers, electoral and party systems, and center-regional relationships. This strategy, as employed by the Kremlin, brought major benefits to Russia's leaders.

Despite the difference in means, the goals of Putin and his associates were nearly the same as those of Vito Corleone and his clan (namely, maximizing their own power and wealth), and it is no wonder that Putin's approach to building his winning coalition also shared some similarities to the actions of *The Godfather*'s characters. In both cases, the power of the dominant actor was based upon personal cronyism and patronage, and multiple clients had no room for maneuvers; there were no alternative patrons and no opportunities for collective action against "the boss." Unlike Yeltsin, who had had to rush to build his own winning coalition atop the ruins of the Communist regime in the 1990s using the materials available at the time, Putin enjoyed the benefits of postrevolutionary conservative stabilization in the early 2000s,[14] when he had enough time and resources to consistently and consciously develop imposed consensus. Over the eight years of his first presidency (2000–2008), Putin promoted his long-standing friends and followers to top positions in politics, government, and business, located or established secure and unimportant niches for precarious and unreliable "fellow travelers," and isolated potential rivals whose disloyalty and resistance might pose a challenge. The reshuffling of the winning coalition under Putin changed the very nature of linkages within the Russian elite. According to the analysis of elite networks in Russia produced by Philipp Chapkovski, in 2000, when Putin took power, he was, so to speak, the first among equals in terms of nodes in intraelite connections; some other key figures of Yeltsin's presidency, such as Anatoly Chubais, had comparable personal influence. However, by 2008, when Putin left presidential office for a while and transferred the role of head of state to Dmitry Medvedev, the structure of the elite networks was completely different. Putin was the only node in the center of the linkages: nobody else among the elite had personal influence even slightly comparable to that of the dominant actor.[15] In a similar vein, other authors have noted that that the rivalry among cliques within the ruling group, known in journalist slang as the struggle between "the Kremlin's towers," was replaced by a highly manageable and centralized hierarchy, which was once compared to a "solar system."[16] While the cliques within the Russian elite did not disappear, and their struggles were often rather fierce, the dominant actor was able to serve as a veto player in the decision-making process, and did not permit his subordinates to go too far in their rent-seeking behavior without being sanctioned by the boss.

Initially, Putin had two major trump cards that allowed him to overcome all real or potential rivals. First, the decisive factor behind the imposed consensus was Putin's great ability to gain electoral legitimacy, by sharp contrast with Yeltsin despite his reelection in 1996. Broadly speaking, while the incumbent vote in the presidential election of 1996 was merely *against* Zyuganov, in 2000 it was a vote *for* Putin even though he had been chosen as a designated successor by his predecessor, and the popular vote just confirmed this choice.[17] Second, after a decade of recession and painful and troubled reforms, the trends of Russian economic development had changed in more positive directions. A favorable alignment of the world market (in other words, high oil prices) allowed Putin and his government to solve—at least in the short term—such problems as the stabilization of public finances, the currency exchange rate, and the payment of pension debts and wage arrears. Under Putin, some liberal-minded economists occupied key positions in the Russian government, and the new directions in policy were oriented toward market reforms in the same way as in the early 1990s. However, the political and economic conditions for these reforms were more comfortable than they had been a decade earlier. The economic changes of the early 2000s (first and foremost, lightening the tax burden on companies and taxpayers) brought major benefits for the country but also empowered Putin,[18] making the "free rein" approach more available to him due to increasing mass support for his leadership.[19] Thus, Putin's claim to the role of dominant actor in Russian politics fell on fertile ground: not only were the Russian elite forced to be loyal to him, but Russian society at large also sincerely perceived him as "the country's boss."

However, the reshuffling of the winning coalition was a necessary but not a sufficient condition for Putin's successful domination. He not only had to replace key actors and to place his followers in prominent positions, but also to change the formal and informal rules of the game, which had partly been inherited from the Soviet period and partly established in the "roaring 1990s." This approach required not only systematic institutional changes, initiated by Putin and his associates in various domains, but also a choice of optimal sequences of moves for building and maintaining imposed consensus. The very first move in this strategic approach was to enforce loyalty among those actors who initially posed major challenges to Putin, namely the parliament, political parties, the regional elite, oligarchs, and the media.

First and foremost, Putin launched his presidency with a forceful commitment to revitalize state capacity. His programmatic rhetoric focused on the keyword "state," reminiscent of the keyword "market" in the rhetoric of liberal economists in the early 1990s, or, if you prefer, the keyword "God" in religious texts.[20] In fact, the military operation in Chechnya and the attempts to use (or

★

abuse) the security apparatus as a major tool in domestic as well as in foreign policy—whether successful or not—had a decisive impact on the remobilization of the state's administrative capacities. While one could trace the roots of this major change in the role of the state to Putin's KGB background,[21] its consequences were much broader than that implies. It meant not only the rise of the military and security elite (who had definitely played a limited role in Russian politics after the Soviet collapse in 1991), as well as their integration into a new mechanism of imposed consensus, but also the rise of security as a powerful tool for the dominant actor. Though costly in economic terms, the security-dominated revitalization of state capacity gave Putin certain opportunities to maintain a balance among the different segments of the elite and to increase his popularity. The drive to impose "order" instead of the chaos and instability of the 1990s was endorsed by the public mood and greatly appreciated by the Russian elite and the general public. But despite this drive, again, Adam Przeworski's bitter statement that "since any order is better than any disorder, any order is established,"[22] mentioned earlier, remained as accurate a description of Russia's political trajectory as in the 1990s.

The next major step toward building imposed consensus brought the Kremlin its first visible success, due to the principal change in the State Duma's loyalty vis-à-vis the executive branch. Between 1993 and 1999, the parliament (both the lower chamber and the upper house) served as a base for opposition(s) of different colors.[23] By contrast, after the 1999 parliamentary elections, the pro-Putin Unity and its allies controlled one-third of the seats, serving as a veto group at minimum.[24] At the very first parliamentary session, Unity and the Communist Party reached an informal agreement on sharing powerful positions within the Duma, with covert support for Putin's administration. The Communists secured the post of chairman of the State Duma, while pro-Putin factions gained control over important committees, and the remaining minor factions received virtually nothing. Although the minority tried to protest against these deals, it was forced to agree with the new institutional arrangements. Moreover, since the minor factions were rewarded later on with posts of secondary importance, they almost always voted in favor of Putin in the State Duma. Soon afterward, Fatherland was forced to join Unity and its allies in a formal pro-Putin grand coalition, and was taken over in the form of a merger under a new label, United Russia (formally established in December 2001). Thus, the Kremlin acquired control over 235 of the 450 parliamentary seats, a secure majority.[25] In practice, this meant that the Duma was able to pass major bills without taking the positions of any opposition parties into account. No wonder, then, that the chamber supported virtually all bills proposed by the president and his government. Finally, in 2002, the pro-Putin coalition (with the support of the minor liberal parties) removed the Communists and their allies from chairmanship of all parliamentary committees, and imposed its unilateral dominance over the State Duma.[26] After this failure, the Communists completely lost their influence in parliamentary politics, and were never able to restore their role. The consequences of this major turn in Russian parliamentary politics were rather contradictory for the State Duma. For the first time in more than ten years, the Kremlin received stable legislative support in terms of the lawmaking process. Major bills devoted to tax, labor, pensions, judicial, and other reforms were enthusiastically adopted by the State Duma thanks to the support of the pro-Putin coalition (as well as the liberals). But at the same time, the political influence of the legislature itself was reduced to rubber-stamp voting for executive proposals regardless of their contents. Kremlin loyalists unanimously voted for Putin's proposals anyway. Overall, while the lawmaking activity of the State Duma increased, its performance in terms of political representation became limited, and it lost political autonomy. It now served mostly as a site for the legal arrangement of policy decisions already adopted by the Kremlin; public discussions were not completely buried in the lower house, but they did become meaningless.[27]

This success with the State Duma was a great help to Putin, who, during the period of his ascendancy to power, was faced with the risk of disloyalty from the other influential autonomous actor, the regional elite. Their attempt to establish an alternative mechanism of coordination during the time of the 1999 parliamentary elections (namely, the Fatherland—All Russia bloc) was perceived as the major immediate threat to Putin, while their wide and unchecked powers were perceived rather negatively by the federal elite and the public. In May 2000, Putin initiated a new agenda aiming to recentralize the governance of the country. He established seven federal districts spanning Russia's entire territory (with each federal district comprising about a dozen Russian regions) and appointed envoys, who were given control over branches of federal ministries, as well as control over the use of federal property and funds from the federal budget. This policy innovation, called "federal reform," pursued the very political goal of weakening regional leaders relative to the federal center in the manner of a zero-sum game: the powers of regional leaders, who had previously enjoyed almost unlimited rule in their fiefdoms, were significantly restrained, although not eliminated.[28] Also, regional leaders were empowered due to the ex officio formation of the upper chamber of the Russian legislature, the Federation Council, composed of chief executives and heads of legislatures from each region. This model was widely criticized for inefficient lawmaking and a lack of democratic accountability.[29] Meanwhile,

Putin proposed a bill on the reform of the Federation Council, with the major goal of removing regional leaders from the upper chamber, thus abolishing their parliamentary immunity. Instead, the new members of the Federation Council were appointed by the regional governments, and most of them were professional lobbyists, absolutely loyal to the Kremlin despite (or because of) their dubious legitimacy. After this bill was implemented in 2002, the Federation Council completely lost its political relevance and turned into a rubber-stamp entity.[30] After yet another bill, Putin gained the right to dismiss regional legislatures and/or fire elected chief executives where they violated federal laws (under some circumstances, even without a court decision). In July 2000, despite sluggish resistance from the Federation Council, the federal reform bills were enthusiastically adopted by the loyal State Duma. Most of the regional leaders were forced to agree to subordinated status or face the risk of major punishments, as happened in the case of Kursk Oblast. The incumbent governor, Alexander Rutskoi, a former rival of Yeltsin and vice president in 1991–1993, was an active opponent of Putin's federal reforms. When he sought reelection in his region in October 2000, he was removed from the ballot list one day before the polls by a court decision. He was accused of violations of electoral law and abuse of incumbency (though any incumbent, including Putin, merited removal from the ballot list for the same reasons). This was a very effective lesson for regional leaders; after that, none of them openly raised his or her voice against Putin or claimed any political autonomy.

Simultaneously, Putin launched attacks on independent media, primarily TV, which had a broad audience and was able to affect public opinion, as the war of Yeltsin's succession had vividly demonstrated. Among the three national TV channels, the state-owned RTR had been politically loyal to Putin from the very beginning. In August 2000, the Kremlin changed the management of Channel 1 (ORT) with its 51 percent of state-owned shares, while the (formally) minor shareholder, tycoon Boris Berezovsky, was forced to sell his shares and leave the country after being intimidated by major criminal charges, and completely lost control over said media resource.[31] The only nonstate national television company was NTV, controlled by yet another tycoon, Vladimir Gusinsky. This channel had backed the OVR during the 1999 parliamentary elections and Yavlinsky during the 2000 presidential race, and was the only national TV channel that openly criticized Putin. In May 2000, the General Prosecutor's Office and the tax police launched a series of attacks on NTV and other Gusinsky-run media outlets. In June 2000, Gusinsky was arrested for alleged violations of law during privatization in the 1990s. Although he was later released, and emigrated to Israel, the harsh attacks on NTV continued. Taking advantage of Gusinsky-run media's excessive debts to the state-controlled joint-stock-holding Gazprom, the Kremlin gave significant aid to Gazprom in order to impose its control over NTV and replace their management. Soon after, NTV news coverage shifted in a more pro-Putin direction. Some of the former NTV journalist team, who had opposed this decision, moved to the Berezovsky-owned channel TV-6, but in late 2001 TV-6 was closed by a court decision. Again, some other media outlets, which had previously claimed independence, learned their lesson and became loyal to the Kremlin.[32]

The pattern of relationships between the state and major business leaders developed on a similar carrot-and-stick model; the Kremlin rewarded its loyalists and threatened those who claimed autonomy. The presidential administration reasserted control over the management of major state-controlled companies (first and foremost, Gazprom), while the prosecutors and the police were able to target anyone for tax evasion, violations of law during the process of privatization, and the like. In June 2000, Putin met with key representatives of large companies (both private and state-owned) at his country residence, and offered Big Business an informal deal, unofficially dubbed the "barbeque agreement."[33] The idea was that the state would not review property rights, and would maintain no favoritism toward the oligarchs, thus preventing any cronyism, while Big Business would have to remain loyal to the authorities, and not interfere in the process of political decision making. The few oligarchs (including Boris Berezovsky) who did not agree to the conditions of this informal deal soon lost their assets and were forced to leave Russia. The remaining representatives of Big Business in Russia simply had no choice under the circumstances. To a certain degree, the barbeque agreement marked a new stage in state-business relationships: the Russian state took a step toward the oligarchs in promoting more favorable conditions for business. Big Business, in its turn, while it did not stop lobbying for its interests in the Russian parliament and in regional legislatures, accepted the institutional arrangements developed by the Kremlin. Furthermore, Big Business actively supported a number of Putin's initiatives, including the recentralization of the state, which destroyed local barriers to business development and was directed toward the formation of a common national Russian market.[34] The Kremlin recognized major associations of Russian entrepreneurs as official junior partners in a framework of what appeared to be a corporatist model of interaction between the state and interest groups in Russia,[35] while business leaders declared their loyalty to the Kremlin.

The same style of relationships between the state and nonstate actors was typical for the "third-sector" NGOs; most of them received funding from the state under the patronage of the presidential administration, and shifted their criticism from the regime as such to specific examples of its policies. In short, in the early 2000s virtually all actors in Russia expressed their loyalty to Putin, and agreed to subordinated status either voluntarily or under pressure.

Thus, during the very first years of his presidency, Putin attained major success in building his political monopoly. The imposed consensus of the Russian elite under Putin was based on the following principles: (1) an implicit taboo on open political contestation among the federal elite (in other words, a taboo on electoral democracy as such); (2) an informal agreement between the dominant and subordinated actors on loyalty in exchange for access to resources and rents; (3) the prevalence of informal and actor-specific particularistic rules of the game over formal and universal norms in the political arena. The latter principle fits the logic of the "dictatorship of law" announced by Putin as a top priority of his political program in July 2000. In fact, the dictatorship of law is very much dissimilar to the principle of the rule of law:[36] it is based on the purely instrumental use of formal institutions, or legal norms, as tools and means of coercion by the dominant actor toward outsiders to the imposed consensus (as in the cases of Gusinsky or Rutskoi). This biased set of rules and norms, as well as their selective enforcement by the coercive apparatus of the state, became an integral part of imposed consensus. It did not lead to the emergence of the rule of law, but rather served as a smokescreen for informal governance[37] based upon the arbitrary rule of the Kremlin and its loyalists.[38] These tools proved to be powerful means for achieving Kremlin's goals, and the ruling group used them effectively in the next stages of building and maintaining imposed consensus.

THE PARTY OF POWER AND THE POWER VERTICAL: FROM COMPETITION TO HIERARCHY

All rulers in the world would like to govern their respective countries without checks and balances. In established regimes, however, they are faced with constraints based upon institutions or other influential actors (both domestic and international). It is no surprise that leaders in newly established states and nations are sometimes more successful in authoritarian regime building from scratch if they are able to avoid or remove these constraints and eliminate alternatives to their governments. But why are some autocrats more successful than others in this respect? Comparative studies of authoritarianism offer a useful distinction between personalist, party-based, and military authoritarian regimes, which form on different power bases and employ different strategies of dominance. Upon the collapse of the Soviet Union, post-Soviet states demonstrated a wide spectrum of personalist authoritarian regimes, although some of them were destroyed in 2003–2005 during the wave of so-called "color revolutions" in Georgia, Ukraine, and Kyrgyzstan. Unlike its neighbors,

Russia exhibited a rather distinctive pattern of authoritarian regime building. While Yeltsin's strategy in the 1990s was largely personalist, despite several unsuccessful attempts to establish pro-Kremlin parties of power,[39] Russia's authoritarian turn under Putin in the 2000s coincided with the spectacular rise of United Russia, the party of power[40] that dominated the electoral and parliamentary arenas by the end of Putin's rule. Over the course of the 2000s, the Kremlin invested deliberate and thorough effort into building a dominant party, which was then able to gain majorities in national and subnational legislatures and greatly contributed to the continuity of Russia's authoritarian regime beyond the leadership succession in 2008.[41] Given that party-based authoritarian regimes are usually the longest-lived in comparison with personalist and military regimes, at first sight this Kremlin strategy of dominant party building seems very rational in the long term, but in the 2010s it proved to be short-lived.

Why did the Kremlin choose this strategy after Putin's unexpected rise to power in 1999–2000? To a great extent, this choice was driven by having learned from Russia's own experience under Yeltsin as well as from other post-Soviet states. Yeltsin's personalist rule was highly unpopular in the eyes of Russia's citizens due to its poor performance, and was faced with a deeply fragmented elite organized around multiple cliques of oligarchs and regional leaders.[42] This arrangement left Yeltsin room to maneuver using "divide and conquer" strategies, but it was rather risky in terms of leadership succession, as the experience of some post-Soviet states (especially the Ukrainian "Orange Revolution") indicates.[43] In Russia, the presidential turnover in 1999–2000 also produced a shift in loyalty among the formerly subordinated elite, and the rise of the loose Fatherland–All Russia coalition on the eve of the parliamentary and presidential elections threatened the very survival of Yeltsin and his entourage. Even though on this occasion the Kremlin had been able to avoid this outcome with successful electoral campaigning and by manufacturing its own political vehicle, Unity,[44] the post-Yeltsin elite had little intention of falling into the same trap. Beyond these short-term considerations, Putin and his associates sought to establish long-term foundations for the stability and continuity of their regime. This task implied that they had to prevent any opportunities for coordinated opposition among the elite through the demolition and/or cooptation of all independent organizational entities (such as parties, interest groups, NGOs, and the media) and to ensure the long-term loyalty of the elite and the masses to the status quo regime, irrespective of its performance, the personal qualities of the leadership, and so forth.

From this perspective, a version of the personalist authoritarian regime that had emerged in Russia by the early 2000s would be the least useful instrument, because regimes of this kind are the most vulnerable to losing their equilibrium compared to other forms of authoritarianism. Thus, Russia's rulers had to choose between two different strategies for long-term authoritarian regime building. One option was a "hard" version of personalist authoritarianism, in the manner of Belarus or Turkmenistan, which would base the loyalty of the elite and society at large on the intense use of violence, coercion, and intimidation. But this strategy would be costly for the Kremlin; quite apart from the need for huge investment in a large-scale coercion apparatus to diminish the threat of major disobedience, such regimes could be faced with the danger of international isolation and political turmoil. Also, given the fact that in hard personalist authoritarian regimes the elite could become victims of repression more often than ordinary citizens, Russia's rulers and subordinated members of the winning coalition had little incentive to launch such a risky enterprise. In Robert Dahl's terms, in Russia's post-Communist setting the costs of repression were incredibly high.[45] A "soft," nonrepressive party-based authoritarian regime looked much more attractive as an alternative for both the Kremlin and the various segments of the Russian elite. It could successfully solve three major problems: the establishment and maintenance of monopolist political control by the rulers, the prevention of alternative coordination among the elite, and the building of long-term loyalty among the elite and the public, while being less coercive and thus less costly for the Kremlin than the hard version of personalist authoritarianism. Indeed, it could lower the regime's costs of tolerating dissent without the risk of losing power due to open political competition.[46] In addition, a soft party-based authoritarianism would be very functional and instrumental for rulers in three other respects: (1) it could enhance the regime's legitimacy through efficient political patronage and the discouragement of alternatives to the status quo;[47] (2) it could effectively and flexibly perform policy adoption and implementation due to the nonideological nature of the dominant party;[48] (3) it would maintain elite loyalty through the mutual reinforcement of both bureaucratic and political mechanisms of control.

While the choice of this strategy for authoritarian regime building in Russia might bring long-term and large-scale benefits to the Kremlin, it also required a significant amount of political investment with a relatively long compensation period. Even though the political environment in Russia in the early 2000s was very advantageous for the Kremlin's authoritarian regime building due to the recentralization of the Russian state, unprecedented economic growth, and the monopolization of state control over major economic assets, political and institutional engineering as well as organizational efforts were nevertheless vital for this venture. The Kremlin had to go beyond avoiding the risk of disloyalty from subordinated actors: it had to offer them full-fledged political and institutional integration into a new self-enforcing hierarchy of decision making led by the dominant actor. The need to transform imposed consensus into a more sustainable mechanism of control over political actors and society at large became more acute after the wave of color revolutions in Georgia, Ukraine, and Kyrgyzstan in 2003–2005. The Kremlin's new strategy included three major components:

(1) Cooptation of subnational "political machines" controlled by regional and local chief executives into a nationwide "echelon" controlled by the Kremlin;[49]

(2) Building a highly controlled party system that could deliver the electoral results desired by the Kremlin, irrespective of the preferences of Russian voters, and leaving both the elite and the voters with no choices unwanted by the Kremlin;

(3) The return of control over major resources and leverages in the economic arena to the state apparatus, thus increasing opportunities for rent-seeking for the regime's loyalists, and decreasing the chances for alternative coordination of real and/or potential opposition.[50]

Although the recentralization of the Russian state, which was launched by Putin in 2000 and dubbed "federal reform" in Russian political jargon, was a great help in restoring the Kremlin's political control over the regional elite, its results were rather partial and incomplete. The restoration of the administrative capacity of the central state, the centralization of the tax system, and the reduction of financial and other resources controlled by regional leaders, as well as the encroachment of nationwide companies into local markets (previously captured by regional bosses and their followers), served as major sticks. The Kremlin was also able to support the reforms with tempting carrots of federal transfers and federal investment projects. Still, despite the recentralization of the Russian state (or perhaps because of it), most of the regional chief executives (hereafter, governors)[51] secured or even strengthened their control over their respective areas in the early 2000s, due to the successful cooptation or sometimes coercion of autonomous subnational political and economic actors. As Grigorii V. Golosov has convincingly demonstrated, while in 1995–1999 regional incumbents won 45 out of 88 gubernatorial elections, in 1999–2003 they retained their posts after 59 out of 88 regional elections; moreover, incumbents lost only 16 gubernatorial races, and abstained from running in 13 electoral campaigns.[52] In some cases the Kremlin had such limited chances of imposing its control over political and economic developments in given regions that it was forced to employ selective individ-

★

ual bargaining with influential regional chief executives. These negotiations led to various outcomes, such as the incumbent's survival and the preservation of the regional political status quo in exchange for the federal election results desired by the Kremlin (as was the case in Bashkortostan in 2003), or Kremlin-driven promotion of the regional governor to a top post in Moscow, with subsequent redistribution of regional power and/or property in favor of the Kremlin. The latter scenario was implemented in Yakutia (Sakha), where the long-standing incumbent declined to participate in new chief executive elections, and received the post of deputy chair of the Federation Council. The Kremlin's nominee won the race, and control over the republic's major asset, its diamond industry, was taken out of hands of the local ethnic elite and given to the central government. In a similar fashion, the governors of Primorsky Krai and St. Petersburg, who had been widely criticized for their inefficiency, left their posts for appointments as federal ministers, and were later replaced by Kremlin-backed candidates.[53] Selective use of sanctions (as in the case of Rutskoi) complemented the Kremlin's practices of individual bargaining with the regional elite; the federal authorities were able to achieve desirable results with minimal agency costs. This approach was very much in line with the implementation of the dictatorship of law, which became nearly universal in the early 2000s;[54] the recentralization of the Russian state was not an exception. Nevertheless, despite the extensive use of administrative tools of control, the Kremlin also actively used elections and political parties to diminish and further eliminate regionalism from Russia's political arena and to achieve vertical integration of subnational politics under its own control.

In 2001, the federal law "On Political Parties" directly prohibited the registration of regional parties, which by and large had previously served as political machines controlled by the regional elites. By that time, most regional legislative elections were largely nonpartisan.[55] After 2003, the Kremlin and the State Duma launched a reform of regional electoral systems in order to improve United Russia's performance in regional legislatures and win centralized political control over the periphery; at least half of the seats were designated for federal political parties. Despite the fact that in 2003–2004 United Russia gained a significant share of votes in many regional legislative elections, and established visible representation in many regional assemblies, this was only a limited success for the party of power; its local branches achieved good results if they were captured by regional governors and served merely as their (rather than the Kremlin's) political vehicle.[56] In addition, governors preferred not to put all their eggs into one basket, and often based their support on parties other than United Russia or on nonparty entities. Thus, reform of regional electoral systems brought partial and inconclusive results in terms of political competitiveness; Perm-based political scientist Petr Panov correctly noted that previously authoritarian regions became even more authoritarian and previously competitive regions remained competitive.[57] As comparative analysis of subnational authoritarian regimes predicts, the Kremlin-driven advancement of party competition in subnational politics could have promoted electoral contestation, and in the medium term undermined the monopoly of regional political machines controlled by the governors.[58] However, such an outcome was hardly desirable for the Kremlin; after all, the federal authorities were mostly interested in preserving and strengthening their own political power, especially in anticipation of the coming national elections in 2007–2008. But this result could only be achieved with the integration of subnational political machines into a nationwide party of power.

The Kremlin adopted the decision to abolish the popular election of regional governors in September 2004 more or less by chance (as a response to a terrorist attack on a school in a small town in North Ossetia), but it was a logical conclusion of the process of political recentralization. The institutionalization of the hierarchy of top-down appointments of regional chief executives (later on extended to many, but not all, major cities) integrated subnational administrations into a centralized power vertical. The Kremlin reduced the political uncertainty of competitive elections in the regions to zero, and reduced its own agency costs. After 2005, regional chief executives were de facto appointed, the institutional arrangements in the regions were more or less unified, and the diversity of regional political regimes was diminished. While in the 1990s their varieties were so many that one could consider regional political regimes and patterns of governance as phenomena more or less autonomous from the federal center,[59] in the 2000s the process of Kremlin-induced bureaucratic rationalization of the rules of the game put an end to this variation. But the centralized imposition of these rules did little to improve the transparency and quality of governance in the most nondemocratic regions of Russia, such as Bashkortostan. Rather, it distorted democratic institutions in the most advanced regions, such as Perm Krai. Some expert analyses came to the conclusion that the average level of democratic credentials of Russian regions had declined by 2005 due to the major nondemocratic drift of the previously politically open and transparent regions.[60] But from the Kremlin's viewpoint, the abolishment of gubernatorial elections brought desirable results: after 2005, United Russia's performance in regional elections greatly improved. Still, in terms of personnel the turn to de facto appointment of regional chief executives changed little; in 2005–2007, in most of the regions, previous governors were reappointed to perform their job.[61] This political continuity was to some extent a side effect of the shortage of capable and experienced officials available to the Kremlin, but also resulted from the Kremlin's risk-aversive strategy, which involved preservation of the status quo in center-regional relations whenever possible. Nevertheless, if one were to leave aside the problems of the ethnic regions of the North Caucasus (which had no plausible solution irrespective of the political centralization of the Russian state), all other Russian regions became completely subordinated to the Kremlin in political, economic, and administrative terms.

In terms of building a Kremlin-controlled party system, the newborn party of power, United Russia, gained a majority in the State Duma from its very emergence, and unequivocally supported virtually all the bills proposed by Putin and his government.[62] Thus, United Russia established its parliamentary dominance. In the December 2003 State Duma elections, the United Russia party list received only 37.6 percent of votes, but the implicit coalition policy of the party of power in single-member districts and further institutional changes to internal parliamentary rules led to the formation of a "manufactured supermajority." United Russia soon acquired more than two-thirds of the seats in the national legislature.[63] Not only was its parliamentary dominance strengthened, but alternatives to United Russia became irrelevant.

The introduction of de facto appointment of regional chief executives changed the bargaining power of the Kremlin vis-à-vis regional leaders, and presented a new solution to the problem of the mutual commitments of the federal and regional elite, which had previously been a major obstacle to turning United Russia into a nationwide dominant party. But after the abolition of gubernatorial elections in early 2005, the incentives were reversed; the appointment and further survival of regional chief executives largely depended on their loyalty to United Russia.[64] It is thus unsurprising that most of them, either willingly or reluctantly, joined the ranks of the party of power. Institutional changes left no room for the diversification of regional governors' political investments: they were forced to be loyal only to United Russia. During the 2007 State Duma elections, 65 out of 85 regional chief executives joined United Russia's list, in a sharp contrast to the 2003 parliamentary elections, where only 39 governors had done so. The Kremlin, in turn, was ready to secure the regional leaders' jobs as long as they were able to deliver votes in both federal and regional elections.[65] The capacity to control the regional electoral process at any cost was the most important resource for the survival of regional chief executives until the end of Putin's first presidency, often irrespective of their performance in other areas. The new formula for political compromise in center-regional relations, "the preservation of the gubernatorial power monopoly in exchange for the 'right' voting results,"[66] became a major element of Russia's political regime. United Russia, in turn, established majorities in almost all regional legislatures and by 2007 achieved regional dominance; with a few exceptions, regional politics no longer produced meaningful alternatives to United Russia.

In 2003, the Kremlin initiated a new wave of institutional changes, which were oriented toward further shrinking the field of party competition. The electoral threshold for parliamentary representation in the State Duma and most regional legislatures increased from 5 percent to 7 percent. The new federal law on political parties dramatically toughened the organizational and membership requirements for political parties, which had to reregister according to the new conditions with no fewer than 50,000 members in two-thirds of Russian regions. This reform significantly raised the entry barrier to Russia's market of party politics: the formation of new political parties became extraordinarily difficult, while only 15 out of the 46 previously existing Russian parties managed to squeeze in according to these rules by 2007 and were able to participate in the December 2007 State Duma election. Furthermore, preelection party coalitions (blocs) were prohibited altogether from 2005, rendering the survival of small party entities very problematic.[67] Finally, the reform of the State Duma election rules in 2007 (the shift from a mixed electoral system to closed party list representation) not only increased United Russia's own party discipline and unequivocal loyalty to the Kremlin,[68] but also helped the party of power to gain electoral dominance during the 2007 parliamentary elections, when the party received 64.3 percent of the votes. While many factors, ranging from unfair campaigns to the high approval rate of Russia's president Vladimir Putin, ensured United Russia's success, no other party could present a viable alternative.

Most political parties worldwide are created by politicians in order to gain public office through the popular vote. The genesis of Russia's parties of power was fundamentally different: United Russia was crafted by top officials in order to maximize their control over political arenas.[69] This distinction undoubtedly affected the major features of Russia's party of power in three important areas—party organization, party ideology, and party government. In terms of party organization, the United Russia model could be best described as Kremlin-based "external governance," independent from official party leadership. While the party officials were merely in charge of everyday routine management, key Kremlin officials served as extraparty rulers who controlled strategic decision making.[70] Thus, the party of power could be compared to a firm whose assets were owned not by its management but by a large multisectoral holding company, which hired its management and personnel and could easily replace them from time to time. From the perspective of corporate control and management within the party, the external governance model was

★

quite efficient; it soon turned the party of power into a highly disciplined and centralized organization. No internal dissent or factionalism was tolerated, and even discussion within the party was strictly regulated by the Kremlin.

The genesis of the party of power also affected its lack of ideology. Top state officials needed United Russia as an instrument for the preservation of the status quo, but not as an instrument of political change. Accordingly, United Russia openly and deliberately manifested its loyalty to Russia's political regime and to Putin personally, while its position on major policy issues remained vague and undefined. During the 2007 State Duma election campaign, the major slogan of United Russia was "Vote for Putin's Plan!" (*Golosui za plan Putina!*) without any specific reference to the content of this "plan." Some critics have argued that party ideology is necessary for long-term regime maintenance;[71] however, in the short term, United Russia's nonideology was an asset rather than a liability, because it contributed to the success of the party of power. Against the background of a decline in transitional uncertainty, the role of ideology as a product on the Russian electoral market has shrunk. The lack of ideology gave United Russia wide room for political maneuver, unlike the fragmented opposition. Indeed, the large policy distance between these parties created major obstacles to the formation of an anti-regime negative consensus coalition, which would include the Communists on the one hand and liberals on the other.[72] From a comparative perspective, opposition parties under dominant party regimes also prefer the preservation of the status quo (i.e., the continuity of dominant party rule) rather than their ideologically distant counterparts breaking through into power;[73] Russia was no exception here.

Finally, the genesis of the party of power doomed it to play a subordinate role in policy adoption and implementation; the top Kremlin officials needed party politicians as obedient followers rather than as autonomous partners. This produced a great asymmetry in terms of party government; while top federal and especially regional executive officials joined United Russia due to their status, rank-and-file party members were only occasionally rewarded with executive posts of secondary importance, based on their personal fortunes rather than party affiliation. Moreover, beyond the parliamentary and electoral arenas, the role of the party of power remained rather limited despite the aspirations of United Russia leaders. Even those members of the cabinet of ministers who joined United Russia held their posts by subordination to the president rather than to the party, and by no means exercised party influence on governmental policies. On the contrary, it was the party of power that pushed governmental policy through the State Duma and was forced to take up the challenge of political responsibility for unpopular policies, such as the social benefits reform launched in January 2005 (after this reform, party performance in regional legislative elections was the lowest ever).[74] United Russia's negligible effect on policy making was to a large degree a byproduct of Russia's institutional design and its notoriously overwhelming presidential power, which diminished the role of other actors and agencies.[75] Putin's approach to government and policy making was ostensibly technocratic, leaving little room for party politics. These features of United Russia as a dominant party—external governance, nonideology, and its secondary role in policy making—produced certain consequences for Russia's political regime. In sharp contrast to the experience of Communist rule, which was best characterized as a "party-state" regime, the new electoral authoritarianism could be labeled "state-party"; not only did the dominant party itself informally serve as a branch of the presidential administration, but in Russia the very party system as such performed the same role.[76]

Post-Communist Russia exhibited a strong record of active involvement of top executive officials not only in the building of dominant parties, but also in the building of loyal and/or fake alternatives to them in the form of Kremlin satellites. These Kremlin-driven "projects" served two basic—and not mutually exclusive—goals: (1) to form a reserve or substitute for the party of power and avoid placing too many eggs in one basket (especially given the background of transitional uncertainty), and (2) to weaken the oppositions of various colors by splitting their votes with spoiler parties.[77] In the 2000s, the Kremlin, facing an oversupply of potential satellite parties, was very active in "inventing the opposition." Under its auspices, small leftist and nationalist parties established the Motherland ("Rodina") coalition before the 2003 elections, led by popular politicians Dmitri Rogozin and Sergei Glaziev. Its well-funded and much-publicized campaign, carried out with nationalist and populist slogans, was oriented toward diluting the Communist vote, and its electoral success exceeded initial expectations: Motherland won 9.1 percent of the eligible vote and established a parliamentary party in the State Duma. Soon after this, however, Motherland's leaders escaped the Kremlin's control; Glaziev ran in the presidential election of March 2004 without permission, and was expelled from the party's ranks. Aggressive nationalist campaigning by Rogozin and his party led to Motherland being denied registration in several regional legislative elections. Finally, in 2006, Rogozin was forced to resign from his post as party leader.[78] Motherland's precipitous rise and fall led the Kremlin into another venture, a satellite party intended to act both as a reserve to the party of power and to split the Communist vote. In 2006, the Kremlin initiated the merger of three previously established satellite parties (including the post-Rogozin Motherland) and the formation of a new party, A Just Russia (Spravedlivaya

Rossiya), which declared a leftist policy position and employed extensive so-cialist rhetoric. This was perceived as a major step toward the establishment of a "managed" two-party system in Russia. Vladislav Surkov, the chief Kremlin political strategist, even announced that while United Russia should remain the major Kremlin vehicle, or its "right leg," Just Russia would act as its substi-tute, like a "left leg," "if the right leg becomes numb." On the eve of the 2007 State Duma elections, polls showed strong potential for electoral support for Just Russia, and the "left leg" party became a Noah's Ark for many politicians with a previous record of partisanship, ranging from Communists to liberals.

Russia's experience of satellite party building in the 2000s was not so unique from a comparative perspective of authoritarian regimes. Besides some other post-Soviet states, such as Ukraine under Leonid Kuchma,[79] one might recall certain Communist regimes in Eastern Europe, which es-tablished loyal peasant or Christian parties in Poland and East Germany as channels of political control over targeted social milieus. Likewise, the Mexican party-based authoritarian regime preferred cooptation over repres-sion in dealing with organized dissent.[80] It also used various channels to pro-mote a number of satellite parties, which aimed to take votes from the real opposition, especially during the process of the PRI's decline in the 1980s and 1990s.[81] However, in Russia, shrinking party competition provided additional incentives for satellite parties. Party politicians outside United Russia were faced with a difficult choice between complete subordination and (relative) autonomy from the Kremlin; in fact, this was a choice between survival and possible extinction. The crisis faced by the liberal parties, such as the Union of Right Forces (which ceased to exist by 2008) and Yabloko (which lost rep-resentation in the State Duma and in regional assemblies), was the most vivid example of the latter threat.

According to several commentators' assessments, the barbeque agreement, which provided a balance of power between the state and Big Business, had a favorable effect both on the policy of economic reforms and on the preserva-tion of political pluralism in Russia during the 2000–2003 period. However, this equilibrium was brought about only by ad hoc arrangements rather than structure-induced, let alone based on formal institutional guarantees.[82] As the barbecue agreement was only a tacit deal, its conditions could easily be revised unilaterally by the Kremlin.[83] The Russian authorities had strong in-centives for such revisions based on both political and economic factors. In economic terms, the rapid rise in world oil prices and the increase of reve-nues from resource rent in the 2000s (especially compared with the 1990s) against the background of the significant increase in the coercive capacity of the Russian state pushed the Russian authorities into a statist economic policy[84] and into re-examining the formal and informal rules of the game in their relations with business.[85] Under these conditions, the further extension of the Kremlin's political monopoly on the economic arena became the logical next step for the Russian authorities, especially as the idea of revising the outcomes of privatization and restoring the predominance of state ownership also had significant support in Russian society.[86] A major revision of property rights in this sense looked like a very rational decision from the Kremlin's perspective, especially in the wake of the 2003 parliamentary election campaign.

On October 25, 2003, Mikhail Khodorkovsky, the majority owner and CEO of Yukos, the biggest Russian private oil company, was arrested on charges of tax evasion and later given a long jail sentence. According to a number of observers, the basic reasons for his arrest were purely political in nature. They were connected with Khodorkovsky's aspiration to lobby his interests in the parliament, and his support at elections of various parties whose lists included his protégés, and also with his intentions to sell his stakes in Yukos to American oil companies (possible buyers named were Chevron and Conoco Phillips), as well as his plans to actively participate in politics himself.[87] Khodorkovsky's arrest soon resulted in Yukos's collapse: the key company shares were sold to pay off its debts. At the same time, the Russian authorities used opaque financial schemes and acted through dummy intermediaries to ensure that major assets of producing and processing enterprises previously belonging to Yukos were placed under the control of the state oil company Rosneft, where the board of directors was headed by Putin's close ally Igor Sechin. At the same time, Yukos's assets were acquired by Rosneft far below their market price. Anders Aslund and Vadim Volkov, analyzing the fate of the Russian oligarchs of the early twenty-first century by comparison with American "robber barons" in the early twentieth century, noted the fundamental differences in the logic of antioligarchic campaigns in the Russian case. As a result of the Yukos affair, the outcome of the conflict between business and the Russian state was not just the bankruptcy and subsequent decay of the oligarchs, initiated by the authorities (as in the case of Standard Oil in the United States, for example), but also a fundamental revision of property rights that was launched in subsequent years.[88] In fact, the Yukos affair was a turning point in the relationship between the Russian state and business, marking a major change from the temporary balance of the barbeque agreement to "business capture" by the Russian state, and the further rise of the "predatory state" model in Russian state-business relationships.[89] In practice, this model meant that state officials gained plenty of opportunities for rent-seeking due to the imposition of direct and/or indirect control over major assets and their owners, and were able to use them as cash cows both for state-directed purposes (such as extraordinary large-scale corporate philanthropy)[90] and for private gains. The Yukos affair greatly contributed to the process of revision of property rights and to the creeping nationalization of a number of profitable assets in various sectors of Russian economy, while Putin's followers became the key beneficiaries of this process.[91]

To summarize, one should evaluate the strategy of Russia's authoritarian regime building under Putin's first presidency in the 2000s as a success story for the Kremlin. By 2007, none of political actors in the country were able to resist Putin. Opposition political parties had been pushed into narrow niches, if not ghettos, and were even regarded as a "dying species".[92] their presence in federal and regional legislatures was symbolic, their capacity for mobilization was weak, and their public support was low. Nonpartisan opposition politics was even less meaningful: regular and loud antisystem protest gatherings in Moscow and other cities brought together mere hundreds of activists, who were justly perceived as an irrelevant minority. And even though numerous instances of local protests, ranging from environmental to cultural protection movements, mushroomed across the country, these movements aimed to avoid politicization of their activism at any cost, and preferred to deal with specific issues rather than blaming the regime as such (as otherwise their goals had zero chance of success).[93] After the Yukos affair, oligarchs were ready to transfer their assets to the Kremlin upon request in exchange for personal freedom and well-being, and tended to avoid any political accent to their business: indeed, they were able to develop their companies successfully due to close connections with federal and regional officialdom. The major media (especially TV) were under the direct or indirect control of the Kremlin, and independent and/or oppositional publications and Internet resources were limited to the relatively narrow niches of their politicized audiences. At the same time, the power vertical went from the regions down to cities and towns, especially after the abolition of popular mayoral elections in some big cities and further shrinking of the political and economic autonomy of local governments.[94] To summarize, the efforts of authoritarian regime building in Russia in the 2000s brought numerous substantive changes, which had a major impact on further political developments.

AUTHORITARIAN REGIME BUILDING: TOWARD AN "INSTITUTIONAL TRAP"

At first glance, the wave of political and institutional changes of the 2000s in Russia should have made the dream of some Kremlin strategists, that of the restoration of a "good Soviet Union," into reality. The Russian authoritarian regime in many ways resembled certain political arrangements of the power monopoly of the Soviet era, without the major deficiencies of the Communist regime. Indeed, centrally managed control over major Russian actors replaced the ungovernable political autonomy that actors had had in the 1990s; the uncertainty of electoral competition was eradicated under unfree and unfair elections; subnational authorities became integrated into the hierarchy of the "power vertical"; and local markets were to some degree taken over by vertically integrated state-owned companies led by Gazprom. Russia's regions and cities were governed by officials de facto appointed from the center, with the formal approval of the subnational elite. Even the forms of "state corporatism" implemented both nationwide and subnationally were similar to that which was present during the Communist period.[95] However, United Russia was not a new reincarnation of the Communist Party, the role of Gazprom and other large companies was very different from the unilateral dominance displayed by Soviet branch ministries, and governors and city mayors did not become "post-Soviet prefects."[96] Although the noncompetitive nature of the political regime and the monopolist economy, based on resource rents, demonstrated striking similarities between the patterns of Soviet and post-Soviet politics, the differences were also crucial. They related to the very heart of the nature of the post-Soviet regime in Russia, the rationale behind its public support, and the nature of its legitimacy, and this is why the claim of the "Sovietization" of politics in post-Soviet Russia is superficial and misleading.[97]

The Soviet authoritarian regime employed "elections without choice," noncompetitive and almost meaningless voting only for the approved candidates, much as in many "classical" authoritarian regimes.[98] Post-Soviet Russian authoritarianism not only was unable to avoid elections, but used this institution as the source of its legitimacy; Putin (like Yeltsin before him) based his rule upon a popular mandate received from the voters. Moreover, elections as such became an unavoidable element of Russian politics, and their results in many ways reflected mass political preferences as well as political formations among the elite. But the very nature of national elections (at least, after 1996 Yeltsin's reelection bid) did not imply any democratic uncertainty: in other words, there was no election outcome that had not been set up by the ruling group well in advance. On the contrary, election outcomes were designed before polls, and the act of voting served as formal voter approval of the decisions taken by the Kremlin. Thus, voter approval did not affect the political regime, government formation or policy making. This was the logic of electoral authoritarianism, which is based upon deliberately designed unfair rules of the game and their heavily biased implementation at all stages of campaigning (including, but not limited to, electoral fraud). This mode of elections under authoritarianism was a typical instance of "virtual politics," as Andrew Wilson labeled this phenomenon (while he called it post-Soviet "faking democracy," it was in fact neither democracy nor specifically post-Soviet).[99] It develops as a byproduct of: (1) the power monopoly of resourceful political elite; (2) the passivity of voters; (3) the control of the rulers over major information streams; (4) the lack of international influence on the conduct of elections. All these conditions for successful authoritarian elections were already in place in Russia in the 1990s, and in the 2000s their influence became even more visible.

Meanwhile, the means of restraining political competition were very different in various electoral authoritarian regimes. Some authoritarian rulers widely employ "hard" methods of exclusion of their rivals from electoral contest (such as selective denial of the registration of candidates and/or party lists in the run-up to campaigns, and/or widespread electoral fraud). But most authoritarian regimes preferred to use (or, rather, abuse) "soft" methods of controlling authoritarian elections. These methods involved blatantly unequal access of candidates and parties to media and political funding, and full-fledged mobilization of the state apparatus to secure the rulers' electoral victory.[100] Although in both instances authoritarian elections are unfair, their consequences are very different. Reliance primarily upon hard methods is a rather risky strategy because it may damage the regime's legitimacy, especially if and when the ruling groups are unable to meet all four above-mentioned conditions. In the case of mass antiregime protests, it could even ruin authoritarian rule, if the costs of coercion of the opposition (both before and after the polls) become excessive. Mass electoral fraud during voting in the cases of Serbia (2000), Georgia (2003), Ukraine (2005), and Kyrgyzstan (2005) contributed to the breakdown of authoritarian regimes against a background of opposition-led mass mobilization. Conversely, soft methods of restraining political competition impose severe costs on the ruling groups during electoral campaigns and polling days, but they allow them to decrease the risk of delegitimation, not to mention the risk of power loss. It is thus natural that that the rulers of electoral authoritarian regimes *ceteris paribus* prefer soft methods over hard ones.

The Russian electoral authoritarian regime in the 2000s was no exception. Although the scope of electoral fraud in Russia, according to numerous studies, became more widespread and its geographical area broadened over time,[101] these issues of Russian electoral politics were more or less the tip of the iceberg. Other institutional and political factors affected the outcomes of authoritarian elections to a greater degree. They included: (1) prohibitively high entry barriers for parties and candidates; (2) one-sided and biased media coverage of elections; (3) direct and indirect state funding of incumbents' electoral campaigns, and informal control over the political funding of other parties and candidates; (4) systematic use of the state apparatus and of the public sector as a whole for incumbents' campaigns, as well as to inhibit opposition campaigns; and (5) biased resolution of election disputes in favor of incumbents. These became undeniable features of elections in 2000s Russia, being typical entries from the broad "menu of manipulations" of many electoral authoritarian regimes in the world.[102]

Some experts even considered the actual voting under Russia's electoral authoritarian regimes not to be elections (even unfair ones), but rather, "electionlike events" which had no electoral relevance.[103] But even without going that far, one should recognize that the regular holding of unfree and unfair elections was greatly useful for the Kremlin in several respects. First, they legitimized the status quo political regime, as in the case of the 2004 presidential elections, when Putin received 71 percent of the vote without any meaningful competition. Second, they legitimized all the ruling group's policy directions, irrespective of voter preferences. Third, they served as a mechanism for elite turnover, not via political competition but through appointing prospective winners of elections long before polling day (similarly to Putin's appointment for the 2000 elections, and later, Medvedev's for the 2008 elections). These electoral practices differed widely from both late-Soviet "elections without choice" and the democratic standards of free and fair elections, and maintained Russia's authoritarian regime as long as the imposed consensus of the elite was effectively managed by the Kremlin and the formal and informal rules of the game preserved a nondemocratic equilibrium.

In sum, by the end of Putin's second term, Russia's rulers were able to accomplish their goals of consolidating an authoritarian regime and successfully building its major institutions, an institutional "core" of the Russian political regime.[104] These institutions are the following: (1) a unilateral presidential monopoly on adopting key political decisions (the regime's personalism); (2) a taboo on open electoral competition among the elite, with unfree and unfair elections (electoral authoritarianism); and (3) de facto hierarchical subordination of regional and local authorities to the central government (the power vertical).

These institutional arrangements, which declared a leftist policy position and are clearly imperfect because for several reasons: their inherent and notorious inefficiency due to extremely high corruption; hidden but fairly stiff competition between interest groups ("the Kremlin towers") for rent access and resource redistribution; and, eventually, the ruling groups' inability to implement policies that could challenge the current equilibrium, which also explains the ineffective attempts at authoritarian modernization of Russia. Nevertheless, if the rules of the game do not fully "serve the interests of those with the bargaining power to devise new rules,"[105] to use Douglas North's well-known phrase, they at least avoid infringing upon those interests today.

However, behind the façade of the political equilibrium, bitter disappointment and growing discontent with the current status quo regime did emerge (as clearly indicated by the 2008 survey of Russia's elite).[106] However, political support of the status quo is not the only reason to maintain political equilibrium. The alternatives to the status quo may look even more unattractive or unrealistic; more importantly, the costs of transition from the existing political order to something else seem prohibitively high. The business community fears new property redistribution, while the employees of state-dependent enterprises are afraid of structural reforms and unemployment; the "systemic" opposition, which remains loyal to the regime, believes that regime change will significantly reduce its influence, and so on. In addition, the bitter memory of the numerous troubles during the triple transition in the aftermath of the collapse of Communism reminds many Russians that a new wave of regime change might be very painful. In short, many of the actors and ordinary people discontent with the status quo see its continuation as a lesser evil in comparison with major regime change. It is unsurprising that, later on, the protests of 2011–2012 received little support even from those social groups that were quite critical of the Russian regime.[107] As long as the costs of the status quo equilibrium do not exceed its current benefits for the ruling groups and society at large, this equilibrium will be endorsed by those who have little incentive to challenge it. Thus, the "institutional trap"—a stable but socially ineffective equilibrium that almost no one wants to break—becomes a fundamental part of Russian politics.[108]

Such political equilibrium may well prove self-enforced—not only due to the lack or weakness of serious actors capable of challenging the regime, but also because of the inertia created by the institutional arrangements that were established in the 1990s and especially in the 2000s. To put it simply, the longer the current status quo regime is maintained, the more costly it is to overcome.

Examples of institutional traps of this kind are ubiquitous in everyday life, but also extensively present in politics. Political stagnation in the Soviet Union under Brezhnev, when virtually the same winning coalition retained power for almost twenty years, was the most prominent experience of the institutional trap in recent Russian history. The winning coalition had no incentives to conduct even minor reforms, to say nothing of major regime changes, while the demand for change among the elite and the general public remained latent at best. No wonder that the time for transforming the Soviet political regime came and went, and when Mikhail Gorbachev initiated its radical revival, the subsequent institutional changes were ill-prepared and inconsistent, finally driving the political regime and the Soviet state to collapse. Although the parallels between Russia's political regime in the 2000s and the late-Soviet stagnation of the 1970s and early 1980s are apparent and widespread in the media and popular books,[109] they are often somewhat superficial. Still, the concept of the institutional trap and its pernicious consequences is relevant for analysis of present-day Russia as much as of the last decades of the Soviet Union.

As a result, Russia finds itself in a situation where even if the elite and the public agree on the urgent need for major institutional changes, the only real incentives for political actors to effect these changes are genuine threats to their political survival. They understand the impossibility of implementing such changes without those who actually launch this meaningful disequilibrium incurring considerable losses. As long as the "stability" offered by the Kremlin is sustained, Russia ends up in a vicious cycle; the longer a status quo regime persists, the smaller the chances of successfully overcoming the institutional trap it has found itself in. In addition, numerous institutional barriers and the fragmentation of political actors hinder collective actions aimed at challenging the current status quo. Indeed, the current political equilibrium effectively creates incentives for the ruling groups to preserve the status quo at any cost as an end in itself; at the same time, the notorious inefficiency of political institutions narrows the time horizons for major actors, making them sacrifice long-term goals for the sake of short-term gains here and now. These incentives hinder even the policies of sectoral reforms, which do not affect the major institutions of the regime as such, and do not directly involve risk-taking and potential threats to its survival. Even if the Kremlin sincerely wishes to improve the quality of governance and/or the rule of law, its efforts face great obstacles caused by the institutional trap. As for the major institutional changes that could result in opening up political competition, they lie beyond the Kremlin's agenda; Russia's rulers have learned from Gorbachev's perestroika experience that politicians who launch political liberalization run a major risk of losing power. Hence, they must place a "No Entry" sign in front of this path. As a result, Russia is in a situation where even if both the elite and society at large understand the deadly need for major regime changes, this has not produced incentives to reject the status quo, given perceptions of almost inevitable significant losses for virtually all political and economic actors and for the country as a whole. This paradox of low-level authoritarian regime equilibrium has also demonstrated its vulnerability to exogenous challenges that could emerge as a byproduct of the changing domestic and international environment. No wonder that the Russian political equilibrium of the 2000s was only partial and became severely shaken (yet not overthrown) in the 2010s—first by the outside pressure of political protests in 2011–2012 and then by the top leadership of the country after 2014.

98 ★

CHAPTER 5

THE UNPREDICTABLE 2010s

RISING CHALLENGES

ON FEBRUARY 21, 2014, Ukrainian president Viktor Yanukovych fled Kiev, leaving his post after three months of large-scale street protests in the center of the capital. These protests began when Yanukovych, under strong pressure from Russia, refused to sign an association agreement with the European Union. The government used various means of countering these protests, including shooting some of the regime's rivals, but in the end the result was the de facto ousting of Yanukovych: the day after his escape, the Ukrainian parliament voted for his removal from the job and called for new presidential elections.[1] As the Kremlin condemned this regime change in Ukraine as a coup d'état plotted by American and European donors (who openly expressed their support for protesters), the Russian authorities considered these developments a major challenge for their own regime. The wave of postelection protests that occurred in the 2000s in a number of post-Soviet countries (including Ukraine), dubbed the "color revolutions," had been a serious warning call for the Kremlin, and served as a reason to diminish political and civic freedoms in Russia in order to remove the possibility of similarly losing power due to mass protests.[2] Although the dangers of a color revolution in Russia were widely exaggerated (and had a limited impact on the regime later on, during the 2011–2012 postelection protests), perceptions of these risks contributed to the Kremlin's politics of preemptive counterrevolution.[3] Ten years on, the consequences of Ukrainian regime change appear much more frightening for the Kremlin: one can easily imagine Putin one day sharing the fate of his Ukrainian counterpart, albeit in somewhat different circumstances.

The reaction from the Kremlin was asymmetrical and far-reaching. Soon after the regime change in Ukraine, Putin initiated annexation of the Crimean peninsula (a region that has belonged to Ukraine since 1954 and is still used as a naval base for the Russian Black Sea fleet). Predictably, the annexation caused a furious reaction both from Ukraine and from Western countries, which placed sanctions on the top Russian and Crimean officials involved in this process. However, Russia did not stop there, and extended its appetites to the entire area of southern and eastern Ukraine, which was considered "Novorossiya" ("New Russia"), heavily populated by Russian-speaking residents and presumably loyal to the Russian rather than the new Ukrainian leadership. These attempts largely failed in many regions of Ukraine. However, in Donbass, the industrial hub of eastern Ukraine, which had previously served as a local power base for Yanukovych, Russia-sponsored separatists proclaimed the emergence of so-called "people's republics" and de facto usurped power. The Ukrainian army and the National Guard (formed from volunteers) launched ground operations against the rebels, who were armed and backed by the Russian military. In July 2014, a Malaysian Airlines Boeing-777 flying from Amsterdam to Kuala Lumpur was shot down over the separatist-controlled zone, presumably by a Russian surface-to-air missile, and almost 300 people were killed. Since the Russian authorities denied accusations and shifted blame to the Ukrainian military, a new round of Western sanctions (which affected not only individuals but also major Russian businesses, including energy and financial sectors) became inevitable. The Kremlin, in turn, only fueled the confrontation with the West, announcing countersanctions in the form of an import ban on many food products from the European Union, the United States, and several other countries. Furthermore, in August 2014, when Ukrainian troops nearly defeated the separatist rebels, Russian military forces encroached into the territory of Donbass and, using heavy arms, pushed the Ukrainians out of the separatist-controlled area.[4] The ceasefire agreement of September 2014 stopped casualties for a while but did not bring peace and stability to these regions of Ukraine.

An analysis of the impact of Ukrainian developments on Russia's foreign policy and on international relations across the globe is beyond the scope of this book. But their impact on Russian domestic politics was remarkable. With the annexation of Crimea, Putin's popularity skyrocketed in the eyes of Russian citizens, who were proud of this vivid demonstration of the Russian state's coercive capacity and military power, especially since even before the annexation many had considered Crimea to belong to Russia.[5] "Then again, Crimea is ours!" ('zato Krym nash!') became the slogan of the season, marked by a "rally around the Russian flag."[6] These changes in public mood gave free rein to the Kremlin, which used the opportunity to target the opposition, suppressing public dissent, toughening regulations, and diminishing the chances of Putin's dominance being undermined from within by the "fifth column" of so-called "national traitors." The Russian media orchestrated an aggressive, furious campaign against the West, its Ukrainian allies, and Western-oriented Russians (portrayed as "fascists"), far exceeding the degree of confrontation during the Cold War. To paraphrase the Boney M song *Rasputin*, which was popular in the 1970s, what the country became in the 2010s under Putin's reign was "Russia's greatest hate machine," dangerous both to the outside world and to its own citizens. At the same time, the Russian regime became more personalist and securitized, its policy making became more spontaneous, and its reliance upon the inner circle of cronies and the security apparatus increased many risks both for the elite and for society at large, making the Kremlin's next moves less and less predictable.[7] By the end of 2014, against the background of increasing economic troubles, rising inflation, and sharp depreciation of the Russian national currency, the quality of policy making at the level of agenda formation, professional expertise, and principal decisions drastically declined. Although some of these tendencies have been observed since 2012, after Putin's return to presidential office,[8] the major shift in Russia's behavior in the international arena has greatly accelerated the drive toward domestic changes.

Nevertheless, by the end of 2014 the electoral authoritarian regime in Russia preserved the same institutional "core," which had emerged in the 1990s and been strengthened in the 2000s. Even so, in the 2010s the regime was increasingly faced with new challenges, both domestically and internationally. These challenges did not only result from exogenous shocks (such as the 2008 global economic crisis or the Ukrainian regime change) or from risky moves initiated by the Kremlin (such as Putin's presidential job swap with Dmitry Medvedev in 2008–2012 or Russia's aggressive confrontation with the West over Ukraine). Rather, they are inherent to many electoral authoritarian regimes around the globe. Even though it is too early to speak of a full-fledged crisis of Russian authoritarianism, let alone the possibility of its failure, the challenges to the regime raised in recent years are fundamental and unavoidable. What was the nature of these challenges, were they inevitable, why did they emerge "here and now," why was the Kremlin able to cope with them, and how might these developments affect the further evolutionary trajectory of Russia's political regime? This chapter is devoted to the search for answers to these questions.

CHALLENGES TO RUSSIAN AUTHORITARIANISM

The belief in the crucial importance of information problems for the survival of authoritarian regimes[9] has become conventional wisdom among scholars. However, the salience of these problems and the mechanisms of their political effects vary greatly in different types of autocracies. While traditional monarchies as well as one-party regimes have been able to develop some plausible solutions, electoral authoritarian regimes face irresolvable problems. In a narrow sense, the very nature of political competition turns unfree and unfair elections into a crucial test for the survival of electoral authoritarian regimes in various parts of the globe.[10] The rulers of these regimes must not only defeat their challengers in unfair elections, but also persuade their fellow citizens and foreign nations to recognize such victories, and muffle the voices complaining about electoral unfairness.[11] But in the broader sense, the source of challenges lies beyond postelection protests, and relates to the rulers' need to maintain a number of institutions that are typical for democracies (not only elections but also parliaments, political parties, NGOs, semi-independent media, etc.) and serve the purposes of securing the authoritarian status quo. This maintenance requires a delicate balance between the three political pillars of authoritarian equilibrium: "lies, fear, and economic prosperity," in the words of Adam Przeworski.[12] If one of these three pillars is questioned, then the rulers' involuntary use of the two others is not always successful—especially for those regimes that previously relied upon carrots rather than sticks: in other words, ones that did not make heavy use of repressions[13] and preferred cooptation rather than coercion as instruments of maintaining their stability.[14] Russia has belonged to this group of authoritarian regimes (and, at present, continues to do so), and responding to various challenges has become an increasingly daunting task for its rulers over time.

When the equilibrium of the "institutional trap" was achieved during Vladimir Putin's second term, the Kremlin faced a dual challenge. In terms of politics, the temporary job swap between Putin and Medvedev during the interregnum of 2008–2012 was a risky game. But in practice, the regime's losses of legitimacy, which initially resembled major cracks in the wall in the wake of the 2011–2012 postelection protests, were short-term and more or less successfully minimized over time. In terms of governance, the idea of major advancement of the country's economic performance and international influence (vigorously advocated during Medvedev's presidency under the label of "modernization") remained wishful thinking at best, due to the lack of institutional mechanisms for implementation of such an ambitious project. To put it simply, political and institutional constraints buried any hopes of turning the Russia of the 2010s into a new South Korea of the 1970s.[15] The path-dependency of the regime's evolutionary trajectory seems unavoidable, and it is no wonder that a number of scholars and experts on Russian politics, economics, and society (including this author) consider inertia-based scenarios of Russia's development to be the most realistic, and deem it inclined to follow the status quo bias, typical of many discussions of that kind.[16]

The gap between ambitions and reality against the background of increasing information problems (especially after the unexpected rise of protests of 2011–2012) contributed to an increased perception of threat by the Kremlin after Putin's return to presidential office in 2012. On the one hand, the Kremlin attempted to avoid the dangers associated with losing legitimacy through the use of cooptation, offering Russian citizens further increases of salaries and pensions (irrespective of the prospects of the country's economic development).[17] On the other hand, further institutional changes were aimed at containing dissent through more tough and repressive regulations of freedom of speech (as well as other freedoms), discrediting and frightening the regime's potential opponents, and selective targeting and coercing of its open rivals. As Russians' relative economic prosperity has served the Kremlin's purposes in the 2010s less effectively than it had in the 2000s, it relies more and more upon lies and fear.

These tendencies had been developing consistently yet relatively slowly until the sudden regime change in Ukraine in February 2014, which accelerated all processes on domestic front. In terms of politics, the "winning coalition" around Putin has been reshuffled, the role of the coercive apparatus has been increased, and the government, formally led by the prime minister, Medvedev, plays only a technical role in decision making in most important policy areas. In addition, the regime has easily contained its domestic challengers: with the Russian public largely enthusiastic about the Kremlin's foreign policy, the political opposition has lost the initiative, and has failed to propose alternative solutions to the country's problems and make them part of the public agenda. As a result, its impact on Russia's agenda has been diminished while the Kremlin's harsh targeting of the "fifth column" has met with little resistance: the strategic and organizational potential of the opposition has been challenged, and its very capacity for organized political dissent is also in question. In terms of governance, the economic doctrine of priorities of state-led capitalist development (which lies behind many policies implemented since 2000)[18] has not been rejected but de facto abandoned for the sake of immediate reactions to external threats, involving not only economic countersanctions but also the militarization and securitization of the economy and society. These strategic changes will aggravate Russia's economic problems in coming years, although the relatively large margin of its strength (which was achieved due to the tremendous growth of 1999–2008) averts the risk of major decline, let alone collapse, in the short term.

While it is too early to predict the consequences of ongoing international and domestic changes on Russia's political regime, it would not be a great exaggeration to argue that by the end of 2014 its state was in sharp contrast to the period of the (in)famous 2000s. During the first two terms of Putin's presidency, electoral authoritarianism in Russia was on the rise, but in the 2010s it experienced a major decline. Yet even a declining trajectory of the life cycle of any regime—especially a nondemocratic one—does not necessarily mean that it will become extinct in the foreseeable future or that it will be inevitably transformed into an "uncertain something else," as Guillermo O'Donnell and Philippe Schmitter described the demise of many authoritarian regimes in the 1980s.[19] Rather, one should focus on analysis of the causes and consequences of this decline: how and why has the developmental trend of Russian authoritarian regime shifted, and to what extent were these shifts driven by exogenous factors as opposed to by Russia's actors themselves? To answer this question, I will reassess the strategy of the Kremlin (and also its domestic rivals, the opposition) in the 2010s, as well as the opportunities and constraints that these strategies met with, and the consequences of major choices by Russia's rulers for the further trajectory of political regime change in Russia.

AUTHORITARIAN "MODERNIZATION": EMPTY ILLUSIONS

Leadership succession is the Achilles's heel of many authoritarian regimes— few of them are able to find a minimally painful solution for dynastic continuity (as in Azerbaijan).[20] But for electoral authoritarian regimes, leadership change is a particularly painful and risky venture in terms of their legitimation, and it can pose major challenges to a regime's survival (the Ukrainian experience in 2004 offers a vivid example of this point).[21] From this perspective, the major intrigue of the 2007–2008 election cycle in Russia was not so much about the voting itself as about the possibilities of the subsequent presidential succession. The limit of the presidential term in office, two four-year periods, as had been included in the 1993 Russian constitution by Yeltsin's liberal advisors, posed a major challenge to Putin, whose second term would expire in the spring of 2008. He faced a difficult dilemma. One option was the revision of the constitution and abolishment (or extension) of presidential term limits, or the adoption of a completely new constitution, or even the elimination of any constitution as a legal set of formal rules of the game for Russia. Putin could openly shift from Yeltsin's above-mentioned concept ("to put it bluntly, somebody had to be the boss in the country; that's all there was to it") to the maxim openly declared by the new chair of the Central Electoral Commission of Russia, Vladimir Churov, appointed in 2007: "Putin is always right." This was an option previously employed by the leaders of several post-Soviet electoral authoritarian regimes (ranging from Alexander Lukashenko in Belarus to Nursultan Nazarbayev in Kazakhstan) or, beyond post-Soviet areas, in regimes such as Egypt under Hosni Mubarak. The alternative to this solution was for Putin to choose a loyal successor as a new head of the state, with his/her further legitimation via popular vote. According to some surveys, public opinion in Russia (which remained unconcerned with democracy as such, but approved elections as a mechanism of legitimation of rulers)[22] was divided over the issue of the continuation of Putin's presidency, and did not decisively object to this option:[23] in terms of the domestic agenda at least, Putin had more or less free rein. In December 2007, after the State Duma elections, when United Russia officially received 64.3 percent of the popular vote and gained 315 out of 450 seats in the legislature, Putin finally announced his decision. As a prospective candidate for a new presidency, he proposed Dmitry Medvedev, the first deputy prime minister and the former chief of his administration, who had often been mentioned as Putin's potential designated successor for a presidential role. Without any meaningful resistance, Medvedev received more than 70 percent of eligible votes during the presidential elections in March 2008, while Putin, according to the openly announced preliminary agreement with his chosen successor, accepted the job of prime minister, thus retaining many leverages of political control. One should note that even though, according to several expert analyses, the 2007–2008 elections in Russia demonstrated an unprecedented level of fraud,[24] they appeared very differently to Russian eyes. As mass survey data demonstrated, most of the voters evaluated the elections as "fair," despite widespread fraud and manipulation,[25] and one of the focus group participants quite naively (or cynically?) noted that "everything was fair . . . but 50 percent of the results were falsified."[26]

We may never be able to answer precisely the question of why Putin and his team chose not to retain all power leverages in their hands "once and for all" and instead decided to transfer formal powers to the designated successor. Such a scheme was risky for Putin, because any successor could behave unpredictably upon acquiring huge constitutional powers, and the threat of disloyalty was unavoidable. But the problem was that the costs of turning the electoral authoritarian regime (with its democratic mimicry) into a naked and unequivocal "classical" form of authoritarianism were quite high because of its dubious domestic and, especially, international legitimacy. Besides the nuisance of being associated with the category of dictators such as Lukashenko and Karimov, in the event of the abolition of presidential term limits, Russia's elite would face major problems legalizing their incomes and property in the West. But most probably, the answer is that status quo electoral authoritarianism largely satisfied the Kremlin's wishes, despite certain costs of maintaining the regime, and the incentives for further major changes were not sufficient. If so, then Putin's dilemma was resolved nearly by default, given the widespread predictions of inertia and the expectation that the domestic and international environment of the regime would be preserved at least during Medvedev's four-year term in office. These expectations related to the continuity of rapid economic growth, to the further rise of global oil prices, and to the political apathy and nonparticipation of many Russian citizens, against the background of a weak opposition and the lack of any meaningful alternatives to the political status quo.

It would seem at first glance that Vladimir Putin's maneuver in 2007–2008, when he picked Dmitry Medvedev to be a loyal successor, a temporary substitute or "acting president" for a mere four years, and secured major leverages by governing the country as prime minister with the expectation of returning to the presidency in 2012, was worth an A+ from the college for dictators. Although these expectations were questioned during the 2011–2012 electoral cycle, which posed certain challenges to electoral authoritarianism in Russia, they were not entirely wrong. To a certain degree, these risks were inevitable and a tolerable price for preserving the continuity of power of the same ruling group. However, several expectations related to maintaining the political status quo in the 2010s did not materialize, for largely unpredictable reasons.[27]

The first major challenge to the regime emerged in the series of protests by Russian citizens in the aftermath of the December 4, 2011, parliamentary elections. The scope of this mass mobilization was unprecedented for the country; no antisystemic political protests since the Soviet collapse had ever had so many participants. These protests strongly contrasted with Russia's previous experience of unfair elections: the public did not refuse to accept the results. So why did some of these voters so dramatically rebel against the status quo four years later and why was this rebellion unsuccessful and short-lived?

The answer can be found through close examination of the interim period of 2008–2011, which was marked by certain efforts to improve the regime's performance and decorate its democratic façade, but in the end contributed to its disequilibrium. On the regime's side, the "ruling tandem" mechanism, where Putin and Medvedev shared executive power as the prime minister and the president respectively, had a few flaws. Although Medvedev was nothing but Putin's puppet, he played the role of a "good cop" and attempted to demonstrate his good intentions by promoting the ideas of economic modernization and political liberalization, thereby giving rise to great expectations of improvement from the domestic and international public. By contrast, Putin partly remained in his shadow as a "bad cop," in charge of routine day-to-day management and retaining major leverages of control in his hands.

Had this mechanism been only an artificial, manipulative façade concealing Putin's full-fledged control over decision making, then it could have brought some benefit to the Kremlin. However, the division of labor within the ruling tandem was imperfect, and the signals the Kremlin sent to Russian society were somewhat inconsistent. Medvedev attempted to present himself as an independent political leader, autonomous from his partner. This led to major uncertainty among both the elite and society at large, especially when Putin's plan to return to the presidency was not disclosed until September 2011. No wonder that the problem of multiple agency (in other words, being servants of two masters) to some extent disoriented the state apparatus, which escaped the political leaders' control and, given the short time horizon, mostly remained passive and demobilized. The Kremlin reacted to this political slackness cautiously, due to the very fact that Medvedev was not able to control his own state apparatus; he placed only a handful of his personal cronies in powerful positions in the Kremlin, and had limited opportunities to fire incompetent and/or corrupt officials in the central government and the presidential administration. Before 2007–2008, the Kremlin invested major resources in building United Russia as a dominant party of power and in strengthening the power vertical through a series of informal contracts with heavyweight regional governors. Later, though, United Russia became merely the legislative and electoral arm of the top officials, with no autonomy from the Kremlin.[28] In addition, the power vertical faced a major overhaul under Medvedev. Several long-serving regional governors were removed and were sometimes replaced by politically inexperienced newcomers, who were often unpopular among both local notables and citizens. Finally, the weakest links of the power vertical, the elected city mayors, were in many cases replaced by nonelected city managers, who came under some criticism from the local elite and urban residents.[29] This Kremlin approach aggravated principal-agent problems in regional and local governance and diminished the role of the power vertical to delivering votes for the Kremlin at all costs, irrespective of the performance of subnational authorities.[30]

Nevertheless, Medvedev also offered a positive agenda for Russia during his presidency, even if it was not implemented. His slogan of "modernization" was loudly proclaimed in numerous public statements as well as in some presidential decrees and laws, but had very little practical effect. The version of Russian modernization advocated by Medvedev was very narrow and self-contained. After all, the process of modernization in the contemporary world (the variety of competing definitions and approaches notwithstanding) includes not only socioeconomic advancements (such as industrialization, urbanization, an increase in well-being, the spread of education, increasing mobility, and the decline of inequality) but also major political changes (such as the promotion of political rights and liberties, competitive elections and party systems, the separation of powers, etc.).[31] However, in Russia under Medvedev the very discussion of political modernization was perceived by the Kremlin as a kind of taboo; at best, it was considered a mid-term goal, but not an urgent matter for the country's development.[32] The Kremlin understood the catchword "modernization" not as a broader agenda of comprehensive change, but rather as a narrow set of policies aimed only at Russia's economic advancement. Its approach is focused on the acceleration of the development of information technology and other high-tech sectors of Russian economy, more active international integration of the country into the globalized world, and improvement of the quality of governance, without implying major steps toward the democratization of Russia's political regime. The political dimension of Russian modernization under Medvedev was deliberately limited to rhetorical liberalization, which assumed no practical implications. In other words, Medvedev's policy agenda was based upon the idea of narrow economic modernization under authoritarianism, both as a goal and as a condition for Russia's successful development.[33]

Although certain experts cautiously expressed some hopes in regard to Medvedev's modernization,[34] most critical observers noted that his loud rhetoric was little more than a demagogical smokescreen, intended to provide domestic and international audiences with illusory prospects of positive change in Russia while in fact it only concerned the preservation of the status quo.[35] Although these accusations are not groundless, and the Kremlin often used modernization slogans for the purpose of manipulative virtual politics, it would be misleading and superficial to consider Medvedev's policy agenda only in this respect. In many ways, this agenda reflected the genuine intentions of the Russian elite, which understood the need for major reforms in terms of economic development and quality of governance in Russia. The notorious inefficiency of the hierarchical power vertical, incredibly high corruption, constant conflicts between "Kremlin's towers" over the redistribution of rents, and Russia's sensitive losses in international arenas became inescapable features of governance in Russia prior to the 2008–2009 global economic crisis (which, in turn, only aggravated these problems). In a sense, Medvedev's rhetoric of modernization merely reflected the elite's major dissatisfaction with these elements of Putin's legacy, and their desire for major improvements in at least some policy areas.[36] But in practice this policy agenda was reduced to words without deeds. And the failure of the very program of authoritarian modernization was filled with principal systemic flaws that made its implementation in post-Soviet Russia impossible.

Critics of the authoritarian modernization agenda often point out that many leaders of authoritarian regimes lack incentives for conscious and consistent socioeconomic reforms; they are rarely inclined toward major changes, and often are incapable of implementing such policies.[37] Yet Medvedev's capacity was severely limited because of constraints imposed on his power of appointment and dismissal, and it is unsurprising that the Russian and international media tended to juxtapose his "reformist" efforts with the ultimate resistance by "antireformist" Putin and his entourage, perceived as new oligarchs.[38] Often, these considerations were not groundless; the large-N survey of Russian subelite groups conducted in 2008 by Mikhail Afanas'ev confirmed the conventional wisdom about strong antireformist sentiments among respondents with military, and especially police and security backgrounds, while a significant share of respondents preferred to go beyond Medvedev's narrow modernization agenda and endorsed the idea of political reforms.[39] But the problem was not only with the personalities of the Kremlin. Even if Medvedev were truly serious in his good intentions of creating a modern economy and efficient system of governance for Russia, he lacked the political instruments to implement these plans into reality while preserving the status quo authoritarian regime.[40]

Yet major policy reforms in any given country (whether democratic or authoritarian) cannot be implemented just because of the good (or bad) will of political leaders, regardless of the contents of these reforms. Leaders have to rely upon major support from their selectorate (which is small under authoritarian regimes)[41] and also make skillful use of the available political instruments that allow them to convert words into deeds in a more or less appropriate way. As for the narrow agenda of authoritarian socioeconomic modernization, the set of political instruments that may be utilized by reformist leaders to achieve these goals is rather limited. They can use one of the three available tools: the bureaucracy, the coercive apparatus, and the dominant party (or a combination). This distinction largely corresponds to the three major types of authoritarian regime in the modern world: bureaucratic, military, and one-party.[42] However, none of these instruments was available for modernization in early twenty-first-century Russia.

Many reflections on bureaucratic authoritarian modernization revolve around dreams of rare success stories such as Singapore under Lee Kwan Yew.[43] However, the bureaucracy in post-Soviet Russia was irrelevant as a major agent of modernization, and had almost nothing in common with that of East Asian bureaucrats. It lacked incentives to conduct major reforms, and the Russian authorities were unable to provide them. Moreover, bureaucratic modernization required not only a critical mass of well-trained, capable, and motivated bureaucrats, but also a high level of state autonomy and insulation of the bureaucracy from special-interest groups, which would allow it to pursue a reform agenda. However, Russian bureaucracy met none of these conditions, and it was unrealistic to expect their emergence under an electoral authoritarian regime. On the contrary, Russian bureaucracy had experienced major institutional decay even before the Soviet collapse, and the multiple reorganizations in the turbulent time of the 1990s had not improved the situation.[44] In the 2000s, against a background of decline in political competitiveness and media freedom, the Russian bureaucracy effectively escaped from political control, while the Kremlin, in its turn, was more interested in the short-term political loyalty of bureaucrats than their long-term efficiency.[45] The results were predictable, as both Putin and Medvedev recognized corrupt officialdom as the most irresolvable problem in the period of their rule.

The use of the Russian bureaucracy as an instrument of modernization was hindered not only by its inefficiency but also by the Kremlin's paramount obsession with the idea of hierarchical centralized control as the major (if not the only) tool of governance; the power vertical was the most vivid example of this approach. For a large and diverse country with a sizable public sector, and in which state bureaucracy was highly important to the economy and in the everyday life of ordinary people, reliance upon these methods of governance led to an incredible increase in agency costs and to further aggravation of the principal-agent problems. The top-down hierarchy was unable to effectively monitor, reward, and punish all the links in the power vertical, while the mid-level bureaucrats systematically misinformed their bosses about their performance. This trap of principal-agent relationships could not be overcome through the occasional use of personnel replacements, nor without major institutional changes, especially given the shortage of reform-oriented officials.[46] Thus, given the lack of public accountability and the increase of centralized control, the Russian bureaucracy had little interest in pursuing a modernization agenda and preferred the preservation of the status quo. Under Medvedev's presidency, the situation hardly improved in this respect.

The "coercive" scenario of authoritarian modernization is often linked to the Chilean experience under Pinochet, which turned out to be a role model for some Russian reformers in the early 1990s.[47] But this arrangement of military rule, with its harsh repression of the opposition and radical market-oriented policy reforms, was exceptional in many ways; the coercive apparatus of the state (i.e., the military, police, and security services) rarely played the role of major agents of modernization.[48] To perform in such a capacity, the coercive apparatus of the state should be run by bright reform-minded leaders, should exhibit a high degree of organizational autonomy, structural integration, and ideological cohesiveness, should be supported by large segments of the elite and the general public, and should not be deeply involved in business activities. This winning combination is unique across the globe, and it was completely absent in Russia. Ever since the Soviet era, the coercive apparatus directly or indirectly exerted control over significant economic resources (ranging from the military industry to the Gulags), and was involved in a bitter interbranch rivalry (as promoted by the political leadership, which employed divide-and-rule tactics),[49] and its limited autonomy was reduced to zero by the time of the Soviet collapse. Therefore, the military remained passive in post-Soviet Russia, and in the 2000s it lost its role as a meaningful actor in domestic politics.[50] As for law enforcement agencies, in the 1990s they became heavily fragmented due to state weakness and excessive decentralization, and were deeply involved in business activities even as political control over them declined.[51] When in the 2000s the status of law enforcers suddenly and dramatically increased, and their political influence significantly expanded,[52] they used these new opportunities mostly for rent-seeking, and had no interest in implementing any modernization agenda. Rent extraction and control over businesses became essential for numerous law enforcement agencies, and this fact greatly contributed to the rise of new conflicts between various actors, while attempts to stop these processes were unsuccessful.[53] The ideological commitments of the representatives of Russia's coercive apparatus were also hardly conducive to modernization.[54] To summarize, not only was this instrument unavailable in Russia, but on the contrary, there was (and still is) an urgent need for the modernization of the coercive apparatus of the state itself.[55] But this major task of state building was not seriously considered as part of Medvedev's agenda, and it remained unresolved after his presidency.

Finally, any hopes of the effective use of a dominant party as an instrument of authoritarian modernization were irrelevant in Russia's case, if one were to consider United Russia in this role. The experience of modernization in the Soviet Union and in post-Mao China, as well as some non-Communist authoritarian regimes (such as Mexico in the 1930s–1980s),[56] tells us that a centralized and well-disciplined dominant party could not only hold power in the long run but also serve as a driving force for major socioeconomic reforms. However, United Russia had no chance to turn into a Russian equivalent of the Chinese Communist Party in China or the PRI in Mexico, because its role in governance and policy making was fairly limited. To some extent, this resulted from Russia's institutional design, with its strong presidential power, as well as from the genesis of the party of power, which was established by top executive officials as their electoral and legislative arm.

But to a certain point, the subordinated status of the dominant party also resulted from the institutional legacy of the Soviet period. Even though the Communist Party of the Soviet Union was able to exert control over the state apparatus and was sometimes labeled a "party-state," the inefficiency of party-led governance in the late-Soviet decades renders impossible any aspirations for a return to this model.

Neither the political leaders of the country, nor their followers, nor mid-range officialdom were interested in turning the party of power into a real site for decision making. United Russia was unable to serve as a major channel for elite recruitment;[57] the career promotion of politicians and officials was based on personal networks rather than party politics. As a result, United Russia, with its low organizational autonomy[58] and the lack of any substantive ideology (which is necessary for conducting policy reforms) was used by the state apparatus only as an instrument of secondary importance, a tool for the maintenance of the status quo. Even if the Kremlin wanted to rely upon United Russia as an instrument of the modernization agenda, it would soon become clear that the party of power had no leverages of influence of its own on either public opinion or the state apparatus; as such, the hypothetical party-driven campaign of modernization was doomed to fail.

Thus, given the lack of efficient political instruments for implementing an agenda of policy reform, the narrow program of authoritarian socioeconomic modernization under Medvedev's presidency was completely useless. If one does not pay heed to the loud rhetoric, which involved some accurate but ultimately empty mantras concerning the need for the rule of law and/or innovative economic development in Russia, then the implementation of this policy was limited to the shallow and partial adoption of some technological innovations. This is why certain Kremlin-led initiatives, such as e-government, resulted in the computerization of some paperwork by street-level bureaucrats, and in the creation of opportunities for ordinary people to set up appointments with these officials or send their complaints via the Internet. Even legal reforms, which were vigorously advocated by Medvedev, were limited to mostly cosmetic institutional changes, such as renaming "militia" as "police." From a cynical perspective, the modernization agenda turned into just a new façade, with the aim of creating a positive image of the Russian leaders in the eyes of domestic and international audiences, and served as a prestigious form of conspicuous consumption by the ruling group. Without exaggeration, one can conclude that Medvedev was able to implement only two of his reforms: he reduced the number of time zones in Russia and abolished daylight saving time.

Meanwhile, the major event of Medvedev's presidency was the global economic crisis of 2008–2009, which harshly struck Russia's economy. The dramatic fall of world oil prices (from $147 per barrel in the summer of 2008 to $35 per barrel in January 2009) not only put an end to Russia's rulers' ambitious claims to future global leadership based on Russia's emerging status as a "world energy superpower," but also posed serious questions in regard to resolving current economic problems. The decline in output during the crisis was deeper in Russia than in other G20 countries, exceeding 8 percent in 2008–2009. While the economic crisis was not that protracted and the Russian authorities were able to minimize its negative consequences with relative success,[59] its major indirect effects were political rather than economic. The Russian public's dominant perceptions of the government and the political regime overall gradually began to change. In the 2000s, many Russian citizens, despite their criticism of the corruption and inefficiency of governance in the country, had considered the political status quo a lesser evil; by the early 2010s the demand for good governance, and therefore the demand for political change, began to emerge in public opinion as a result of increasing dissatisfaction with the status quo.[60]

While the practice of governing the country encountered multiple problems, virtual politics under Medvedev continued, and Kremlin-induced manipulations evolved to a new stage: instead of a (mostly virtual) "tightening of the screws" under Putin, a new "virtual thaw"[61] was offered to the Russian public in the form of many statements about liberalization, political openness, transparency, and the like (Medvedev's "freedom is better than nonfreedom" was a prime example of this). This discursive liberalization, however, resulted only in minor if not cosmetic institutional changes. In essence, this discursive liberalization served to conceal steps taken in the opposite direction; amendments to the Russian constitution, adopted in 2008, extended the term of office for the Russian president and the State Duma to six and five years respectively.[62] Nevertheless, even manipulative discursive liberalization existing in speech only had major unintended consequences for the Kremlin. It contributed to the rise of public expectations about the regime's liberalization in real terms (which would be undermined later on, after the announcement of Putin's return to the presidency in September 2011) and to the extension of the scope of public self-expression and the decline of self-censorship in the media. In other words, the deceitful rhetoric of the authorities itself provoked a further increase in demand for the rule of law and good governance among the Russian elite and the public, but the Kremlin was not interested in turning words into deeds, and considered these words to be empty shells. Thus, discursive liberalization became a Potemkin village, a façade that covered up authoritarianism, arbitrary rule, and corruption. The gap between rising societal demand for changes and the Kremlin's continuing supply of the status quo increased over time, and contributed to disloyalty among the voters, which became evident during the 2011 parliamentary elections.[63]

The "virtual thaw" also contributed to other unintended consequences. Upon acquiring its political monopoly and after coopting all relevant political, economic, and societal actors into the framework of imposed consensus, thus keeping them as loyal allies, the Kremlin paid little attention to its rivals, the nonsystemic opposition, which was pushed into a seemingly hopeless ghetto. Its chances were slim because almost all attempts to establish new opposition parties were effectively blocked at the stage of registration, almost all political protests were brutally oppressed by the police, and almost all opposition leaders were heavily discredited in the media (indeed, often they discredited themselves). However, discursive liberalization under Medvedev somewhat changed the political opportunity structure for new public initiatives and contributed to their further politicization.[64] The spontaneous emergence of numerous civic initiatives (mostly at the local level), ranging from environmentalists to cultural protection movements and defenders of drivers' rights,[65] encountered resistance from state officials: at certain points these groups realized that the only way to achieve their goals was to turn their specific concerns into political demands. Thus, civic activism, which in the 2000s served as a substitute for political activism, in the 2010s not only turned into a major school of political participation, but also offered a new recruitment pool for the opposition.[66]

At the same time, the opposition camp underwent a generational change of leaders and activists. Gradually, those leaders who had entered the political arena during the period of Gorbachev's perestroika (or even earlier) were replaced by new activists, who had grown up—both as people and as public figures—during the two post-Soviet decades.[67] The older generation tended to perceive current developments in Russia as more or less a continuation of their previous battles (which had often lost relevance over time), and the general public—correctly or not—identified them as dubious heroes of the "roaring 1990s." But the new generation aspired to a political career in new conditions, and exhibited forward-looking rather than retrospective assessments of new political developments. By contrast with its predecessors, the new generation of opposition leaders was more inclined to develop a negative consensus against the status quo regime, without regard for ideology. The most vivid example of this trend was Alexei Navalny, a charismatic anticorruption activist and a very popular blogger, who positioned himself as a liberal and a nationalist simultaneously and soon became the most visible public figure among his generation.[68]

The Kremlin was well aware of these changes, but its preemptive moves were rather inefficient; the previously arranged political and institutional settings of an electoral authoritarian regime were reproduced over time, and the few attempts at reshuffling the informal winning coalition around Putin under the new label of the All-Russia People's Front (and the downplaying of the United Russia brand name) had no serious impact. Discursive liberalization imposed certain constraints, because the transition from virtual politics to real violence could become more costly over time, and the authorities used only low-scale coercion against their rivals.[69] Even though open antisystemic protests were broken up by the use of coercion, public criticism of the authorities and of the regime as such was more or less tolerated. When the authorities made some minor concession to civic activists, it raised the stakes for the participants and encouraged them to go beyond local protests. But when the authorities denied requests made by the angry public, they contributed to the politicization of activism and pushed participants into the ranks of the opposition. In addition, the Kremlin mostly attempted to discredit opposition activists rather than killing or imprisoning them. Whereas in 2007–2008 the Kremlin had harshly preempted any danger of a color revolution (a danger that was greatly overestimated), before the 2011–2012 elections the seeds of future protests germinated without major resistance.

In conclusion, during Medvedev's presidency the Russian authorities mostly invested their political efforts into painting the façade of the regime rather than paying attention to the potential threats to electoral authoritarianism from within. They probably expected that the second substitution of rulers would tear down the façade almost automatically. The Potemkin village, however, turned out to be populated by Russian citizens not particularly susceptible to coercion and/or cooption. As a result, the Kremlin-induced balance of positive and negative incentives for loyalty tipped; sticks were used rarely and selectively, and carrots remained insufficient. These factors contributed to what happened after the elections.

THE TIME OF TROUBLES, 2011–2012

Postelectoral protests have often posed major challenges that can be incompatible with regime survival, as the experience of the color revolutions from Serbia to Kyrgyzstan tells us. Although Russia's electoral authoritarian regime in 2011–2012 did ultimately succeed in fending off these challenges, it had to pay a price for political survival, and its domestic legitimacy was placed in doubt to some degree. Indeed, authoritarian regime failure as a result of unfair elections is not an entirely new phenomenon. Samuel Huntington, in his famous analysis of the "third wave of democratization" in the 1970s and 1980s, coined the term "stunning elections," those that authoritarian rulers held to renew their legitimacy, but that undermined their regimes and sometimes paved the way for full-fledged democratization.[70] The 1989 Soviet parliamentary election serves as a paradigmatic case in this respect; although unfree and unfair, it allowed Soviet citizens to express their rejection of the political regime and contributed to mass mobilization and to the subsequent rise of an antisystemic opposition, and played an important role as one of several "turning points" in the collapse of Communist rule.[71] The causes of "stunning elections," however, remain insufficiently explained. While they are not considered a kind of *deus ex machina*, most analysts tend to be deterministic in their ex post explanations. They often emphasize the key influence of socioeconomic modernization and cultural changes, which give birth to political demands among the rising urban middle class and to the latter's appearance in the political arena.[72] Other experts have pointed out the major impact of information technology, especially the role of the Internet and social media in speeding up political communications, reducing authorities' control over information streams, and accomplishing the tasks of mobilization and coordination of mass protests through the mechanism of "connective action."[73]

The logic of these and other structural explanations is related to major shifts in public demand in the political market. These shifts, in turn, often depend upon the effects of various exogenous changes (such as major economic shocks or dynamics of international influence) on domestic public opinion,[74] which are hardly predictable, especially given the ways in which the general public's preferences are falsified under authoritarianism.[75] Without denying such possibilities, one should note that none of these factors, alone or in combination, can explain why at certain critical junctures some electoral authoritarian regimes survive (with major losses or without them) whereas others do not. An analysis of the supply side of political markets therefore seems useful. Under electoral authoritarianism, the political supply comes, more or less, from the ruling group (the regime) and its rivals, the opposition. Their influence on the survival and failure of electoral authoritarianism has become a hot topic, especially in lively discussions of the causes of the color revolutions. Some scholars have noted in this regard the crucial influence of oppositional efforts in mass antisystemic mobilization, the successful cooperation of various segments of the opposition, its broad international support, and its political strategies. In the aftermath of unfair elections, the combination of these factors dealt the final blow to electoral authoritarianisms from Serbia to the Ukraine.[76] However, these scholars' opponents have pointed out the vulnerability of authoritarian regimes due to their lack of insulation from Western influence, the weak coercive capacities of their states and/or their inability to establish strong dominant parties, and their inability to establish full-fledged control over the electoral process at all stages, from the nomination of the "right" candidates to the "correct" counting of votes.[77]

The troubles of electoral authoritarianism in Russia in 2011–2012 might be perceived through both these lenses. Regime's strategists oriented their expectations retrospectively and without sufficient sensitivity to changing political realities, and the Kremlin offered a rather imperfect package of carrots and sticks as incentives to its fellow citizens and to the opposition. The 2011 parliamentary electoral campaign opened a narrow window of opportunity for the opposition, which successfully used it to undermine the regime from within. The regime's reaction was delayed and sluggish, and the opposition not only came out of its ghetto but even took the initiative, as it established certain forms of cooperation and organized antisystemic mass mobilization and collective action. Although the protests did not overthrow Russia's electoral authoritarianism, they posed a threat to the regime, which had to change its tactics and achieved its desired results only after serious setbacks.

Before the parliamentary elections of 2011, the political landscape seemed unthreatening to the Kremlin; all the systemic parties remained loyal to the authorities, the degree of public support for the regime had decreased only slightly, analysts' concerns about rising public discontent were not taken seriously, and the Russian economy had recovered after the 2008–2009 global crisis. As a result, the authorities expected that the political status quo would be secured almost by default, and the risks involved in Putin's return to the presidency were not perceived as crucial. The Kremlin's strategy rested on three pillars: (1) unhesitating use of the state apparatus to maximize the United Russia vote by all available means (ranging from workplace mobilization to shameless fraud);[78] (2) genuine support of the status quo regime on the part of peripheral voters (rural/small-town residents, the elderly, the poor, public-sector employees); and (3) the apathy and nonparticipation of "advanced" voters (educated, young, upwardly mobile residents of large cities).[79] But these expectations proved to be wrong.

Before the campaign, various segments of the opposition were bitterly divided over electoral strategy; some activists suggested a boycott, claiming that participation in the act of voting would legitimate the regime, while others argued in favor of the systematic spoiling of ballot papers at the polling stations (although this approach had proved ineffective in the 2007–2008 elections), and others proposed support for systemic opposition parties such as the Communists or the liberal Yabloko as a lesser evil. In the end, the strategy advocated by Navalny and other young leaders—"vote for any party but United Russia"—became the most successful option. First, it enhanced the negative consensus that united not only various streams of the opposition but also different groups of voters, and left no room for the regime's divide-and-rule tactics. Second, United Russia became an ideal target for protest votes, because it was perceived only as a mindless arm of the ruling group, had no ideology other than preservation of the status quo, identified with corrupt officialdom, and was unpopular among advanced voters anyway; moreover, the lame duck Medvedev as the head of the United Russia party list made the situation even worse. Past discursive liberalization was now considered to be conscious deception of voters, and his rhetoric about modernization and the rule of law was perceived as empty words. Disillusionment with Medvedev was exceptionally deep.[80]

With limited access to television, the opposition creatively and successfully used the Internet as a campaigning tool. While some observers have argued that the Internet and online media played a decisive role during postelection protests in the recent wave of social movements,[81] the Russian experience demonstrates the importance of the Internet at the initial stage of the campaign, as a means of politicization and active involvement of previously uninterested voters. YouTube, rather than Twitter or Facebook, served as the most important tool in this respect. With the opportunity to post information available to everyone (not just to users of social media), hundreds of video and music clips, and poetry mocking United Russia and the regime as a whole flooded the Web and reached numerous apolitical voters, thus subverting the regime. The YouTube video of the March 2011 debate between Navalny and a member of the State Duma from United Russia, Yevgeniy Fedorov, during which the party of power was nicknamed "the party of swindlers and thieves" by Navalny, received 600,000 hits in just over a week,[82] and this label for United Russia soon turned into its brand name. In the period of the electoral campaign, Navalny even proposed a competition among Internet users to produce the best negative campaign material for use against the "party of swindlers and thieves"; this provoked an explosion of mass creativity. It also contributed to the rise of interest in the elections among previously apolitical Internet users, and increased the share of votes against United Russia. The landscape of the campaign began to change, especially given the dull public appearance of United Russia and its leaders. At the same time, the systemic opposition parties realized that they would benefit from the "vote for any party but United Russia" campaign, and raised their voices against Putin's return to the presidency and against the regime as such more loudly, thus presenting a niche alternative to the status quo.[83] In some cases, these parties offered their labels to be used by volunteers who wished to be independent election observers; their

★

numbers dramatically increased in comparison to the 2007–2008 elections, especially in large cities.

The regime counteracted the opposition in a number of ways, but its moves were delayed and sometimes even fueled protest sentiments. Multiple instances of street-level bureaucrats promising various benefits to their subordinates for boosting the United Russia vote by all possible means, and issuing various threats if the party did poorly, caused a host of scandals.[84] In the period of the campaign, the Kremlin offered voters no new carrots, while after the experience of the "virtual thaw" the promises of sticks were not taken seriously. Moreover, even subnational officials themselves often demonstrated a desire to minimize their own campaign efforts rather than maximizing United Russia votes. The power vertical underwent extraordinary stress as some regional governors and city mayors proved incapable of coordinating subnational political machinery smoothly enough, especially in cases where elections to regional and local assemblies were held simultaneously with the State Duma campaign.

All these trends coincided with one another, and greatly contributed to the effect of the "stunning elections" in December 2011. Despite almost ubiquitous instances of vote fraud, many of which were detected by observers and widely announced via the Web, United Russia officially received 49.3 percent of the vote and 238 of 450 parliamentary seats. In fact, it lost heavily, and several data sources demonstrated that the actual United Russia results were much lower than the official numbers (in the city of Moscow, the gap between exit polls, performed by Kremlin's contracting firm, FOM, and actual results reached 20 percent,[85] while other analysts considered electoral fraud in Moscow polling stations to account for about 11 percent of the total vote).[86] The opposition could nevertheless celebrate a certain victory, because (1) United Russia could not secure a majority of votes despite all the means used to maximize its results; (2) the regime was greatly discredited in the eyes of advanced voters; and (3) the negative consensus that had emerged during the campaign deepened after the polls. This success gave rise to large-scale postelection protests, which were larger than any in post-Soviet election history, and soon exceeded the technical limits of police coercion. The public's demonstrative rejection of the status quo contributed to the shift in previously hidden public preferences and had a snowball effect on the protest.[87] Lies and fear, which had previously supported authoritarian equilibrium in Russia alongside economic growth,[88] no longer served as efficient tools for maintaining the political status quo.

The Kremlin was poorly prepared for such developments. The regime perceived the electoral failure merely as a minor bump in the road rather than a systemic challenge. Using coercion against the protesters amid declining mass support for the regime was a risky strategy. The option of coopting some moderate opposition figures and arranging a major government reshuffle was unavailable, because it might cause further dissatisfaction within the ruling group and could be perceived by Kremlin loyalists as a sign of weakness on the part of the leadership and of the regime as a whole. Instead, all personnel changes initiated by the Kremlin were more or less a rotation of the same figures. This fact contributed to the spread of collective action and to the increasing numbers of its participants, while Putin's harsh rhetoric toward the opposition only enhanced the negative consensus and personalized Putin as their major target, changing the key slogan of the protests from "For Fair Elections!" to "Putin, Go Away!"[89]

The inertia and delay in the reaction of the authorities, who refused to rely upon sticks but did not offer the protesters enough carrots, contributed to the spatial diffusion of collective action, the increase in the numbers of participants, and the change in their repertoires.[90] Only after a new series of demonstrations in late December 2011 did the Kremlin propose some bills aimed at liberalizing the registration of new political parties and reinstating the popular election of regional governors. These measures aimed to pacify the opposition, which demanded new elections. But the proposals clearly did not satisfy the protesters, who perceived them as half-measures rather than as full concessions. Even though the membership threshold for the registration of new political parties was reduced from 45,000 to 500 people, the Kremlin retained its leverages of control over parties' access to elections. The proposals also included some dubious clauses, such as the "municipal filter": the nomination of candidates for gubernatorial elections would require the official support of 10 percent of municipal councilors, which would allow the Kremlin to effectively ban unwanted candidates from regional elections. But the most important issue was related to the fact that implementation of all of these institutional changes could affect the election and the party system, as well as regional government, only after the next election cycle, and did not respond to the protesters' immediate demands.

Despite some efforts, the few attempts to build bridges between the regime and the opposition failed. The regime's moderate supporters within the ruling group, as well as the systemic opposition parties, remained loyal to the status quo despite challenges to the regime; the risk of losing out as a result of (possible) major regime changes outweighed their dissatisfaction with the status quo. From a broader perspective, the time for an elite settlement or pact,[91] somewhat similar to the 1989 roundtable talks in Poland or the Moncloa Pact in post-Franco Spain, was not yet ripe in late 2011 and early 2012 in Russia. All successful negotiated democratic transitions of this kind have emerged out of unsuccessful previous attempts at one-sided coercion and the inability to achieve a zero-sum game, resulting from the conflicting sides' perceptions of the relative balance of forces and their unwillingness to repeat a past experience.[92] Numbers played a decisive role in this respect, because even though the Russian opposition was able to mobilize around half a million supporters in total, by the most optimistic assessments, this was more or less trivial by comparison with Solidarity in Poland, whose membership reached 9 million in 1981 (though roundtable talks occurred only eight years later).[93] Russia after the 2011 parliamentary elections was a long way from these conditions, and political opportunities for bargaining between an organizationally unified (although politically declining) regime and an organizationally weak (if politically rising) opposition were largely illusory. The incentives for bargaining were insufficient, and trust between the regime and the opposition was minimal, to put it mildly. It is too early to say whether negotiated transition as a mode of overcoming authoritarianism will ever occur in Russia, but in 2011–2012 both the regime and the opposition proceeded to the next round of political battle.

The Kremlin's dominant strategy was very simple: since none of Putin's challengers could defeat him in the presidential elections, the regime put all its effort into ensuring his victory. The list of candidates included the leaders of three loyal systemic parties and the billionaire Mikhail Prokhorov; the anti-systemic opposition had no chance to compete. On this occasion, the Kremlin mobilized all the leverages of the power vertical in a more coherent and consistent way than in the State Duma elections. It developed a more aggressive media campaign based on vicious attacks against opposition leaders, who were accused of being Western agents. It intimidated voters with threats of a new color revolution in Russia and presented the status quo as the only way to preserve "stability." It fired lower-level officials, ranging from regional governors to chiefs of electoral commissions, who had produced poor results for United Russia in December 2011. Finally, it organized an aggressive campaign of countermobilization of hundreds of thousands of peripheral voters for pro-Putin meetings, which aimed to demonstrate wide public support for the incumbent.[94] Returning to the soccer game analogy, one can view this strategy as the equivalent of an aggressive and dirty play, designed to secure victory at any cost before the end of the match.

At the same time, the opposition expanded the negative consensus under the slogan "No Votes for Putin!" and encouraged the public to vote for anyone but the former (and the future) president. But the major problem for those who challenged the political status quo was the very fact that they could not offer a positive alternative. The liberals, leftists, and nationalists who had combined their efforts since the postelection protests in December 2011 differed widely in terms of their political and economic views, and could not offer a joint action plan. Navalny's public statement that his economic program was limited to combating corruption provided clear evidence for the lack of a positive agenda.[95] But the Kremlin's refusal to bargain with the opposition united the ranks of the protesters. Even though each ideological camp within the opposition would have considered the hypothetical rule of its antisystemic comrades-in-arms to be worse than the status quo, the issue of supporting (or rather, not supporting) the regime became more salient not only for opposition leaders but also for some advanced voters. As the experience of many countries (ranging from Mexico under the last years of the PRI[96] to Serbia before the fall of Milošević)[97] suggests, the strengthening of the negative consensus among a regime's opponents is a necessary, albeit not sufficient, factor in democratization.

On the eve of the presidential elections, however, the opposition demonstrated its organizational and strategic weaknesses. Antisystemic protest mobilization was not based on strong and influential organizations (which do not exist in Russia) but rather exploited the "weak ties"[98] and "connective actions"[99] of Internet networks and social media. Although easy to mobilize for postelection protests, these ties and actions were insufficient for a large-scale nationwide campaign that could overthrow the regime. The scope of mass protests barely reached most cities beyond Moscow and St. Petersburg; in most parts of the country, it remained symbolic. Even though the opposition recruited several thousand supporters as election monitors on voting day, this number could not cover most polling stations even in large cities. Worse, numerous voters (and not only peripheral ones) perceived the preservation of the status quo as the lesser evil in comparison with major regime changes that could impose major costs on them. Furthermore, systemic opposition parties and other moderate supporters of the Kremlin retained their loyalty and were not inclined to join the ranks of the protesters because the hypothetical fall of the regime could make their political survival very questionable.[100] The opposition's strategy, in turn, was short sighted and limited to preparing the next protest actions; they lacked the time and/or the resources to look ahead while the regime launched its counteroffensive. Last but not least, the lack of available opposition-backed candidates made the slogan "No Votes for Putin!" less attractive to voters. In sum, the creativity and passion of the opposition leaders and their supporters could not replace organizational potential and strategic planning.

If the time lag between the parliamentary and the presidential elections had lasted more than three months, the opposition would probably have been able to overcome these inherent weaknesses. But the campaign's schedule favored the regime, which took the initiative and responded using every possible means. In the March 2012 election, the Kremlin achieved its goals thanks to (1) the employment of a combination of intimidation and promises to mobilize supporters of the status quo (mainly, but not exclusively, among peripheral voters); (2) the use of local political machinery in a full-scale and consistent manner; and (3) the effective implementation of various types of vote fraud, ranging from letting the same people vote multiple times at different polling stations to blatantly rewriting the official voting results.[101] The Kremlin got what it wanted (63.6 percent of votes for Putin), even though the spread of electoral dissent was meaningful enough; Prokhorov, the only viable alternative to the status quo, received more than 20 percent of votes in Moscow and 15 percent in St. Petersburg (and about 8 percent nationwide). But none of the candidates posed a decisive threat to Putin, and the systemic opposition and its supporters, voluntary or involuntary, agreed to Putin's return to the presidency.

THE KREMLIN STRIKES BACK

The disequilibrium of Russia's political regime that occurred during the 2011–2012 elections seemed to be exhausted soon after Putin's return to a new presidency. The Kremlin was able to redistribute key spoils and rents among members of the winning coalition after a slight reshuffling. The regime's loyal moderate supporters, including "systemic" opposition parties, businesspeople, and part of the reform-minded public who had joined the camp of protesters in 2011–2012, willingly or unwillingly agreed to the preservation of the political status quo. The wave of protest mobilization in Moscow was over; the intensity and quantity of antigovernment rallies and meetings decreased, although they did not vanish entirely. Some liberal concessions promised by the Kremlin, such as a return to the popular election of regional chief executives, were so decisively emasculated that they seemingly could not provoke major risks for the regime.[102] Although the economic slowdown (the growth rate in 2013 being less than 2 percent) has been widely perceived as a major challenge, no immediate threats to the political regime emerged at that time.

To some extent, these trends look like a natural political aftermath of the turbulent uproar of 2011–2012. But their main causes were related to the nature of the confrontation between the Kremlin and its emerging rivals, the opposition; both sides of the conflict learned some lessons from the experience of the protests, and attempted to reach their goals anew. Russia's authorities, quite naturally, desired to restore the previous regime's equilibrium, while the opposition, even if it was unable to subvert the regime, tried to inflict maximum damage on the Kremlin. However, both sides of the conflict were faced with major constraints inherited from the previous trajectory of Russia's political regime; in many ways, their actions were path-dependent.

Putin promised to "tighten the screws" immediately after the March 2012 presidential elections. Indeed, the Kremlin took a number of demonstrative steps in this direction in the subsequent months. They included, first and foremost, a shift in legal regulations: raising fines for participation in prohibited protest actions, restoring criminal charges for libel in the media,[103] labeling NGOs with foreign funding as "foreign agents," and the like. They also included pressure on opposition leaders and activists; apart from public discrediting of opposition leaders, several major figures, such as Alexei Navalny and Sergei Udaltsov, were faced with manufactured criminal investigations, while some rank-and-file activists were accused of clashes with police in May 2012 and imprisoned, becoming examples of the risks of disobedience. Furthermore, the pressure extended to those representatives of the subelite who expressed their public support for the opposition. In May 2013, the rector of the New Economic School, Sergei Guriev, who had been involved in drafting some economic proposals for Medvedev and had also openly donated money to Navalny, after a number of interrogations and searches of his office by criminal investigators flew to Paris and announced that he would not return to Russia. Last but not least, the Kremlin initiated a "culture war" on several fronts, ranging from the imprisonment of the members of female punk group Pussy Riot, who had performed an anti-Putin show in a major Orthodox cathedral in Moscow, to a legal ban on "homosexual propaganda," the prohibition of adoption of Russian orphans by Americans, and the introduction of criminal charges for offending religious feelings.

These actions have been perceived by some observers as a major shift toward repression, if not toward the "Stalinization" of Russian politics,[104] while others noted that the repressions were conducted more or less in "velvet gloves."[105] In fact, the regime was still far from being truly harsh and bloody. Independent media and websites continued to exist and even expanded their audience, few NGOs were labeled as "foreign agents" despite numerous raids and inspections by law enforcement agencies, and Navalny, who had been accused of criminal charges, was released and placed under house arrest. The reasons for these incomplete and inconsistent moves were twofold. On the one hand, after the successful experience of building a nonrepressive authoritarian regime, Russia's rulers had little incentive to turn to full-fledged repression.[106] On the other hand, the Kremlin did not overestimate the scope of the protest mobilization of 2011–2012, and perceived its threat to the regime as less than crucial. Thus, the Kremlin now approached the politics of fear primarily in terms of preventing the further spread of antiregime activism, rather than its total elimination; it perceived this as a more feasible and less costly task. This task also required the intimidation of the opposition's potential new recruits, as well as discrediting the opposition, and inflicting selective repressions on some of the most visible and/or most hated enemies (such as homosexuals or foreign spies). In a sense, this approach somewhat resembled the tactics employed by the Soviet authorities against the dissident movement in the USSR in the 1970s and 1980s; they successfully restricted the scope of open antiregime protests despite the rise in distrust of the authorities and the Communist regime as a whole.[107] At that time, major challenges to the status quo were postponed, and the temptation to repeat this experience in the twenty-first century was very natural for the Kremlin.

At the same time, the liberalization of registration rules for political parties and the restoration of the popular election of regional governors seemed to open a new window of opportunity for the opposition, which also had to deal with the challenge of an electoral struggle. The problem not only related to the fact that carefully crafted formal and informal rules of the game made elections under authoritarian regimes heavily biased and unfair[108] (for example, the "municipal filter" made the nomination of candidates for gubernatorial elections impossible without the support of United Russia).[109] In addition, opposition parties and the candidates themselves faced the trap of falling into an electoral niche, receiving votes only from a narrow base of core supporters with little hope of attracting broader political constituencies. Given that the opposition lacked strong organization and had limited public support, this move seemed a reasonable minor concession from the regime; it did not undermine the status quo, but rather enhanced the legitimacy of elections and the regime, and averted the risk of antiregime contagion in terms of taking protests from polling stations to the streets.

As for the general public, it more or less agreed with the restoration of Russia's political equilibrium. The degree of mass support for Russia's regime and its leader largely stabilized; while it did not reach (and most probably will never reach again) the extraordinarily high level seen in the "good old days" of the 2000s,[110] it did not fall as rapidly and dramatically as it had during the last months of 2011.[111] However, the decline of mass support for the regime and the rise of public discontent did not automatically benefit the opposition; Russians did not perceive the political rivals of the Kremlin as a viable alternative to the status quo. Thus, the partial equilibrium of "resigned acceptance" of Russia's authoritarian regime remained unchallenged and survived over time.[112] Moreover, even the public demand for change was rather different from the democratic slogans of the 2011–2012 protests: requests for good governance and better provision of public goods and services (such as education, public health, infrastructure, and the like)[113] were generally not linked to demands for democratization. Even supporters of the protests wanted to oust Putin and replace him with another strong (but supposedly more efficient) leader without major regime changes, making critical analysts skeptical of the democratic potential of mass support for protests.[114] However, the very commitment of many Russians to elections as the only acceptable way to choose their rulers (which was consistently demonstrated by numerous past studies) was considered to be a fundamental preference for democracy, even if in the most basic sense.[115] Yet the same commitment to choosing rulers through a popular vote might be relevant for electoral authoritarian regimes as well.

Nevertheless, the increasing gap between the public demand for changes and the supply of the status quo by the Kremlin provided some grounds for political entrepreneurship by the opposition. In 2013–2014, opposition-backed candidates won mayoral elections in Yekaterinburg, Petrozavodsk, and Novosibirsk. The major breakthrough occurred in the Moscow mayoral elections in September 2013. The incumbent, Sergei Sobyanin (a former head of Putin's presidential administration) expected an easy victory; surveys predicted no serious competition, and even his major would-be rival Navalny, the most popular and capable leader of the new generation of the opposition, initially had the support of no more than 10 percent of Moscow voters.[116] These expectations were very favorable for the Kremlin; a landslide victory in fair elections would greatly enhance the regime's legitimacy, discourage the opposition, and show voters that there were no viable alternatives to the status quo. This is why Navalny, who was undergoing a criminal trial during the campaign, was registered as a candidate. Apparently, the Kremlin wanted to sacrifice Navalny after the polls, but it underestimated his potential; the thirty-seven-year-old lawyer organized a very active electoral campaign based around young, dynamic, creative, and energetic staff, attracted a large number of devoted volunteers, effectively used crowdfunding techniques, and mobilized a lot of voters beyond the opposition's core supporters. The election results exceeded virtually all predictions: officially, Navalny received 27 percent of votes, and even though Sobyanin's result (51 percent) allowed him to escape the runoff, perceptions of fraud in his favor were unavoidable. Despite Navalny's electoral defeat, he reached extraordinary success at the polls, gaining more than 600,000 Muscovite votes. Still, these developments were indicative of the increasing troubles facing the Russian authorities; it became clear that major challenges for electoral authoritarianism in Russia lay ahead.

From this perspective, the Ukrainian crisis of 2014 should be perceived as a trigger event that accelerated the Kremlin's existing trend when it came to changing the domestic political agenda. The resulting changes greatly affected the regime's real or potential rivals: the opposition was bitterly divided, its previous "negative consensus" against the regime was undermined (if not disintegrated), and the Kremlin effectively pushed it back to the periphery of the political arena by discrediting, harassing, and intimidating its members. Competition in subnational elections was almost eliminated, so their new round in September 2014 more closely resembled a "hegemonic" (or "classical") version of authoritarian regimes than previous practices of electoral authoritarianism.[117] Independent media outlets reduced their levels of criticism, and vicious attacks on civic activists and dissenters became showcases of the politics of fear. Not only were the prodemocratic protests of 2011–2012 nearly forgotten, but the very rhetoric of democracy was abandoned by the Russian authorities, and the ultimate and demonstrative rejection of Western institutions became a mainstay of official propaganda. Against this background, Russian society did not demonstrate any serious resistance to its rulers. Quite the opposite, the mass public applauded Russia's aggressive foreign policy and appreciated the rising confrontation with the West, and Putin's approval rate reached its highest-ever level of more than 80 percent, according to numerous surveys.[118] At least for a while, the Russian leadership received *carte blanche* in the eyes of its fellow citizens, and used this support to strengthen its dominance. One may expect that the shortening of the time horizon for all domestic and international actors, as well as the regime's personalism and securitization, will further affect the trajectory of changes in politics and governance.

It is too early to discuss the consequences of the Ukrainian crisis for Russia's domestic agenda, but some effects are very visible; most probably, by the end of 2014 they will have become irreversible. First and foremost, the economic slowdown (which was observed even before the annexation of Crimea) is likely to turn into a full-fledged and severe decline. The foreign sanctions, Russian countersanctions, and increased military burden are only part of the story. Most importantly, economic issues lost their priority in the Kremlin's decision-making process, and the very mode of governance quickly deteriorated, since the security apparatus took the upper hand in agenda-setting for Russia's rulers. The project of "authoritarian modernization," which was launched under Putin in the early 2000s[119] and loudly announced under Medvedev, was sacrificed for the sake of the militarization and securitization of the country. Second, the regime's rising personalism in major policy directions (even the annexation of Crimea was a surprise for a part of Putin's inner circle) and the decline of auxiliary political institutions—not only parliament, political parties, and regional authorities, but even the federal government—is likely to turn into a principal feature of the Russian regime.[120] Even though the mode of ruling the country under Putin is far from that described in *The Autumn of the Patriarch* by Gabriel García Márquez (at least as of yet), the drive in this direction is strong and striking. Third, the information problems that contributed to the wave of protests in 2011–2012 are increasingly acute and likely to become exacerbated over time. The regime, which heavily relies upon lies as the primary instrument of politics, is at constant risk of wrong decisions due to misperceptions by its rulers. In fact, Russia's foreign policy toward Ukraine (both during the Orange Revolution and in the wake of regime change in 2014) might be considered a prime example of these misperceptions. No doubt similar risks in domestic politics will increase over time.

To summarize, one may consider the balance of the political pillars of the Russian authoritarian regime to be undergoing increasing disequilibrium. While economic prosperity has become a matter of the past, lies and fears are under stress from rising challenges. These challenges have come not only from outside the country, and even not only from the Russian citizens, but also from the Kremlin's top leadership. While these rising challenges could be considered as signs of the regime's decline, it would be premature to expect it to end soon in one way or another: as numerous examples of authoritarian regimes around the globe suggest, their rulers often hold power for a long while—not despite their poor economic performance, inefficient governance, arbitrary decisions, and systematic misinformation, but precisely because of some (or even all) of these features.[121] To what extent Russia will join this list of long-standing authoritarian regimes remains to be seen. But what kind of political future might we expect for Russia, and what lessons might we learn from the Russian experience of authoritarian regime building after the Soviet collapse?

CHAPTER 6

THE AGENDA FOR TOMORROW

FOR SOCIAL AND POLITICAL scientists, there is probably nothing more in demand, and at the same time more speculative, than the business of predicting the future. Just as economists are expected to predict global oil prices and the dynamics of stock exchanges, political scientists are valued in the eyes of politicians as well as the public primarily for their forecasts of domestic and international politics, rather than for their theoretical explanatory schemes and/or methodological sophistication. And if someone is able to make assumptions that prove to be factually correct over time, and then he or she may be rewarded irrespective of the substantive grounds for their predictions. With regard to Russian studies, the case of Hélène Carrère d'Encausse is probably the best-known example of predictions of this kind. In 1978, she published a book in which she argued that the Soviet Union would collapse by 1990 due to the rise of the Muslim population in Central Asia, which would cause Islamic revolt and a drive for independence from the Soviet empire.[1] Yet when the Soviet Union collapsed in 1991 for different reasons to those she had suggested,[2] she received outstanding academic recognition and became a permanent secretary of the French Academy, despite (or perhaps because of) the fact that the academic value of her forecast was dubious at best.

The problem, however, is not that so-called political experts actually producing political forecasts no more precise and substantively grounded than predictions made by an "average Joe." Virtually all political forecasts of this sort—whether made by professionals or amateurs—are based on projection of a current state of affairs into the future, with certain corrections and reservations, adjusting for either positive or negative exogenous factors. Meanwhile, real world developments often follow a different logic, one that is not always clearly understood, especially considering "wild cards"—unexpected and sometimes unpredictable factors that alter possible scenarios. It is no surprise that forecasting can turn into a lottery, and this is one of the major reasons why the business of predicting Russia's development—especially in the post-Soviet environment—is such a controversial and vague enterprise.[3] This is especially true given the acceleration of all political developments in Russia after the annexation of Crimea in 2014, which led to the shortening of time horizons in both domestic and international politics.

So are there any reasons for quasi-scientific debates about the prospects of Russian politics? Even given the above factors, it appears that discussing the political future still makes sense, and one can agree with Daniel Treisman, who believes that "even if one cannot say which of many paths history will go down, it is still useful to think about the layout of the paths, their forks and intersections. If nothing else, this prepares one to interpret rapidly what is happening as events unfold. At the same time, the attempt to think systematically about the future imposes a certain discipline and perspective that are helpful for understanding the present. One is forced to think about how different aspects of current reality fit together."[4]

Using this rationale, I will first discuss the conditions and constraints that prevent fundamental regime change, thus preserving the political status quo in Russia and the prospects for the regime's political stagnation, Then, I will turn to the possible alternatives, such as the rise of a more repressive version of authoritarianism (the "iron fist" option), the sudden collapse of the regime, and finally the gradual ("creeping") democratization trajectory, each with its opportunities and risks. Next, I will discuss the implications of analysis of post-Soviet authoritarianism for the study of the politics of regime changes around the globe. Possible implications for the evolutionary logic of Russia's political development will be considered in the conclusion.

Taking Russia's current regime—electoral authoritarianism with a low degree of repression—as a point of departure for further discussions, one should consider whether Russia can reject it and establish new institutional arrangements. If so, will these new rules become more democratic or, instead, will the country drift further toward a hegemonic (classical) model of authoritarianism or toward a more repressive regime (or both)? The answers to these questions are not clear, at least in the short term. It is true that, as the experience of various countries suggests, major regime changes are often the result of impacts from exogenous shocks such as wars, ethnic conflicts, revolutions, and economic crises. However, predicting such developments is an impossible task by definition and speculating on the possible impact of exogenous shocks on politics and society in Russia (and beyond) is counterproductive almost by definition, especially against the background of Russia's major confrontation with the West over Ukraine and increasing challenges and troubles on both domestic and international fronts. One should also not underestimate the risk that exogenous shocks might have an adverse effect on political development in some mid-developed countries: instead of becoming a driver of major changes (in whatever direction), they could be insufficient for altering the previous political regime's trajectory and inhibit any potential shifts. Russia could fall into this trap of seemingly endless regime continuity.

Another problem when analyzing possible directions for the regime's trajectory is the impact of its economic, social, and international environment, which imposes important structural constraints on regime change but does not determine political outcomes. For instance, some experts believe that the nature of the Russian political regime and the trajectory of its possible changes is more or less a byproduct of economic development.[5] This claim produces expectations that a possible economic recession in Russia brought on by domestic causes or by global economic developments may provoke major disequilibrium, which will lead to open competition among elites and revision of the rules of the game toward a more democratic direction. While such developments are possible, one has to bear in mind that authoritarian regimes do not always respond to economic crises in this way; they often demonstrate an involution tendency toward turning in on themselves, losing their capacity to change for a long period of time. Also, according to some studies, economic incentives for regime change are indirect and depend not only on the length of an economic decline but also on its depth; one can imagine that short-term economic shocks (similar to those of 2008–2009) as well as protracted but not so deep recessions may not affect political regimes, and their impact is sometimes insufficient to effect major changes. The same caution should be applied to the assumption that long-term and sustainable economic growth will inevitably lead to an increasing demand for democratization among the expanded urban middle class, thus triggering political reforms.[6] Although such a line of reasoning is quite logical and can be proven by the experience of numerous countries, there are no guarantees that this demand will play a major role at a particular critical juncture. On the contrary, one might argue that long-term and sustainable growth (similar to what Russia experienced in 1999–2008) can be conducive to the survival of any political regime, regardless of its nature.

Therefore, in further analysis I will attempt to avoid discussion of exogenous shocks and their possible impacts in terms of assumptions along the lines of "if A, then B." No doubt the economic and international environment of the Russian political regime is ever-changing and will change in one way or another. But one should not evaluate political developments only as a projection of social, economic, and international conditions; politics in any given country (including Russia) is a relatively autonomous arena. This is why I will focus primarily on the role of domestic political factors on the continuation and/or change of the Russian political regime, while related economic, social, and international factors will be viewed not as alternative explanations but rather as a background to political continuity and/or changes. With this approach in mind, I will consider a number of alternative paths for the Russian political regime's evolution in the short term:

- preservation of the current political regime in Russia (to use Soviet-era terminology, further "decay" of the Russian regime),
- increasing trends toward hegemonic and/or repressive authoritarianism as a result of the ruling groups' reaction to challenges to their dominance (the "iron fist" mechanism),
- a wild card—a sudden collapse of the current political regime under certain conditions (not necessarily caused by powerful external shocks), and
- a gradual and, most probably, inconsistent creeping democratization of the political regime under societal pressure.

Even though it is impossible to evaluate the probability of these paths, none of them should be dismissed. The regime's actual trajectory may not fit these ideal types but represent a combination of some of these trajectories and/or involve inconsistently alternating between some of their individual components. I will look at different perspectives of analysis, discussing each of these political development paths one by one in order to understand their potential constraints and risks.

"POLITICAL DECAY": THE ART OF MUDDLING THROUGH

Many observers of Russian politics assume that the rising dissatisfaction with the status quo regime (whatever status quo meant at any given moment) creates incentives for major political changes in a certain direction practically by default. Nothing could be further from the truth; the logic of political development that posits the preservation of the status quo as an end in itself for the ruling groups and for society at large can best be expressed by the maxim "stay away from trouble." Indeed, provided that in the foreseeable future roughly the same arrangement of key actors and their incentives, and capabilities will persist, and granted that opposition and protest movement pressure on the regime has been brought back to a level predating late 2011, one should not expect Russian ruling groups to fully revise the rules of the game and change the institutional core of the political regime. An inertia-based trajectory of muddling through, in the manner of a "political decay" that preserves the current constellation of actors and set of political institutions with some insignificant changes, looks to be the Kremlin's preferred choice compared to both political liberalization and a shift to more repressive authoritarianism.

However, the inefficient political equilibrium cannot maintain itself automatically; it will require substantial effort on the part of the Kremlin. Besides the skillful use of the carrots and sticks, the authorities will most certainly be forced to resort more actively to targeted and strictly limited repressions and fears thereof against the regime's opponents and its "fellow travelers" from the elites and correct both formal and informal rules of the game in order to consolidate, rather than simply preserving, the institutional core of the political regime. Some examples of such behavior can be clearly seen in the steps the Kremlin took during Putin's third term in office. These were the politics of fear: crackdowns on protest actions, jailing activists, increasing fines and sanctions for violations of the rules on meetings and rallies, and a number of other frightening moves were accompanied by the partial liberalization of party registration procedures and a return to the popular election of regional chief executives. But institutional engineering became even more manipulative than before the 2011–2012 protests. While the use of the municipal filter in gubernatorial elections and very arbitrary enforcement of the new party and electoral rules effectively prevented all unwanted candidates from seeking nomination, the intended shift from a proportional electoral system in State Duma elections back to a mixed disconnected system (as used in Russia in 1993–2003) was intended to compensate for the decline of United Russia's support with the help of "independent" candidates in single-member districts.[7] In fact, the partial revision of the rules of the game was intended to entrench and reinforce the electoral authoritarianism, though in a new guise. In short, these changes are oriented toward consolidation of the regime by making it less vulnerable; in other words, they represent an "authoritarian correction" of mistakes and a rectification of certain excesses of the previous stage of authoritarian regime building in Russia.[8] In this respect, even some shallow institutional changes might be instrumental for the Kremlin in terms of coopting some of its potential rivals and isolating others.

A preservation of the status quo that involves further regime consolidation and rearrangement will not be able to solve the problems of poor-quality governance in Russia, and will most likely exacerbate them. The path to political decay will lead to further aggravation of the principal-agent problems in central-regional-local relations, as well as to an increase in corruption at all levels and to permanent conflicts over rent redistribution among interest groups. This political decay will also lead to sharp increases in the costs of maintaining the political equilibrium, due to the rising payoffs that the Kremlin will have to offer various political and economic rent-seekers as well as numerous social groups as side payment for their loyalty.

And what about the general public? As of yet, the Kremlin is able to satisfy demand for change to a certain extent through some concessions on second-order issues, through the effective cooptation of some moderate opponents of the regime, and through the relatively successful resolution of certain issues, or in some instances it may simply remain at the level of minor discontent. Even numerous local "rebellions" driven by socioeconomic issues do not pose a major threat to the Kremlin as long as a significant part of society may react to institutional decay through a passive individual "exit" rather than through a collective and open "voice," as Albert Hirschman terms it.[9] The exit can take different forms (such as emigration from Russia), but it will pose no danger to the authorities, since not only does it not challenge the status quo as such, but it also increases the cost, for protesters, of overcoming the regime's resistance. One should not expect major changes without cumulative and relatively protracted societal pressure on the regime. If the scope and time frame of this pressure is insufficient, the institutional decay may last until the costs of maintaining the status quo become prohibitively high for the Kremlin, or even until the current generation of Russian leaders simply becomes extinct, akin to the generation of Soviet leaders of the Brezhnev period, thus postponing a major revision of the regime's institutional core into the indefinite future. Yet while the preservation of the status quo regime and the lack of further bad news from Russia may postpone major changes, it cannot avert them entirely.

Although political decay might be treated as the basis for considerations about Russia's political future, there are two important constraints to this scenario in Russia. First, in order to maintain political equilibrium, the Kremlin will require a constant and substantial rent inflow that will ensure the loyalty of major political and economic actors and society at large. Certainly, Russia's economic trends are hardly conducive to fulfilling these requests, especially given its major disequilibrium that launched in 2014. Second, the regime's manipulative strategy with the use of lies and fear may become less efficient over time, recalling Lincoln's remark that one cannot fool all the people all the time. Thus, attempts to preserve the regime through institutional decay are very questionable, to put it mildly.

THE "IRON FIST": AN OPTION FOR THE DICTATOR?

An alternative path for Russian political development assumes that the ruling group will face an increase in actual and potential challenges to its domina-

tion, which may involve various threats that could be considered very dangerous by the Kremlin. The risk perception of "rebellion" by some of the regime's
current loyalists as well as the risk of mass protests might increase, and the
Kremlin's potential for their cooptation and/or the use of the politics of fear
for maintaining loyalty might be exhausted. The experiences of some other
authoritarian regimes in different parts of the world (ranging from the South
Korean regime's massacre at the student uprising in Gwangju in 1980 to the
introduction of martial law in Poland in 1981) suggest that under such circumstances, their leaders tend to pick up a stick and use it without restraint. In
the long term this strategy rarely proves successful for initially nonrepressive
authoritarian regimes (especially if these regimes do not enjoy mass support
and the scope of protests increases over time).[10] However, in the short term
such a reaction to political crises may postpone negative consequences for the
regime, despite the resulting increase in violence and potential conflict in the
future. Thus, in order to maintain their domination, the Russian authorities
may possibly opt for an "iron fist" response, requiring them to partially or
completely dismantle the democratic façade of some current institutions of
electoral authoritarianism, and replace them with openly repressive mechanisms through various means of coercion, while retaining the regime's institutional core. Even if the "iron fist" option may appear suicidal, a delayed or
postponed self-annihilation and its possible political consequences still merit
serious consideration.

It is hard to predict the Kremlin's steps along this path, which presumes
further concentration of power in the hands of Putin and his cronies and the
increased role of the security apparatus; they may impose major restrictions
on elections, political parties, and NGOs, a radical overhaul of legislation and
practice that expands the powers of law enforcement agencies and security services and further restricts individual rights and liberties, new vicious attacks
on independent media, greater pressure on public dissent, and so on (some of
these tactics were already in place in the process of tightening the screws after
the 2011–2012 protests and, especially, after Russia's annexation of Crimea in
2014). This path may logically result in the adoption of a new Russian constitution stripped of declarations of individual rights and liberties, denying
the supremacy of Russia's international obligations over domestic legislation,
and eliminating other liberal statements as remnants of the "roaring 1990s."
One can consider abolishment of presidential term limits, possible elimination of elections and/or turning them into elections without choice as logical
extensions of this turn from an electoral version of authoritarianism toward
its hegemonic or "classical" form. The possible design of new institutions, as
well as the scale and scope of repression, would depend upon *perceptions* of

threats or challenges and associated risks to the ruling groups rather than the actual danger they pose.

However, the reliance upon repressions (and/or upon the threat thereof), even in the form most favorable to the authorities, would allow the latter to cope with symptoms of the regime's troubles but not their underlying causes. It is hard to expect that they would be able to enhance the regime's legitimacy, which thus far has been almost exclusively output-based and has relied upon mass perception of the regime's performance.[11] However, the possible shift toward an iron fist would hardly be productive for these purposes, and one should not expect these measures to increase regime performance. Corruption, the struggle for rent redistribution among the Kremlin's cronies, and the growing principal-agent problems would not disappear but would take other forms. Rather, one might expect the iron fist option to lead to a sharp increase in the cost of maintaining political equilibrium in the country. The ruling groups will not only have to significantly increase agency costs, but will also need to dramatically raise payoffs to the coercive apparatus to reward its loyalty. The risk of becoming a hostage to the coercive apparatus can be a problem for any repressive regime, and, in Russia's case, law enforcement agencies and security services have exhibited notoriously poor quality of service[12] and do not enjoy significant support in Russian society. Given that the security apparatus of the Russian state (unlike the army in military regimes) cannot perform the functions of governance in an appropriate way, a turn toward this path would only exacerbate many of the Kremlin's problems, especially against the background of economic crisis.

However, one should not expect that this change (if and when it helps the Kremlin tame protests and reduce immediate threats to the regime) will provoke political disequilibrium in and of itself, even if the increasing threats of repression pose a major challenge to a large number of former Kremlin loyalists or other potential dissenters. For at least as long as the "advanced" segment of Russian society considers the exit option (via leaving the country by emigration) a preferable alternative to the voice option (that is, protests against the status quo), the risk of public disobedience will not be excessively high for the ruling groups.[13] The experience of Belarus under Alexander Lukashenko also tells us that, given a lack of viable alternatives, repressive authoritarian regimes of this kind may be able to maintain political equilibrium, at least for a while, without major risk.

In Russia's case, there are other risks for the Kremlin if it opts for an iron fist authoritarian policy. First, international experience suggests that authoritarian regimes that initially refrain from repression rarely become significantly more repressive. Using a stick is quite a difficult task for the Kremlin after a long and successful distribution of carrots. Second, the international consequences of a shift toward repressive authoritarianism will probably be even more negative than the current conflict with the West over Ukraine. Finally, repressive authoritarianism threatens to open the door to the use of violence as an instrument for the resolution of rising conflicts within the ruling groups, and may aggravate problems for the Kremlin, especially given the poor performance of the coercive apparatus. The unsuccessful use of repressions may in turn bring about the collapse of the authoritarian regime, as happened after the August 1991 coup in the Soviet Union. Due to the unpredictable consequences of such developments, the iron fist, far from being a "dictator's solution," may prove to be one of the possible causes of regime collapse. Thus, the chances for successful implementation of this scenario are rather dubious.

THE REGIME'S COLLAPSE: A CLEAN-CUT vs. A FESTERING WOUND?

At first glance, the collapse of the political regime—a sudden, rapid, and complete breakdown that implies major replacement of actors and institutions— appears increasingly likely in present-day Russia, given the rising challenges for the regime and the unpredictability of the Kremlin's behavior in both the domestic and the international arena. Yet such a collapse is hindered by the conspicuous lack of any signs of a "revolutionary situation" in Russia, at least for now.[14] The degree of cohesion of the ruling groups and their allies is still high enough to avoid these risks. One should also take into account that even the emergence of a revolutionary situation does not necessarily lead to a revolutionary outcome to the political process. Rather, such developments quite frequently occur in spontaneous, sometimes even mostly accidental, combinations of events at a certain critical juncture. Neither the February 1917 uprising that ended the monarchy in Russia nor the fall of the long-standing authoritarian regime in Tunisia in early 2011 that launched the "Arab Spring" were inevitable and predetermined. Therefore, although it is clearly impossible to predict, one cannot rule out the possibility of regime collapse, especially given the increasing difficulty faced by the authorities in maintaining a political equilibrium.

A clean cut is better than a festering wound, as the conventional wisdom goes. However, this notion is rather questionable when it comes to the collapse of nondemocratic regimes. Regime collapses sometimes lead to the replacement of one authoritarian regime with another, and the risk that the new regime will become even more repressive is reasonably high. The experience of both the 1917 collapse of the monarchy and the 1991 collapse of Soviet Communism are probably the most telling in Russian history. After a regime's collapse, power can be seized by political entrepreneurs who build their monopolies on the ruins of the previous political order (Lukashenko in Belarus can be regarded as a prime example among post-Soviet leaders), and zero-sum conflicts between would-be new rulers (similarly to the 1993 clash between Yeltsin and the parliament in Russia) are also possible. Due to these risks, even the restoration of the previous authoritarian regime after its collapse might be perceived as a preferable option for the elite and society at large. The problem is that a regime's collapse is similar to a sudden death; usually nobody is prepared for this shift, and given the shortage of time and high uncertainty, major actors often make poor choices, and the public is deceived by false promises and expectations. If, after the collapse of the current authoritarian regime, Vladimir Putin were simply replaced by a new authoritarian leader, it would probably not bring about the country's democratization, but would instead signal a regime change from bad to worse. Moreover, attempts to retain power at any cost in the process of the regime's collapse might be suicidal not only for the Kremlin but also for the country as a whole. Although a situation where Putin threatens to use nuclear weapons as a response to mass protests against his rule now looks like the opening of a thriller rather than a realistic political scenario, real life is sometimes more dramatic than any invented horrors.

However, it is also plausible that Russia may successfully capitalize on the unexpected chance for democratization, if and when such a chance appears, upon the regime's collapse. As Mancur Olson has noted, "autocracy is prevented and democracy is permitted by the accidents of history that leave a balance of power or stalemate—a dispersion of force and resources that makes it impossible for any leader or group to overpower all the others."[15] However, such a situation is hardly likely to emerge by default, and be followed by successful democratization, without special efforts by political actors and society as a whole; thus, relying on such an option is as reasonable as relying on a winning lottery ticket. While the degree of harm that would be done by a sudden political collapse of the Russian regime is quite high, the probability of immediate positive outcomes is very small.

"CREEPING DEMOCRATIZATION": OPPORTUNITIES AND RISKS

Creeping democratization is a complex, incremental, and sometimes quite lengthy process of transition from authoritarianism to democracy through a series of strategic interactions between the ruling groups and the opposition, who adjust their strategies in response to each other's moves.[16] Ruling groups may agree to partial regime liberalization under pressure from the opposition against a background of rising public discontent, and then—given increasing pressure and the regime's inability to eliminate liberalization—accept the extension of room for political participation, which, in turn, leads to increasing divisions within ruling groups and the involvement of the opposition in the political process. Further developments may involve several different options, among which are a compromise between the reform-minded part of the ruling groups and the moderate segments of the opposition (also known as pacts or elite settlements, like the Polish roundtable in 1989),[17] as well as the ruling groups' efforts for democratization, which allow them to maintain power upon beginning competitive elections (as in South Korea in 1987).[18] Finally, the process may develop into a series of electoral competitions with a more level playing field in national and subnational electoral arenas over time, guaranteeing a peaceful transfer of power to the opposition (as in Mexico in 1997–2000).[19] Such trajectories have resulted in success stories of democratization in some countries, and there is no reason to rule them out in the case of contemporary Russia. However, at the moment conditions for such a shift appear unlikely, given that by the end of 2014 Russia's regime has increased its international isolation and strengthened its coercive capabilities as well as state control over the economy.[20] However, the very existence of democratic institutions in Russia (irrespective of their current functions of maintenance of electoral authoritarianism)[21] does not preclude this possibility. Bearing these prospects in mind, one can consider the 2011–2012 protests (despite their failure) to be the first—necessary but insufficient—steps toward creeping democratization in Russia. Of course, it is equally likely that Russia will turn away from this path and witness a restoration of the status quo, and/or have the regime's trajectory switch to other forms of authoritarianism; creeping democratization often turns out to be inconsistent and may involve numerous attempts.

As a rule of thumb, one can argue that the Kremlin's strategy of maintaining electoral authoritarianism may change only due to simultaneous and cumulative pressures from all directions: not only from outside the country but mostly from within; international influence will change little if domestic pressure is not strong enough.[22] This will occur only if various social groups and political actors, both the opposition and the general public, are able to consolidate and mobilize a large number of their supporters on the basis of a negative consensus against the status quo over a reasonably long period of time. At the moment, however, the Russian opposition has very limited potential, resulting not only from its organizational weakness but also from the very fact that a large part of Russian society does not perceive the opposition as an attractive and realistic alternative to the status quo political regime—at least for now.[23] To put it bluntly, the decline of public support for the regime, if and when it occurs, will not empower the opposition by default. Much will depend upon the Russian opposition itself. The experience of creeping democratization in a number of countries, from Latin America to post-Communist Europe (including those of the color revolutions),[24] suggests the crucial importance of the opposition's organizational consolidation in the struggle against a common enemy based on a negative consensus; in order to reach their goal, the regime's rivals would require cooperation between different segments of the opposition and the mutual support of potential allies.[25] This cooperation need not necessarily mean organizational unity, but various segments would have to seek the support of different cross-sections of the public. Another important element of cooperation is a taboo on open and deep disagreements among the opposition; its leaders and activists would have to refrain from publicly attacking one another to accomplish their principal goal. In addition, they would have to demonstrate their ability to reach tactical compromise, their willingness to be ideologically flexible, and their capacity to act together. At the moment, the opposition in Russia is very far from this developmental stage; it must learn a great deal from the experience of the opposition in other authoritarian regimes and from its own errors, but there are no grounds to consider such an evolution completely impossible.[26]

Besides different forms of mass protest activism, elections serve as the major institution capable of undermining the current authoritarian equilibrium in Russia. This does not mean that Russia's transition to democracy—if and when it happens—will come as a result of the opposition's electoral victory over the Kremlin; as long as the electoral authoritarian regime is preserved, it will not just go away by itself. But the ambiguity of elections under authoritarianism due to their central role in maintaining the regime's legitimacy contributes to the stunning elections effect,[27] similar to what was observed in the December 2011 State Duma vote. The problem that the Kremlin also learned from its own errors and tries to avoid these risks using any possible means makes elections less and less competitive and meaningful in the eyes of its fellow citizens. Still, one cannot exclude the possibility that at a certain point national elections may become a key challenge to preservation of the status quo, especially as they are happening under highly uncertain conditions.

However, successful democratization does not happen by default when the authoritarian regime is overthrown. It becomes possible, but is not guaranteed, if and when the key political actors are able to accept the new institutional arrangements and, more importantly, ensure they are successfully implemented. In other words, these rules should both act to prevent power monopoly and provide more efficient governance than was established under authoritarian rule—otherwise, the regime's trajectory could be reversed and return to the previous order, and democratization as such could be discredited. Such rules are not always easily adopted and implemented; not only Russia's experience immediately after the collapse of Communism in 1991, but also that of Ukraine after the "Orange Revolution," might be perceived as classic examples of failures in democratic institution building.[28] In Ukraine's case, the constitutional reform aimed at limiting presidential powers was adopted in the wake of mass postelection protests in 2004.[29] However, power-sharing between the president and the prime minister was vague and fluctuating, the party system was unable to maintain an effective balance of political actors, and rivalry between major leaders caused great trouble in politics and governance. It is no surprise that this experience was widely considered to be negative, and after Viktor Yanukovych's electoral victory in 2010 this reform was abolished, and the previous institutional arrangements, which had been widely criticized before 2004, were restored as a lesser evil. Thus, the institutional effects of democratization in Ukraine were greatly diminished, and these trends contributed to a new round of political conflicts, which led to the overthrow of Yanukovych after the series of protests in 2014.[30] This is why politicians concerned about democratization in Russia will have to learn from these failures, including from Russia's own experience of the 1990s and 2000s.

In fact, most political institutions built in Russia after the collapse of the Soviet Union cannot be improved through partial revisions and corrections. However, their thorough overhaul will bring not only new opportunities but also new risks. These risks, while inevitable, can and should be minimized. New rules of the game are more likely to be accepted in the process of dismantling an authoritarian regime or immediately after its collapse; the experience of certain postauthoritarian transformations tells us that new institutions are most likely to emerge because of a change in the balance of resources and interests of various actors. This is why, at the moment, designating new democratic institutions in Russia as the opposition's first priority seems like putting the cart before the horse. Nevertheless, a minimal consensus among the elite and society at large will be necessary to avoid abuse of power by the chief executives, establish a workable system of checks and balances, ensure political accountability, and prevent monopolization of power in both national and subnational politics, but at the same time to avert the risk of major policy deadlocks and ensure efficient decision making. A number of bright ideas for reforming executive-legislative and center-regional-local relations, electoral and party systems[31] and reorganization of law enforcement agencies[32] were recently proposed in Russia, and there is little doubt that at least some of them will be demanded if and when democratization occurs in Russia. It is still too early to outline the specific institutional solutions that will be sought in the wake of democratization, but one should be ready for a possible comprehensive rewriting of the rules of the game in various arenas of Russian politics and government; a chance to ensure democratic change should not be missed again, as happened in Russia in the early 1990s. And even though efficient institutional design is not in itself a guarantee of successful democratization in Russia or elsewhere, it may reduce its risks.

Overall, a number of observers would agree that creeping democratization is the most desirable trajectory for the Russian regime in the future. But at the moment it seems to be just wishful thinking, since almost no signs of movement in this directions has been observed in Russia in the wake of the "tightening the screws" launched during Putin's third term in office, and especially after the 2014 annexation of Crimea and subsequent events.[33] It does not preclude these possibilities for Russia but there is little ground to expect "creeping democratization" in the foreseeable future.

UNKNOWN VARIABLES AND WHY THEY MATTER

Any attempts at political forecasting are faced with the unavoidable problem of multiple unknown variables, which cannot necessarily be defined and measured even at a given moment, let alone making reasonable estimations of how they may change in the future. Therefore, evaluations of the probability of each of the four regime trajectories outlined above—political decay, iron fist, regime collapse, and creeping democratization—appear all but pointless. None of them can be ruled out, nor can we predict their combination or succession, and this makes analysis even more difficult.

The list of unknown variables that might contribute to a particular trajectory, or to a combination of trajectories or shifts between them, is extremely long and not country-specific. Thus, there is no need to list all the factors whose impact is known to be unpredictable by definition. However, at least three unknown variables are especially important in the context of present-day Russia, and the direction of a possible political regime trajectory, inter alia, is highly contingent upon their dynamics.

First of all, there is the possibility of unpredictable changes in the public opinion of Russians—at the level of both the elite and the general public—and in the political behavior of citizens. There is no need to underline the ultimate role of these changes as such, but their assessment and prediction are especially difficult under the conditions of authoritarian regimes, since survey data are systematically distorted by the "preference falsification effect" first discovered in East Germany in 1989[34]—in other words, instead of being truthful in inter-

★

views and polls, the average citizen provides responses that are socially acceptable in the eyes of the regime. To use a colloquial term, people often "give the authorities the finger" behind their backs. Hence the problem of preference falsification for electoral authoritarian regimes is twofold. On the one hand, false results in surveys greatly contribute to electoral fraud; when many people openly lie to pollsters that they support the regime, survey results become an easy target for the state officials responsible for delivering votes to rulers by every possible means.[35] On the other hand, those people who routinely lie while answering questionnaires may decide to "give the authorities the finger" out in the open at the most unexpected critical juncture. At times, the sudden appearance of mass preference changes (which may initially be hidden) may lead to the collapse of the authoritarian regime (East Germany in 1989 serves as a prime example of this), but very often the finger may remain behind the back for quite a while, and the public's true preferences are unknown until new challenges to the status quo emerge seemingly out of the blue. Since an ostensibly stable authoritarian regime may be toppled at any critical juncture, the actual behavior of all political actors at these points is certainly unpredictable. This means that the authorities can overestimate or (more often) underestimate the risks entailed by the shifting preferences of both the elite and society at large, while the opposition sometimes considers the failure of the authoritarian regime to lie in the too-distant future, and remains unprepared for major regime changes if and when they suddenly occur.[36]

Second, the key issue for the survival of any authoritarian regime is the capacity and willingness of the ruling groups to use violence and repression against their challengers, and also the consequences of such moves. This issue is particularly salient in Russia's case. Indeed, repressive regimes habitually use violence in the case of even relatively minor threats to their survival, and sometimes even killing their own citizens is just a routine affair. Among post-Soviet countries, the Andijan massacre in Uzbekistan in 2005 is an example of coercion of this kind.[37] However, nonrepressive authoritarian regimes, which mostly rely upon preemptive politics of fear rather than upon actual use of violence, may face the tough choice of a change from carrot to stick. In addition, the turn toward large-scale violence against the people is very rare among authoritarian regimes in modernized middle-income countries.[38] Russia is no exception in this respect, given the previous record not only of the post-Soviet regime but also of the Soviet Union after Stalin. Even if turning in this direction does not cause immediate political consequences for the regime, it determines ruling groups' strategy for many years to come (as was the case with the Novocherkassk massacre of 1962 in the Soviet Union, after which using the army to shoot citizens became taboo for the

Communist regime, and the regime turned from an ex post to a preemptive strategy of coercion).[39]

In reality, the key question "to beat or not to beat?" (referring to the choice between using violence against antiregime protests and refraining from it) is often answered based on past experience of using mass violence. The 1989 China example demonstrates that the use of force against the protesters on Tiananmen Square became possible because the veterans of the revolution, who took the dominant positions in Chinese leadership and had been accustomed to killing their fellow citizens since the time of the Communist Party's struggle for power, prevailed over their less harsh rivals during the decision-making process.[40] Russia is a special case in this respect, not only due to the low repressiveness of the regime but also because the means of mass repression are unreliable; the security apparatus is largely lacking authority, too heavily involved in rent-seeking, and too hungry to usurp major leverages of power. Yet Russia's rulers lack moral constraints on the use of mass violence; in the cases of the hostage crises in Moscow (2002) and Beslan (2004) they never apologized after killing hundreds of people alongside the terrorists, and probably did not even concern themselves with saving their lives.[41] But it would probably be incorrect to reduce the issue of potential repressions to one of technical constraints to repressive capabilities, which become excessive if and when mass protests reach a certain scale (as the chief of the East German security services noted to Erich Honecker in 1989, "we can't beat hundreds of thousands of people").[42] Rather, the questions should be posed in a different sequence: (1) will the Russian leaders resolve to order mass-scale use of violence against citizens in the case of real or imaginary threats to their political survival? (2) If so, will the order be successfully carried out, and will violence be able to eliminate the threat? (3) If so, will the Russian leaders end up being hostages to the executors of this order? The answers to these questions are unclear, and one can only hope that they do not become part of Russia's actual political agenda.

Third, we still do not know to what extent the country is manageable (or, rather, unmanageable) for the Kremlin. This problem does not refer to any instances of organized sabotage, regional separatism, or ethnic conflicts that the Kremlin considers a nightmare—these are rather unlikely at the moment. But under the conditions of a highly corrupt authoritarian regime, the power vertical hierarchy simply cannot handle even relatively small overloads and emergency situations, given the rise of principal-agent problems over time.[43] For example, when it comes to natural disasters, the federal government has to deal with local issues through "manual control," while the lower links of the power vertical consistently and systematically misinform the higher authorities. In the worst case, the impact of natural and technological disasters on governability crises in Russia may be similar to those of the Chernobyl nuclear catastrophe in 1986, which dealt a huge blow to the Soviet Union and ultimately contributed to Gorbachev's great shift to glasnost. Given the recent trend of personalization and securitization of decision making in Russia, the rise of threat perceptions among the Kremlin's leadership, the diminishing salience of the economic agenda,[44] and the increasing risks attributed to the regime's information problems,[45] even relatively manageable issues might contribute to a major governability crisis. One cannot predict the possible consequences of such developments in present-day Russia, but given the preservation of the current political regime and the attempts to maintain the status quo at any cost, the inefficiency of the entire hierarchical chain of command and the rising principal-agent problems will probably only be exacerbated. This means that certain challenges may arise at any moment and suddenly bring about a new critical juncture in Russia's regime trajectory.

We have seen, then, that even a short list of unknown variables affecting possible regime changes in Russia would be rather impressive in scope, featuring such items as (1) preference falsification and the unpredictability of Russians' political behavior, (2) the degree of the ruling groups' willingness and capability to suppress mass protests through the use of mass violence, and (3) the degradation of governance and inability to implement anticrisis policies. However, understanding the regime's possible trajectory requires more focus on the overall logic of Russia's post-Soviet political evolution, which will help in understanding the logic of authoritarian regime building across the globe. It will also allow one to see the larger picture of the evolutionary trends of Russian politics beyond the details of current events.

LESSONS FROM RUSSIA'S EXPERIENCE: POLITICAL HANGOVER AND WRONG SIGNALS

Although the current state of Russia's authoritarianism might look gloomy, for political scientists there should be no grounds for sloth in terms of a scholarly agenda. On the contrary, present-day Russia can be perceived as a kind of El Dorado for experts in the study of numerous instances of "bad politics," such as clientelism, corruption, and institutional decay. From this perspective, post-Soviet Russian authoritarianism offers evidence for the testing of existing theories and the development of new approaches. Instead of condemning post-Soviet Russia as an example of unfulfilled promises, with its failed democratization and authoritarian drift, we have to answer the major scholarly question "why?" from the viewpoint of lessons that might be learned from Russia's experience of post-Soviet regime changes.

The core argument of this book is based upon the statement that Russia's post-Soviet experience is a textbook example of power maximization by politicians, who faced few constraints to achieving their aspirations. International influence, irresolvable elite conflicts, mass political involvement, and ideologically driven perceptions of leadership were all insufficient to build barriers that could not be crossed by post-Soviet Russian rulers. And while Yeltsin's power maximization strategy was limited by circumstances such as state weakness after the Soviet collapse, and the economic troubles of the 1990s, Putin almost always had free rein and acted as a more effective power maximizer: even bumps on the road such as the wave of protests of 2011–2012 and the Ukrainian crisis of 2014 have not yet significantly constrained him.

This statement, however, covers only a part of the story. Indeed, if we turn back to the first page of chapter 1, which began with the collapse of Soviet Communism, we will be surprised to see that at that time some of the potential barriers were in place: during the years of perestroika under Gorbachev, the Soviet Union experienced a great opening toward international influence, an ideologically driven shift toward liberalization and political pluralism, mass political involvement, and numerous elite conflicts both nationwide and subnationally.[46] Why did all these factors, which were so vividly observed *before* the end of the Communism and certainly played a decisive role in the Soviet collapse,[47] become so negligible *after* the dissolution of the Soviet Union and the elimination of the Communist regime? Although, as I argued in the previous chapters, major elite conflicts in post-Soviet Russia have always been resolved in a zero-sum manner, where have the West, the masses, and the ideas gone?

While a complete answer to this question would require an entire additional book, one might argue that the nonemergence of constraints to unchecked power maximization in post-Soviet Russia in a way reflected the failure of the democratization project launched under Górbachev. Indeed, many electoral authoritarian regimes in post-Soviet Eurasia and beyond have appeared as byproducts of failed democracies.[48] Whatever the causes of these failures, the experience of perestroika, which started as a project of reforming the Soviet system but resulted in the collapse of both the regime and the state, offered an example of the wrong path in every possible sense to the actors and citizens of the post-Soviet period. For the masses, the major lesson learned from perestroika and the first years after the Soviet collapse was bitter disillusionment in the upheaval of social and political activism, which brought them few (if any) benefits. For domestic political and economic actors, the power of any and all ideas was heavily discredited in the wake of this disillusionment. In addition, the process of generation change and the associated decline of the sixties (*shestidesyatniki*), with their ideationally driven agenda, greatly contributed to this shift.[49] From both perspectives, the very agenda of democratization was considered at best as one possible tool for achieving economic prosperity; it is no wonder that in the 2000s, when Russia experienced economic growth without democratization, this agenda was easily abandoned.

While some scholars, especially in the 1990s, discussed whether the economic shock in Russia after the Soviet collapse was excessively strong or more or less natural, and whether the country successfully coped with it,[50] there was also the post-Soviet political shock, which presented different problems for the further trajectory of regime change. The shock of the failure of democratization after the Soviet collapse caused a political hangover syndrome, which produced a number of wrong signals for Russia's political actors and for society at large, and thence contributed to the country's authoritarian drift. Moreover, each step away from democratization taken at certain critical junctures of the post-Soviet trajectory—the rejection of building new democratic institutions in 1991, the disbanding of parliament in 1993, the unfair presidential elections in 1996, the zero-sum "war of Yeltsin's succession" in 1999–2000, the "authoritarian modernization" project in the 2000s, or the Putin–Medvedev job swap game in 2008–2012—only further aggravated the "flight from freedom" trend. The antidemocratic trajectory became path-contingent over time, such that the menu of choices for political actors was limited by what they (or their political predecessors) had chosen during previous episodes.[51] Like a drinker who cannot (and/or does not wish) to change self-destructive behavior, even while repeatedly intoxicated, and after each shot of vodka gradually becoming an alcoholic, none of Russia's actors after the Soviet collapse had sufficient incentives for democratization; faced with the risk of major losses, they exacerbated antidemocratic trends, thus turning the trajectory of authoritarian regime building in Russia into a dead end, if not a vicious circle.

The first wrong signal, which can be considered both a product and a cause of the post-Soviet political hangover syndrome, was related to the dilemma of simultaneity, which in the Russian case was resolved in favor of economic reforms over democratization and state building. This choice, made by Russia's self-interested rulers, greatly favored Yeltsin and the loyal part of his winning coalition. However, at the moment of Soviet collapse this choice was also welcomed by some domestic observers and by Russian society at large.[52] The extraordinary salience of economic problems against the background of a major recession was not the only reason to reject the democratization agenda. The previous negative experience of perestroika, when rapid democratization without major economic reforms greatly contributed to violent ethnic conflicts and the subsequent demise of the Soviet state, also played an important role in this choice. It provided the Russian elite and the general public with the perception that democratization was not an overly urgent goal; it could be sacrificed for the sake of much-needed economic reforms and postponed to better times. Indeed, the political freedom that seemingly emerged in Russia in the wake of the Soviet collapse was at the time perceived by a number of observers as a benefit of secondary importance that could be used only after resolving more acute problems.

In fact, this perception was wrong. Not only did immediate democratization and rapid economic reforms in Eastern Europe mutually reinforce each other and bring positive results in both arenas,[53] but the rejection of the democratization agenda in Russia also coincided with the economic reforms' numerous troubles. Even though the deep and protracted recession of the 1990s finally changed to the tremendous growth of the 2000s, major economic institutions such as the rule of law and the protection of property rights have still not emerged in Russia after more than two decades; in the end the crony capitalism run by the Kremlin's inner circle can hardly be considered a success story.[54] The increasingly nondemocratic political environment in the context of post-Soviet Russia greatly contributed to these evolutionary trends of economic institutions. Without entering into endless debates on whether democracy causes economic development or vice versa,[55] one might argue that electoral authoritarianism in Russia and beyond has made economic progress more problematic, to put it mildly. As Russia's experience demonstrates, this regime has combined all the obstacles that hinder economic growth in democracies (such as political business cycles[56] and the dominance of distributional coalitions)[57] with politicized control of leaders over the economy, the arbitrary use of the coercive apparatus,[58] and the use of patronage as a tool of politics and policy making.[59]

The second wrong signal resulting from the political hangover syndrome after the Soviet collapse is related to the role of the legacy of the past in terms of political changes and institution building.[60] The Soviet economic model was so heavily discredited that in post-Soviet Russia no one seriously proposed going "back to the USSR": all discussions on economic policy since the Soviet collapse revolved around various approaches to markets, but not the adaptation, let alone restoration, of the Soviet institutional legacy.[61] By contrast, in the political arena the Soviet legacy has been increasingly considered as a role model (especially under Putin) and constantly used as a set of building blocks for the making of post-Soviet institutions. As Brian Taylor has convincingly argued, this fact played a major role in the remaking of law enforcement agencies in post-Soviet Russia—it is from the Soviet past that they inherited their centralized hierarchy, lack of political and societal accountability, supremacy of secret services, and arbitrary use of coercion for protecting the state against its citizens.[62] The same logic might be applied to the building of the hierarchical power vertical of subnational governance, which by and large was a Soviet-type solution to post-Soviet problems and inherited the same kind of notorious inefficiency against a background of increasing principal-agent problems.[63] In a sense, the reliance upon late-Soviet practices of politics and governance became a byproduct of the rejection of the democratization agenda: in the absence of viable alternatives, it was the only role model readily available to Russia's rulers and society at large.

The third wrong signal from the experience of the Soviet collapse and early post-Soviet developments was addressed to the West. Because the Soviet Union ceased to exist after 1991 and Russia (like other post-Soviet states) was no longer perceived as a source of major potential threat, the victors of the Cold War considered their goal achieved and paid little attention to political developments in Russia ever since. There were no incentives to offer Russia comprehensive economic aid during the transformation recession in the 1990s,[64] let alone to take advantage of the opening window of opportunities for full-scale use of prodemocratic leverage. Yet international influence is complementary rather than substitutive for domestic actors, and no one believes that even immediately after the Soviet collapse the West would have been able to impose its set of institutions on domestic actors the way it did in West Germany after the Second World War. While in post-Communist Eastern Europe and in some states of post-Eurasia (such as Ukraine and Moldova) the West played a major role and actively used certain leverages in pushing forward a democratization agenda,[65] in Russia this impact was negligible after the Soviet collapse, and declined over time even before the Kremlin's efforts to counter Western influence on Russia. To put it bluntly, American and European actors made few rhetorical concessions to Russia, and simply did not consider the advancement of democratization in Russia a priority.[66] Even so, the irreversibility of the political changes in Russia after the Soviet collapse was overestimated, while the risks associated with the rise of new post-Soviet authoritarianism were not taken seriously enough by many observers and by Western actors.

The fourth wrong signal of the political hangover syndrome was related to mass politics, which had not entirely lost its influence when it came to post-Soviet regime changes in Russia, but certainly played a secondary role in the process of authoritarian regime building. If one puts aside the brief but highly visible wave of political protests in 2011–2012, then for the purposes of post-Soviet politics Russian citizens might at best be considered mere resources in the hands of a self-interested elite, as some studies have vividly demonstrated.[67]

These tendencies have not resulted only from elite manipulations (although a great deal of "virtual politics" has flourished since the 1990s)[68] but also from the very fact that post-Soviet Russian citizens had few (if any) incentives for activism and political involvement. In a context marked by deeply entrenched "patronal politics,"[69] they learned that political involvement could not bring them any benefits; the manipulative campaigns aimed at boosting pro-Yeltsin mass support in 1993 and in 1996 increased this perception. Even the social activists of the 2000s deliberately turned away from politicization, while their engagement in protests in 2011–2012 was hardly productive in achieving their particular goals of resolving certain issues.[70] As for ordinary citizens, they soon realized that no political changes were likely to improve their well-being and/or life opportunities, but they could easily make things much worse. This is why even those Russians who were highly critical of the authorities often supported the political status quo and sought to avoid the risks that would come with major changes.[71] They thus preferred maintenance of political order in any form, which they still perceived as a lesser evil than disorder.[72] As a recent study demonstrated, even major exogenous shocks (such as natural disasters) have led to an increase in mass political support for leaders and for the regime as such, rather than to the rise of antiregime political stances.[73] Mass political conformism and obedience have become a rational construct for post-Soviet Russian citizens. Given the shrinking menu of political supply in post-Soviet Russia, these risk-averse mass political demands, once portrayed by Samuel Greene as the "aggressive immobility" of Russian society,[74] have also greatly contributed to authoritarian regime building in Russia.

All the four wrong signals that resulted from the post-Soviet political hangover—(1) a low (and decreasing) salience of the democratization agenda in the eyes of the elite and the masses; (2) a conscious search for Soviet solutions for post-Soviet problems and the use of Soviet legacies as building blocks for a post-Soviet political and institutional order; (3) a nearly total lack of Western agenda of promoting Russia's democratic development; and (4) a rationally constructed mass political passivity and disengagement—made building barriers to self-interested power maximizers in Russia impossible. From this viewpoint, one might expect that if the protracted political hangover syndrome continues and deepens in coming decades, it will make Russia's possible return to the trajectory of democratization more difficult and complex, if not impossible.

But Russia's post-Soviet experience of authoritarian regime building does not have to be interpreted only as a "pure" case of power maximization by self-interested political actors who met little resistance to their aspirations. It has also called into question some other explanations of trajectories of regime changes, which have been widely discussed in the literature. First and foremost, a popular argument attributes democratization to a side effect of economic development, which causes the rise of demands for political freedoms among more affluent citizens.[75] Looking at Russia's political trajectory, however, one might consider that at least in the short term, this link is not so straightforward, and that if and when economic development reaches a certain level, it might contribute to the stability not only of democratic but also of nondemocratic regimes (Russia's experience of economic growth in the 2000s might well be such a case).[76] From this perspective, economic development should be perceived as a *factor* in possible democratization but not as its immediate *cause*. In a similar way, the discussion about state weakness as a major impediment to democratization[77] might be reoriented toward an explanation of the major problems of authoritarian regime building. The inefficiency of the winning coalition around Yeltsin in the 1990s and the permanent struggle among various cliques, which resulted in the zero-sum "war of Yeltsin's succession," was not an example of "protracted transition" and "unconsolidated democracy" as some experts suggested then,[78] but rather of unconsolidated authoritarian regime building.[79] On the other hand, the strengthening of the Russian state during Putin's first two terms, and the rise of its coercive as well as distributive capacity, greatly contributed to the "success story" of authoritarian consolidation in the 2000s.

Finally, the Russian experience added a new dimension to the long discussion on the role of institutions in regime changes. Until very recently, this discussion primarily focused on the effects of formal institutions, such as varieties of presidential rule or different types of electoral systems.[80] Although these formal institutions produced certain incentives to influence the behavior of political actors in Russia,[81] one should not perceive them as causes of the trajectory of authoritarian regime building. Quite the opposite: the Russian rulers effectively used manipulative institutional engineering by designing some formal institutions to achieve their goals: the parliamentary electoral system switched from mixed to proportional and back, and gubernatorial elections were abandoned and later reinstalled, yet they did not dramatically change the regime's trajectory, and only helped the Kremlin. Judging from the perspective of authoritarian regime building, one might say that formal institutions under authoritarianism could be analyzed as epiphenomena of power politics, which merely serve to allow the winning coalition to adjust to real and/or potential challenges.[82] It is thus no surprise that any changes to these formal institutions have scarcely affected the authoritarian regime, but rather have become instruments of its fine-tuning.[83]

At the same time, some recent studies have underlined the primary role of informal institutions in post-Soviet authoritarian regime building, though they have mostly focused on their path-dependent nature with regard to the legacies of the Soviet (or even pre-Soviet) past.[84] Without denying the importance of these legacies, one should also pay attention to the politics of informal institution building, which lies at the heart of constructing authoritarianism.[85] Russia's post-Soviet experience might be considered a key case in this regard. Behind the façade of ever-changing formal institutions, three major informal institutions, namely (1) the ruler's unilateral monopoly over the adoption of key political decisions, (2) a taboo on open electoral competition among the elite, and (3) the de facto hierarchical subordination of regional and local authorities to the central government (the power vertical), were deliberately and consciously built, cultivated, and consolidated by the Kremlin, and drive the country along the path of the post-Soviet regime trajectory. These key rules of the game form the institutional core of the authoritarian regime in present-day Russia, and their fundamental revision and peaceful replacement will be the major task of Russia's shift to redemocratization, if and when the country turns in this direction.

IN LIEU OF A CONCLUSION: RUSSIA WILL BE FREE

The collapse of the Communist regime and the breakup of the Soviet Union occurred in 1991, when many observers believed that the worldwide process of an ultimate transition to democracy (then regarded as "the third wave of democratization")[86] that had launched in Southern Europe and Latin America and gone on to reach Eastern Europe[87] would also affect the post-Soviet states, which were doomed to become democratic nearly by default. These naïve expectations proved to be wrong. The Russian post-Soviet experience tells us that democracy cannot emerge by default because of the end of an authoritarian regime, even if and when social, economic, cultural, and other structural conditions are not unfavorable for the country's evolution in a democratic direction. Post-Soviet authoritarian rulers were able to use all available means to maximize their powers when none of the major constraints that prevent monopolization of power played a decisive role—conflicts among the elite were resolved as zero-sum games, the public as a whole remained passive and disengaged from politics (at least until very recently), international influence was (and remains) relatively insignificant, and ideology did not matter much. As a result, what was considered the emergence of a new post-Soviet democracy in Russia after the end of Communism actually turned into the rise of a new post-Soviet authoritarianism, which, in turn, has been part of a global trend that affects many countries and regions of the world.[88] But does this mean that authoritarianism in Russia should be considered the heart of its political regime's endless trajectory, perhaps a vicious circle, and that any attempts at democratization can be perceived as mere partial and temporary deviations?

If one shifts from analyzing politics to observing everyday life, there is no reason to think that even a major defeat closes the path to success once and forever; many people achieve successful marriages after disastrous divorces, many writers publish bestsellers after their previous novels are excoriated, and so on. And even if one were to look at the historical trajectories of many present-day democracies, the Russian post-Soviet and even Soviet experience should not be regarded as exceptional. Even though each of these trajectories is fairly specific, having several unsuccessful attempts at democratization is not unique. France twice ended up a dictatorship after the revolutions of 1789 and 1848, and only after the painful failure of Napoleon III's highly corrupt regime in 1870 did democratization occur—not only because of the arrangement of forces at a certain critical juncture, but also because of the transformation of the French political regime, the elite, and the wider society, as well as the major evolutionary trends of European democratization in the nineteenth century.[89] Argentina in the twentieth century shifted back and forth several times from democracy to dictatorship in a dramatic sequence of coups, violence, and repressions until the military regime finally collapsed and civilian rule was installed. Parallels between Russia under Putin and the French regime of Napoleon III,[90] as well as references to Russia as "the Argentina of the North,"[91] are fairly common in the media, but they provide some hope that the authoritarian regime in Russia may be overcome sooner or later, although nobody guarantees that this process will inevitably result in a success story. In sum, from a historical perspective Russia deserves to be judged as a slow developer, not as an outlier of political regime change.

I would argue that the failure of Russia's first experience of post-Communist democratization attempts after 1991 by no means indicates that democracy is always doomed to fail in this country, or that a new attempt at democratization—if and when it takes place—will lead to a new cycle of flight to authoritarianism, or, say, to a vicious cycle of conflicts, crises, and violence (although these possibilities cannot be ruled out). At first glance, it seems that after almost a quarter century of authoritarian regime building the ruling groups have been able to shut the window of opportunity for democratization. However, the situation in Russia is likely to change over time due to the benefits of learning from the recent past and the effects of generational change. A growing comprehension of the dead end of the current regime and the need for new rules of the game will lead to a desire for political changes among different segments of Russian society.[92] The trial-and-error political experience of post-Soviet development has not been in vain, despite the fact that the political conditions for such a transition seem gloomy at the moment and are certainly less favorable today than immediately after the fall of the Communist regime. The public demand for political changes, though currently rather low and to a certain degree not oriented toward democratization,[93] can grow over time. This possibility offers some "bias for hope"[94] that Russia will not jump out of the frying pan and into the fire, as happened in the 1990s and especially in the 2000s. Therefore, the major slogan of the opposition rallies—"Russia Will Be Free!"—may be perceived not just as a call for action but also as a key item on Russia's political agenda in the not so distant future. Russia will indeed become a free country. The question is exactly when and how this will happen, as well as what the costs of Russia's path to freedom will be.[95]

NOTES

PREFACE

1. See *Authoritarian Brazil: Origins, Policies, and the Future*, ed. Alfred Stepan (New Haven, CT: Yale University Press, 1973); *Democratizing Brazil: Problems of Transition and Consolidation*, ed. Alfred Stepan (Oxford: Oxford University Press, 1989).

CHAPTER 1. REGIME CHANGES IN RUSSIA

1. For detailed descriptions, see *Russia at the Barricades: Eyewitness Accounts of the Moscow Coup*, ed. Victoria Bonnell, Ann Copper, and Gregory Freidin (Armonk, NY: M. E. Sharpe, 1994).

2. See Francis Fukuyama, *The End of History and the Last Man* (New York: Free Press, 1992).

3. A wide range of critical assessments of current developments and trajectories in Russian politics can be found in the annual reports of numerous international NGOs, such as Human Rights Watch (www.hrw.org), Amnesty International (www.thereport.amnesty.org), and especially *Nations in Transit* by Freedom House (www.freedomhouse.org).

4. On crucial cases in political research, see Harry Eckstein, "Case Studies and Theory in Political Science," in *Handbook of Political Science*, vol. 7. eds. Fred Greenstein and Nelson Polsby (Reading, MA: Addison-Wesley, 1975), 79–138. For a criticism, see John Gerring, "Is There a (Viable) Crucial-Case Method?" *Comparative Political Studies* 40, no. 3 (March 2007): 231–53.

5. See Giovanni Sartori, Fred Warren Riggs, and Henry Teune, *The Tower of Babel: On the Definition and Analysis of Concepts in the Social Sciences* (Pittsburgh, PA: International Studies Association, 1975).

6. See Robert Dahl, "The Concept of Power," *Behavioral Science* 2, no. 3 (June 1957): 202–3.

7. See John Higley and Michael Burton, *Elite Foundations of Liberal Democracy* (Lanham, MD: Rowman and Littlefield, 2006).

8. See Thomas Hobbes, *Leviathan*, chapters 13–14.

★

9. See Douglass North, *Institutions, Institutional Changes, and Economic Performance* (Cambridge: Cambridge University Press, 1990), 3.

10. See Sue S. E. Crawford and Elinor Ostrom, "A Grammar of Institutions," *American Political Science Review* 89, no. 3 (September 1995): 584.

11. See, for example, Matthew Shugart and John S. Carey, *Presidents and Assemblies: Constitutional Design and Electoral Dynamics* (Cambridge: Cambridge University Press, 1992).

12. See Juan Jose Linz, *Totalitarian and Authoritarian Regimes* (Boulder, CO: Lynne Rienner, 2000).

13. This definition of political regime, in fact, is close to the one used in the seminal book *Transitions from Authoritarian Rule*: "the ensemble of patterns, explicit or not, that determines the forms and channels of access to principal governmental positions, the characteristics of the actors . . . and the resources and strategies that they can use to gain access." Guillermo O'Donnell and Philippe Schmitter, *Transitions from Authoritarian Rule: Tentative Conclusions about Uncertain Democracies* (Baltimore, MD: Johns Hopkins University Press, 1986), 73.

14. See North, *Institutions, Institutional Changes, and Economic Performance*, 89.

15. An equilibrium is understood here as "a state in which no actor, acting individually, can improve his outcome by changing his action. That is, no actor has an incentive to change his action. The equilibrium is a result of this absence of incentive to change." See James Coleman, "A Rational Choice Perspective on Economic Sociology," in *The Handbook of Economic Sociology*, eds. Neil Smelser and Richard Swedberg (Princeton, NJ: Princeton University Press, 1994), 168

16. On the advantages of the use of dichotomies in analysis of political regimes, see David Collier and Richard Adcock, "Democracy and Dichotomies: A Pragmatic Approach to Choices About Concepts," *Annual Review of Political Science* 2 (June 1999): 537–65; Matthijs Bogaards, "How to Classify Hybrid Regimes? Defective Democracy and Electoral Authoritarianism," *Democratization* 16, no. 2 (April 2009): 399–423.

17. See Joseph Schumpeter, *Capitalism, Socialism, and Democracy* (New York: Harper and Row, 1947), 269.

18. For some arguments, see Adam Przeworski, "Minimalist Conception of Democracy: A Defense," in *Democracy's Value*, eds. Ian Shapiro and Casiano Hacker-Gordon (Cambridge: Cambridge University Press, 1999), 23–55.

19. Adam Przeworski, *Democracy and the Market: Political and Economic Reforms in Eastern Europe and Latin America* (Cambridge: Cambridge University Press, 1991), 10.

20. See Robert A. Dahl, *Democracy and Its Critics* (New Haven, CT: Yale University Press, 1989).

21. See, for example, the titles of two well-known books: Barrington Moore Jr., *Social Origins of Dictatorship and Democracy: Lords and Peasants in Making of the Modern World* (Boston: Beacon Press, 1966); Daron Acemoglu and James A. Robinson, *Economic Origins of Dictatorships and Democracy* (Cambridge: Cambridge University Press, 2006).

22. See Barbara Geddes, *Paradigms and Sand Castles: Theory Building and Research Design in Comparative Politics* (Ann Arbor, MI: University of Michigan Press, 2003), 47–88.

23. For a detailed analysis, see Bruce Bueno de Mesquita, Alastair Smith, Randolph M. Siverson, and James D. Morrow, *The Logic of Political Survival* (Cambridge, MA: MIT Press, 2003).

24. See Steven Levitsky and Lucan Way, *Competitive Authoritarianism: Hybrid Regimes After the Cold War* (Cambridge: Cambridge University Press, 2010); *Electoral Authoritarianism: The Dynamics of Unfree Competition*, ed. Andreas Schedler (Boulder, CO: Lynne Rienner, 2006); Yonatan L. Morse, "The Era of Electoral Authoritarianism," *World Politics*, 64, no. 1 (January 2012): 161–98.

25. See *Elections without Choice*, ed. Guy Hermet, Richard Rose, and Alain Rouquie (London: Macmillan, 1978). For more on differences between "classical" (hegemonic) and electoral (competitive) versions of authoritarianism, see Mark Morje Howard and Philip G. Roessler, "Liberalizing Electoral Outcomes in Competitive Authoritarian Regimes," *American Journal of Political Science*, 50, no. 2 (April 2006): 365–81.

26. For more on this country, see Sebastien Peyrouse, *Turkmenistan: Strategies of Power, Dilemmas of Development* (Armonk, NY: M. E. Sharpe, 2011).

27. See Levitsky and Way, *Competitive Authoritarianism*, chapter 2.

28. For more on a long-standing electoral authoritarian regime in Mexico, see Beatriz Magaloni, *Voting for Autocracy: Hegemonic Party Survival and Its Demise in Mexico* (Cambridge: Cambridge University Press, 2006); Kenneth Greene, *Why Dominant Parties Lose: Mexico's Democratization in Comparative Perspective* (Cambridge: Cambridge University Press, 2007).

29. For more on varieties of post-Soviet electoral authoritarian regimes, see Lucan Way, "Authoritarian State Building and the Sources of Regime Competitiveness in the Fourth Wave: The Cases of Belarus, Moldova, Russia, and Ukraine," *World Politics* 57, no. 2 (January 2005): 231–61; Henry Hale, "Regime Cycles: Democracy, Autocracy, and Revolution in Post-Soviet Eurasia," *World Politics* 58, no. 1 (October 2005): 133–65; Vladimir Gel'man, "Out of the Frying Pan, into the Fire? Post-Soviet Regime Changes in Comparative Perspective," *International Political Science Review* 29, no. 2 (March 2008): 157–80. The most up-to-date comprehensive analysis is offered in Henry E. Hale, *Patronal Politics: Eurasian Regime Dynamics in Comparative Perspective* (Cambridge: Cambridge University Press, 2014).

30. See Barbara Geddes, "Why Elections and Parties in Authoritarian Regimes?" Paper presented at the APSA annual meeting, Washington, DC, 2005.

31. See Beatriz Magaloni, "The Game of Electoral Fraud and the Ousting of Authoritarian Rule," *American Journal of Political Science* 54, no. 3 (August 2010): 751–65.

32. See, for example, Valerie Bunce and Sharon Wolchik, *Defeating Authoritarian Leaders in Postcommunist Countries* (Cambridge: Cambridge University Press, 2011).

33. For more on Ukraine, see Olexiy Haran, "From Viktor to Viktor: Democracy and Authoritarianism in Ukraine," *Demokratizatsiya: The Journal of Post-Soviet Democratization* 19, no. 2 (April 2011): 93–110.

34. A listing of just the major books in this field would fill several pages. Among many contributions, I would emphasize O'Donnell and Schmitter, *Transitions from Authoritarian Rule*; Przeworski, *Democracy and the Market*; Samuel P. Huntington, *The Third Wave: Democratization in the Late Twentieth Century* (Norman, OK: University of Oklahoma Press, 1991); and Juan Jose Linz and Alfred Stepan, *Problems of Democratic Transition and Consolidation: Southern Europe, South America, and Post-Communist Europe* (Baltimore, MD: Johns Hopkins University Press, 1996).

35. See Wolfgang Zapf, "Modernization Theory and the Non-Western World," *Wissenschaftszentrum Berlin für Sozialforschung Discussion Papers*, P 2004–003 (2004), http://www.econstor.eu/bitstream/10419/50239/1/393840433.pdf.

36. For a similar criticism, see Levitsky and Way, *Competitive Authoritarianism*, chapter 1.

37. For a criticism of this approach, see Vladimir Gel'man, "Post-Soviet Transitions and Democratization: Toward a Theory-Building," *Democratization* 10, no. 2 (Summer 2003): 87–104.

38. See, for example, Lilia Shevtsova, *Yeltsin's Russia: Myths and Reality* (Washington, DC: Carnegie Endowment for International Peace, 1999); Lilia Shevtsova, *Russia—Lost in Transition: The Yeltsin and Putin Legacies* (Washington, DC: Carnegie Endowment for International Peace, 2007); Fiona Hill and Clifford C. Gaddy, *Mr. Putin: Operative in the Kremlin* (Washington, DC: Brookings Institution Press, 2013).

39. The essence of this approach is presented in Anthony Downs, *An Economic Theory of Democracy* (New York: Harper, 1957); Mancur Olson, *Power and Prosperity: Outgrowing Communist and Capitalist Dictatorships* (New York: Basic Books, 2000); Bueno de Mesquita et al., *The Logic of Political Survival*.

40. See Ruth Bernice Collier and David Collier, *Shaping the Political Arena: Critical Junctures, the Labor Movement, and Regime Dynamics in Latin America* (Princeton, NJ: Princeton University Press, 1991).

41. See Claus Offe, "Capitalism by Democratic Design? Democratic Theory Facing the Triple Transition in East Central Europe," *Social Research* 58, no. 4 (December 1991): 865–92.

42. "Institutions . . . are created to serve the interests of those with the bargaining power to devise new rules." North, *Institutions, Institutional Changes, and Economic Performance*, 16.

43. See Levitsky and Way, *Competitive Authoritarianism*, chapter 2.

44. See Henry E. Hale, *Why Not Parties in Russia? Democracy, Federalism, and the State* (Cambridge: Cambridge University Press, 2006); Stephen Hanson, *Post-Imperial Democracies: Ideology and Party Formation in Third Republic France, Weimar Germany, and Post-Soviet Russia* (Cambridge: Cambridge University Press, 2010).

45. See Graeme Robertson, *The Politics of Protest in Hybrid Regimes: Managing Dissent in Post-Communist Russia* (Cambridge: Cambridge University Press, 2010).

46. See Richard Rose, William Mishler, and Neil Munro, "Resigned Acceptance of an Incomplete Democracy: Russia's Political Equilibrium," *Post-Soviet Affairs* 20, no. 3 (July–September 2004): 195–218.

47. For detailed analyses, see Richard Rose, William Mishler, and Neil Munro, *Popular Support for an Undemocratic Regime: The Changing Views of Russians* (Cambridge: Cambridge University Press, 2011); Daniel Treisman, "Presidential Popularity in a Hybrid Regime: Russia under Yeltsin and Putin," *American Journal of Political Science* 55, no. 3 (August 2011): 590–609; Daniel Treisman, "Putin's Popularity since 2010: Why Did Support for the Kremlin Plunge, and Then Stabilize?" *Post-Soviet Affairs* 30, no. 5 (September–October 2014): 370–88.

48. See, for example, Graeme Robertson, "Protesting Putinism: The Election Protests of 2011–2012 in Broader Perspective," *Problems of Post-Communism* 60, no. 2 (April 2013): 11–23; Samuel A. Greene, "Beyond Bolotnaya: Bridging Old and New in Russia's Election Protest Movement," *Problems of Post-Communism* 60, no. 2 (April 2013): 40–52.

49. My approach to the supply and demand sides of Russian politics is somewhat similar to the view presented in Rose, Mishler, and Munro, *Popular Support*.

CHAPTER 2. RUSSIA'S FLIGHT FROM FREEDOM

1. There is numerous evidence of electoral misconduct in Russia, and it has been covered in much detail by observers, journalists, and scholars. The NGO *Golos* ("Voice"), which has been notoriously and viciously harassed by the Russian authorities since 2012, has probably gathered the most extensive data on various unfair electoral practices in Russia. See, for example, *Assotsiatsiya Golos: Dostoverno o vyborakh s 2000 goda,* http://archive.golos.org/; *Dvizhenie v zashchitu prav izbiratelei "Golos,"* http://www.golosinfo.org/.

2. See Richard Rose and William Mishler, "How Do Electors Respond to an 'Unfair' Election? The Experience of Russians," *Post-Soviet Affairs* 25, no. 3 (July–September 2009): 118–36; Kenneth Wilson, "How Russians View Electoral Fairness: A Qualitative Analysis," *Europe-Asia Studies* 64, no. 1 (January 2012): 145–68.

3. See, for example, certain *Golos* reports (note 1) as well as several documents of the Organization of Security and Co-operation in Europe (by the Office for Democratic Institutions and Human Rights), http://www.osce.org/odihr/elections/75352. On the 2007 State Duma elections, see especially Miklos Haraszti, *Cases of Media Freedom Violations During the Electoral Campaign to the State Duma of the Russian Federation, 2007,* http://www.osce.org/fom/29576.

4. See Elinor Ostrom, *Governing the Commons: Evolution of Institutions for Collective Action* (Cambridge: Cambridge University Press, 1990), 53.

5. For an overview, see, for example, Jorgen Elklit and Andrew Reynolds, "A Framework for the Systematic Study of Election Quality," *Democratization* 12, no. 2 (April 2005): 147–62; on electoral misconduct in post-Communist states, see Sarah Birch, "Electoral Systems and Electoral Misconduct," *Comparative Political Studies* 40, no. 12 (December 2007): 1533–56; Sarah Birch, "Post-Soviet Electoral Practices in Comparative Perspective," *Europe-Asia Studies* 63, no. 4 (June 2011): 703–25.

6. See Douglass North, *Institutions, Institutional Changes, and Economic Performance* (Cambridge: Cambridge University Press, 1990), 89–93.

7. See Lawrence Harrison, *Who Prospers? How Cultural Values Shape Economic and Political Success* (New York: Basic Books, 1992).

8. See Kenneth Jowitt, *The New World Disorder: The Leninist Extinction* (Berkeley, CA: University of California Press, 1992).

9. See Richard Pipes, *Russia Under the Old Regime* (New York: Scribner, 1974).

10. See Richard Rose, "Living in Anti-Modern Society," *East European Constitutional Review* 8, no. 4 (1999): 68–75.

11. See Samuel P. Huntington, *The Clash of Civilizations and the Remaking of World Order* (New York: Simon and Schuster, 1996).

12. The essence of this view is presented in Alena Ledeneva, *Can Russia Modernise? Sistema, Power Networks and Informal Governance* (Cambridge: Cambridge University Press, 2013).

13. See *Sovetskii prostoi chelovek: Opyt sotsial'nogo portreta na rubezhe 80-kh–90-kh*, ed. Yuri Levada (Moscow: Mirovoi okean, 1993); Yuri Levada, *Ishchem cheloveka: Sotsiologicheskie ocherki 2000–2005* (Moscow: Novoe izdatel'stvo, 2006).

14. See James C. Scott, *Weapons of the Weak: Everyday Forms of Peasant Resistance* (New Haven, CT: Yale University Press, 1985).

15. See Irina Denisova, Markus Eller, Timothy Frye, and Ekaterina Zhuravskaya, "Who Wants to Revise Privatization? The Complementarity of Market Skills and Institutions," *American Political Science Review* 103, no. 2 (May 2009): 284–304.

16. See, for example, Lev Gudkov, Boris Dubin, and Alexei Levinson, "Fotorobot rossiiskogo obyvatelya," *Mir Rossii* no. 2 (2009): 22–33, and numerous other writings of these authors.

17. See, for example, the dataset of the World Values Survey, http://www.worldvaluessurvey.org/.

18. See, for example, Henry Hale, "The Myth of Mass Russian Support for Autocracy: The Public Opinion Foundation of a Hybrid Regime," *Europe-Asia Studies* 63, no. 8 (October 2011): 1357–75.

19. See Gretchen Helmke and Steven Levitsky, "Informal Institutions and Comparative Politics: A Research Agenda," *Perspectives on Politics* 2, no. 4 (December 2004): 727.

20. On some details, see Vladimir Gel'man, "Subversive Institutions, Informal Governance, and Contemporary Russian Politics," *Communist and Post-Communist Studies* 45, no. 3–4 (December 2012): 295–303.

21. For a critique, see Vadim Volkov, *Violent Entrepreneurs: The Use of Force in the Making of Russian Capitalism* (Ithaca, NY: Cornell University Press, 2002), 17–18.

22. See Andrei Shleifer and Daniel Treisman, "A Normal Country," *Foreign Affairs* 83, no. 2 (April 2004): 20–38.

23. See Vladimir Mau and Irina Starodubrovskaya, *The Challenge of Revolution: Contemporary Russia in Historical Perspective* (Oxford: Oxford University Press, 2001).

24. See North, *Institutions*, 89.

25. See Stephen Holmes, "What Russia Teaches Us Now: How Weak States Threaten Freedom," *American Prospect* 33 (July–August 1997): 30–39.

26. See Vitalii Naishul', "Vysshaya i poslednyaya stadiya sotsializma," in *Postizhenie*, ed. Tatyana Notkina (Moscow: Progress, 1991), 31–62.

27. See Steven L. Solnick, *Stealing the State: Control and Collapse in Soviet Institutions* (Cambridge, MA: Harvard University Press, 1998).

28. See Russell Bova, "Democratization and the Crisis of the Russian State," in *State-Building in Russia: The Yeltsin Legacy and the Challenge of the Future*, ed. Graham Smith (Armonk, NY: M. E. Sharpe, 1999), 17–40.

29. For some detailed descriptions, see Chrystia Freeland, *Sale of the Century: The Inside Story of the Second Russian Revolution* (Boston, MA: Little, Brown, 2000); David Hoffman, *Oligarchs: The Wealth and Power in the New Russia* (New York: Public Affairs Books, 2002).

30. See Kathryn Stoner-Weiss, *Resisting the State: Reform and Retrenchment in Post-Soviet Russia* (Cambridge: Cambridge University Press, 2006).

31. See David Woodruff, *Money Unmade: Barter and the Fate of Russian Capitalism* (Ithaca, NY: Cornell University Press, 1999).

32. See Volkov, *Violent Entrepreneurship*, chapters 4 and 5.

33. See, for example, Yakov Pappe and Yana Galukhina, *Rossiiskii krupnyi biznes: pervye 15 let, Ekonomicheskie khroniki 1993–2008* (Moscow: State University—Higher School of Economics, 2009); Thane Gustafson, *Wheel of Fortune: The Battle for Oil and Power in Russia* (Cambridge, MA: Belknap Press of Harvard University Press, 2012).

34. See Vladimir Gel'man, "Leviathan's Return? The Policy of Recentralization in Contemporary Russia," in *Federalism and Local Politics in Russia*, eds. Cameron Ross and Adrian Campbell (London: Routledge, 2009), 1–24.

35. See Volkov, *Violent Entrepreneurship*, chapter 6.

36. See Theda Skocpol, "Bringing the State Back In: Strategies of Analysis in Current Research," in *Bringing the State Back In*, eds. Peter Evans, Dietrich Rueschemeyer, and Theda Skocpol (Cambridge: Cambridge University Press, 1985), 3–37.

37. See Arthur Stinchkombe, "Ending Revolutions and Building New Governments," *Annual Review of Political Science* 2 (1999): 49–73.

38. See, for example, the arguments of leading Russian experts: Yaroslav Kuzminov, Vadim Radaev, Andrey Yakovlev, and Yevgeny Yasin, "Instituty: ot zaimstvovaniya k vyrashchivaniyu," *Voprosy ekonomiki* 5 (May 2005): 5–27.

39. See, for example, Vladimir Gel'man and Sergei Ryzhenkov, "Local Regimes, Sub-National Governance, and the 'Power Vertical' in Contemporary Russia," *Europe-Asia Studies* 63, no. 3 (May 2011): 449–65.

40. See Douglass North, *Structure and Change in Economic History* (New York: W. W. Norton, 1981).

41. See David Kang, *Crony Capitalism: Corruption and Development in South Korea and the Philippines* (Cambridge: Cambridge University Press, 2002).

42. Although the realist approach to politics presented in this book is not related to the realist school in international relations (associated with big names of such scholars as Hans Morgenthau and Kenneth Waltz), their epistemological foundations are rather similar.

43. I use "his" instead of the standard "his/her" because there are not yet female dictators in the contemporary world.

44. See Adam Przeworski, *Democracy and the Market: Political and Economic Reforms in Eastern Europe and Latin America* (Cambridge: Cambridge University Press, 1991), 10.

45. See North, *Institutions*, 16.

46. On details of establishing the institutional arrangements in Russia's electoral governance, see Vladimir Gel'man, "The Unrule of Law in the Making: The Politics of Informal Institution Building in Russia," *Europe-Asia Studies* 56, no. 7 (November 2004): 1021–40.

47. See Margrit Cohn, "Fuzzy Legality in Regulation: The Legislative Mandate Revisited," *Law and Policy* 23, no. 4 (December 2001): 469–97.

48. Gel'man, "The Unrule of Law," 1034.

49. Author's personal observations (August 1994).

50. See Vladimir Gel'man, Sergei Ryzhenkov, and Michael Brie, *Making and Breaking Democratic Transitions: The Comparative Politics of Russia's Regions* (Lanham, MD: Rowman and Littlefield, 2003), 121.

51. See Grigorii V. Golosov, "Regional Roots of Electoral Authoritarianism in Russia," *Europe-Asia Studies* 63 (June 2011): 623–39.

52. See Bruce Bueno de Mesquita and Alastair Smith, *The Dictator's Handbook: Why Bad Behavior Is Almost Always Good Politics* (New York: Public Affairs Books, 2011).

53. For a typology and analysis, see, for example, Ronald Wintrobe, *The Political Economy of Dictatorship* (Cambridge: Cambridge University Press, 1998).

54. International datasets use diverse indicators and methodologies, but their assessments of Russia are not widely different. See, for example, *Freedom House,* http://www.freedomhouse.org; *Polity IV,* http://www.systemicpeace.org/polity/polity4.htm; *Worldwide Governance Indicators,* http://info.worldbank.org/governance/wgi/index.asp.

55. See Przeworski, *Democracy and the Market*, 19.

56. See Otto Kirschheimer, "Confining Conditions and Revolutionary Breakthroughs," *American Political Science Review* 59, no. 4 (December 1965): 964–74.

57. See Adam Przeworski, Michael E. Alvarez, Jose Antonio Cheibub, and Fernando Limongi, *Democracy and Development: Political Institutions and Well-being in the World, 1950–1990* (Cambridge: Cambridge University Press, 2000).

58. See Alvin Rabushka and Kenneth Shepsle, *Politics in Plural Societies: A Theory of Democratic Instability* (Columbus, OH: Merrill, 1972).

59. See Ruth Berins Collier, *Paths Toward Democracy: Working Glass and Elites in Western Europe and South America* (Cambridge: Cambridge University Press, 1999).

60. See Bueno de Mesquita and Smith, *The Dictator's Handbook*, chapter 1.

61. See Daron Acemoglu and James A. Robinson, *Economic Origins of Dictatorship and Democracy* (Cambridge: Cambridge University Press, 2006).

62. See Barrington Moore Jr., *Social Origins of Dictatorship and Democracy* (Boston, MA: Beacon Press, 1966).

63. See Acemoglu and Robinson, *Economic Origins*, chapter 1.

64. On "winning coalitions," see Bruce Bueno de Mesquita, Alastair Smith, Randolph M. Silverson, and James D. Morrow, *The Logic of Political Survival* (Cambridge, MA: MIT Press, 2003); see also Bueno de Mesquita and Smith, *The Dictator's Handbook*.

65. See John Higley and Michael Burton, *Elite Foundations of Liberal Democracy* (Lanham, MD: Rowman and Littlefield, 2006).

66. See Douglass North and Barry Weingast, "Constitutions and Commitment: The Evolution of Institutions Governing the Public Choice in Seventeenth-Century England," *Journal of Economic History* 49, no. 4 (December 1989): 803–32.

67. See Richard Guntner, "Spain: The Very Model of 'Elite Settlement,'" in *Elites and Democratic Consolidation in Latin America and Southern Europe*, eds. John Higley and Richard Guntner (Cambridge: Cambridge University Press, 1992), 38–80.

68. See, for example, Steven Levitsky, and Lucan Way, *Competitive Authoritarianism: Hybrid Regimes After the Cold War* (Cambridge: Cambridge University Press, 2010); *Electoral Authoritarianism: The Dynamics of Unfree Competition*, ed. Andreas Schedler (Boulder, CO: Lynne Rienner, 2006).

69. See Levitsky and Way, *Competitive Authoritarianism*, chapter 2. For a similar argument on the impact of European Union influence on undermining patrimonial political practices in Eastern Europe (but not in the former Soviet Union), see Henry E. Hale, *Patronal Politics: Eurasian Regime Dynamics in Comparative Perspective* (Cambridge: Cambridge University Press, 2014).

70. See Samuel P. Huntington, *The Third Wave: Democratization in the Late Twentieth Century* (Norman, OK: University of Oklahoma Press, 1991), 174–80.

71. See Stephen E. Hanson, "Gorbachev: The Last True Leninist Believer?" in *The Crisis of Leninism and the Decline of the Left: The Revolution of 1989*, ed. Daniel Chirot (Seattle, WA: University of Washington Press, 1991), 33–59.

72. On the role of information problems in authoritarian regimes, see, for example, Milan Svolik, *The Politics of Authoritarian Rule* (Cambridge: Cambridge University Press, 2012).

73. See M. Steven Fish, *Democracy Derailed in Russia: The Failure of Open Politics* (Cambridge: Cambridge University Press, 2005).

74. See Przeworski et al., *Democracy and Development*.

75. On the importance of these issues for democratic stability, see, for example, Tatu Vanhanen, *Prospects of Democracy: A Study of 172 Countries* (London: Routledge, 1997); Acemoglu and Robinson, *Economic Origins*.

76. See Thomas Remington, *The Politics of Inequality in Russia* (Cambridge: Cambridge University Press, 2011).

77. See M. Steven Fish, *Democracy from Scratch: Opposition and Regime in the New Russian Revolution* (Princeton, NJ: Princeton University Press, 1995); Michael Urban, with Vyacheslav Igrunov and Sergei Mitrokhin, *The Rebirth of Politics in Russia* (Cambridge: Cambridge University Press, 1997).

78. On these developments, see Anastassia Alexandrova and Raymond Struyk, "Reform of In-kind Benefits in Russia: High Cost for a Small Gain," *Journal of Euro-*

pean Social Policy 17, no. 2 (May 2007): 153–66; Susanne Wengle and Michael Rasell, "The Monetisation of L'goty: Changing Patterns of Welfare Politics and Provision in Russia," *Europe-Asia Studies* 60, no. 5 (July 2008): 739–56.

79. See Graeme Robertson, "Strikes and Labor Organization in Hybrid Regimes," *American Political Science Review* 101, no. 4 (November 2007): 781–98.

80. See Debra Javeline, *Protest and the Politics of Blame: Russia's Response to Unpaid Wages* (Ann Arbor, MI: University of Michigan Press, 2003).

81. See Samuel A. Greene, "Russia: Society, Politics, and the Search for Community," in *Russia in 2020: Scenarios for the Future*, eds. Maria Lipman and Nikolay Petrov (Washington, DC: Carnegie Endowment for International Peace, 2011), 459–75.

82. See, for example, Vladimir Gel'man, "Cracks in the Wall: Challenges for Electoral Authoritarianism in Russia," *Problems of Post-Communism* 60, no. 2 (April 2013): 3–10; Graeme Robertson, "Protesting Putinism: The Election Protests of 2011–2012 in Broader Perspective," *Problems of Post-Communism* 60, no. 2 (April 2013): 11–23; Samuel A. Greene, "Beyond Bolotnaya: Bridging Old and New in Russia's Election Protest Movement," *Problems of Post-Communism* 60, no. 2 (April 2013): 40–52.

83. See Jerry F. Hough, *Democratization and Revolution in the USSR, 1985–91* (Washington, DC: Brookings Institution Press, 1997); Urban, *The Rebirth of Politics in Russia*; Michael McFaul, *Russia's Unfinished Revolution: Political Changes from Gorbachev to Putin* (Ithaca, NY: Cornell University Press, 2001), chapter 2.

84. See Adam Przeworski, "Some Problems in the Study of the Transition to Democracy," in *Transitions from Authoritarian Rule: Comparative Perspectives*, eds. Guillermo A. O'Donnell, Philippe C. Schmitter, and Lawrence Whitehead (Baltimore, MD: Johns Hopkins University Press, 1986), 59.

85. See Martin Gilman, *No Precedent, No Plan: Inside Russia's 1998 Default* (Cambridge, MA: MIT Press, 2010).

86. See William Zimmerman, Ronald Inglehart, Eduard Ponarin, Yegor Lazarev, Boris Sokolov, Irina Vartanova, and Ekaterina Turanova, *Russian Elite—2020: Valdai Discussion Club Grantee Analytical Report* (Moscow: RIA Novosti and Council on Foreign and Defense Policy, 2013), http://vid-1.rian.ru/ig/valdai/Russian_elite_2020_eng.pdf. See also Eduard Ponarin, "Russia's Elites: What They Think of the United States and Why," *PONARS Eurasia Policy Memo Series* no. 273 (August 2013), http://www.ponarseurasia.org/sites/default/files/policy-memos-pdf/Pepm_273_Ponarin_August2013.pdf.

87. For an overview, see Vladimir Gel'man, "Mediocrity Syndrome in Russia: Domestic and International Perspectives," *PONARS Eurasia Policy Memo Series* no. 258 (June 2013), http://www.ponarseurasia.org/sites/default/files/policy-memos-pdf/Pepm_258_Gelman_June%202013_0.pdf.

88. See Stephen E. Hanson, *Post-Imperial Democracies: Ideology and Party Formation in Third Republic France, Weimar Germany, and Post-Soviet Russia* (Cambridge: Cambridge University Press, 2010).

89. See Henry Hale, *Why Not Parties in Russia: Democracy, Federalism, and the State* (Cambridge: Cambridge University Press, 2006).

90. See Arthur Denzau and Douglass North, "Sharing Mental Models: Ideologies and Institutions," *Kyklos* 47, no. 1 (1994): 3–31.

91. For an overview of some of these discussions, see Grigore Pop-Eleches, "Historical Legacies and Post-Communist Regime Change," *Journal of Politics* 69, no. 4 (November 2007): 908–26; Hale, *Patronal Politics*.

92. See Huntington, *The Third Wave*, 55.

93. See Jennifer Gandhi, *Political Institutions under Dictatorship* (Cambridge: Cambridge University Press, 2008).

94. For a classical analysis of the role of the costs of tolerance and costs of repression as determinants of political regimes, see Robert A. Dahl, *Polyarchy: Participation and Opposition* (New Haven, CT: Yale University Press, 1971), chapter 1. For the overview of the role of repressions in maintaining political order in various regime settings, see also Christian Davenport, "State Repression and Political Order," *Annual Review of Political Science* 10 (2007): 1–23.

95. See Vladislav Surkov, *Suverenitet—eto politicheskii sinonim konkurentosposobnosti* (February 7, 2006), http://www.intelros.org/lib/doklady/surkov1.htm.

CHAPTER 3. THE ROARING 1990s

1. For this qualification of Russia's political development in the 1990s, see, for example: *Growing Pains: Russian Democracy and the Election of 1993*, eds. Timothy J. Colton and Jerry F. Hough (Washington, DC: Brookings Institution Press, 1998).

2. The best-known source on Russian-language usage, Vladimir Dal', *Explanatory Dictionary of the Living Great Russian Language*, dated back to the mid-nineteenth century, defined the entry *likhoi* as a "double-meaning word," both "valiant, grasping, lively, alert . . . courageous, and resolute" and "angry, spiteful, vindictive, evil," http://slovardalja.net/word.php?wordid=15013. In the context of the Russian experience of the 1990s, both interpretations look reasonable.

3. See Claus Offe, "Capitalism by Democratic Design? Democratic Theory Facing the Triple Transition in East Central Europe," *Social Research* 58, no. 4 (Winter 1991): 865–92.

4. See, for example: Anders Aslund, *Building Capitalism: The Transformation of the Former Soviet Bloc* (Cambridge: Cambridge University Press, 2003); Milada Anna Vachudová, *Europe Undivided: Democracy, Leverage, and Integration after Communism* (Oxford: Oxford University Press, 2005); Timothy Frye, *Building States and Markets after Communism: The Perils of Polarized Democracy* (Cambridge: Cambridge University Press, 2010); *Central and East European Politics: From Communism to Democracy*, eds. Sharon L. Wolchik and Jane L. Curry (Lanham, MD: Rowman and Littlefield, 2010).

5. Among the voluminous literature on Russia's economic reforms in the 1990s and the 2000s, see, for example: Andrei Shleifer and Daniel Treisman, *Without a Map: Political Tactics and Economic Reforms in Russia* (Cambridge, MA: MIT Press, 2000); *The New Russia: Transition Gone Awry*, eds. Lawrence R. Klein and Marshall Pomer (Stanford, CA: Stanford University Press, 2001); Peter Reddaway and Dmitri Glinski,

The Tragedy of Russian Reforms: Market Bolshevism Against Democracy (Washington, DC: United States Institute of Peace, 2001); *Russia's Post-Communist Economy*, eds. Brigitte Granville and Peter Oppenheimer (Oxford: Oxford University Press, 2002); *Russia Rebounds*, eds. David Owen and David O. Robinson (Washington, DC: International Monetary Fund, 2003); Anders Aslund, *Russia's Capitalist Revolution: Why Market Reforms Succeeded and Democracy Failed* (Washington, DC: Peterson Institute for International Economics, 2007); Daniel Treisman, *The Return: Russia's Journey from Gorbachev to Medvedev* (New York: Free Press, 2011).

6. On troubles with the rule of law (or lack thereof) in post-Soviet Russia, see, for example: *The Rule of Law and Economic Reforms in Russia*, eds. Jeffrey D. Sachs and Katharina Pistor (Boulder, CO: Westview, 1997); *Assessing the Value of Law in Transition Countries*, ed. Peter Murrell (Ann Arbor, MI: University of Michigan Press, 2001); Kathryn Hendley, "Assessing the Rule of Law in Russia," *Cardozo Journal of International and Comparative Law* 14, no. 2 (2006): 347–91; Peter Solomon, "Law and Public Administration: How Russia Differs," *Journal of Communist Studies and Transition Politics* 24, no. 1 (March 2008): 115–35. The most up-to-date empirical analyses of the lack of the rule of law in Russia and its consequences are presented in numerous studies conducted by the Institute for the Rule of Law at the European University at St. Petersburg, http://www.enforce.spb.ru/.

7. On these developments, see, for example: M. Steven Fish, *Democracy from Scratch: Opposition and Regime in the New Russian Revolution* (Princeton, NJ: Princeton University Press, 1995); Archie Brown, *The Gorbachev Factor* (Oxford: Oxford University Press, 1996), chapter 5; Michael Urban, with Vyacheslav Igrunov and Sergei Mitrokhin, *The Rebirth of Politics in Russia* (Cambridge: Cambridge University Press, 1997); Michael McFaul, *Russia's Unfinished Revolution: Political Changes from Gorbachev to Putin* (Ithaca, NY: Cornell University Press, 2001), chapter 2.

8. For a detailed analysis of the economic aspects of the decline and collapse of the Soviet Union, see Yegor Gaidar, *Collapse of an Empire: Lessons for Modern Russia* (Washington, DC: Brookings Institution Press, 2007).

9. This practice of hierarchical appointments of subnational chief executives (under various institutional arrangements) is also known in Russia as the "power vertical." For some details, see Vladimir Gel'man and Sergei Ryzhenkov, "Local Regimes, Sub-National Governance, and the 'Power Vertical' in Contemporary Russia," *Europe-Asia Studies* 63, no. 3 (May 2011): 449–65.

10. The term "Washington consensus" was initially coined in 1989 to describe a set of economic policy prescriptions for crisis-wracked developing countries, but later it evolved into a symbolic label for all market-oriented transformations. See John Williamson, "What Should the World Bank Think About the Washington Consensus?" *World Bank Research Observer* 15, no. 2 (2000): 15–24.

11. See Jeffrey D. Sachs, "Crossing the Valley of Tears in East European Reform," *Challenge* 34, no. 5 (September–October 1991): 26–34.

12. On various critical arguments about economic reforms in Russia in the 1990s and the political constraints of economic policies, see, for example: Joel Hellman,

"Winners Take All: The Politics of Partial Reform in Post-Communist Transitions," *World Politics* 50, no. 2 (January 1998): 203–34; Shleifer and Treisman, *Without a Map*; Frye, *Building States and Markets*.

13. For analyses of the emergence of parliamentary politics in Russia in the early 1990s, see Thomas F. Remington, *The Russian Parliament: Institutional Evolution in a Transitional Regime 1989–1999* (New Haven, CT: Yale University Press, 2001); Josephine Andrews, *When Majorities Fail: The Russian Parliament 1990–1993* (Cambridge: Cambridge University Press, 2002); Viktor Sheinis, *Vzlet i padenie parlamenta: Perelomnye gody v rossiiskoi politike (1985–1993)*, vols. 1 and 2 (Moscow: Moscow Carnegie Center, Fond INDEM, 2005).

14. For more detailed analyses, see Lilia Shevtsova, *Yeltsin's Russia: Myths and Reality* (Washington, DC: Carnegie Endowment for International Peace, 1999), chapters 2 and 3; Shleifer and Treisman, *Without a Map*, chapter 2; McFaul, *Russia's Unfinished Revolution*, chapter 3.

15. See, for example: "Zhestkim kursom . . . analiticheskaya zapiska Leningradskoi assotsiatsii sotsial'no-ekonomicheskikh nauk," *Vek XX i mir* no. 6 (June 1990): 15–19.

16. For this argument with regard to the Latin American experience, see Stephan Haggard and Robert Kaufman, *The Political Economy of Democratic Transitions* (Princeton, NJ: Princeton University Press, 1995). For criticism of idea of "insulation" of the government from public demands in the wake of market reforms, see Adam Przeworski, *Democracy and the Market: Political and Economic Reforms in Eastern Europe and Latin America* (Cambridge: Cambridge University Press, 1991), 163–90; Offe, "Capitalism by Democratic Design?"

17. On these issues see, for example: Dmitry Gorenburg, *Minority Ethnic Mobilization in the Russian Federation* (Cambridge: Cambridge University Press, 2003); Elise Guiliano, *Constructing Grievance: Ethnic Nationalism in Russia's Republics* (Ithaca, NY: Cornell University Press, 2011).

18. One should also take into account that Yeltsin was popularly elected in June 1991 as a subnational leader (the president of the biggest Soviet Union republic), and enjoyed genuine high public support at that moment.

19. For this document, see Aleksandr Sobyanin, Dmitry Yur'ev, and Yuri Skorinov, "Vyderzhit li Rossiya eshche odni vybory v 1991 godu," *Nevskii kur'er* no. 11 (1991): 4–5; see also McFaul, *Russia's Unfinished Revolution*, chapter 3.

20. See Adam Przeworski, Michael E. Alvarez, Jose Antonio Cheibub, and Fernando Limongi, *Democracy and Development: Political Institutions and Well-being in the World, 1950–1990* (Cambridge: Cambridge University Press, 2000), 54.

21. The analysis of the ideological agenda of Russian reformers under Gorbachev and Yeltsin is presented in our book: Vladimir Gel'man, Otar Marganiya, and Dmitry Travin, *Reexamining Economic and Political Reforms in Russia, 1985–2000: Generations, Ideas, and Changes* (Lanham, MD: Lexington Books, 2014).

22. For detailed analyses of this conflict, see Yitzhak Brudny, "Ruslan Khasbulatov, Aleksandr Rutskoi, and Intraelite Conflict in Postcommunist Russia, 1991–1994," in *Patterns in Post-Soviet Leadership*, eds. Timothy J. Colton and Robert C. Tucker

(Boulder, CO: Westview, 1995), 75–101; Shevtsova, *Yeltsin's Russia*, chapter 4; Andrews, *When Majorities Fail*; Timothy J. Colton, *Yeltsin: A Life* (New York: Basic Books, 2008), chapter 10.

23. For various analyses of the political crisis of September–October 1993 in Russia see, for example: Archie Brown, "The October Crisis of 1993: Context and Implications," *Post-Soviet Affairs* 9, no. 3 (1993): 183–95; George Breslauer, "The Roots of Polarization: A Comment," *Post-Soviet Affairs* 9, no. 3 (1993): 223–30; *Osen'-93: Khronika protivostoyaniya* (Moscow: Vek XX i mir, 1993); Reddaway and Glinski, *The Tragedy of Russian Reforms*; Sheinis, *Vzlet i Padenie Parlamenta*, vol. 2; Oleg Moroz, *Tak kto zhe rasstrelyal parlament?* (Moscow: Rus'-Olimp, 2007); Colton, *Yeltsin: A Life,* chapters 10 and 11.

24. On the conduct of the 1993 elections, see Michael Urban, "December 1993 as a Replication of Late-Soviet Electoral Practices," *Post-Soviet Affairs* 10, no. 2 (April–June 1994): 127–58; Vladimir Gel'man and Vitalii Elizarov, "Russia's Transition and Founding Elections," in *Elections in Russia, 1993–1996: Analyses, Documents, and Data,* eds. Vladimir Gel'man and Grigorii V. Golosov (Berlin: edition sigma, 1999), 19–46.

25. The Constitution of the Russian Federation, http://www.constitution.ru/en/10003000–01.htm. For a criticism of extended and unchecked presidential powers, see Stephen Holmes, "Superpresidentialism and Its Problems," *East European Constitutional Review* 2, no. 4 (Fall 1993)/3, no. 1 (Winter 1994): 123–26; M. Steven Fish, "The Pitfalls of Russian Superpresidentialism," *Current History* 96 (October 1997): 326–30. For a different analysis, see Timothy J. Colton and Cindy Skach, "The Russian Predicament," *Journal of Democracy* 16, no. 3 (July 2005): 113–26.

26. See *Izvestiya* 1993, November 16.

27. Boris Yeltsin, *Struggle for Russia* (New York: Times Books, 1994), 6. This statement was not much different from Sobchak's understanding of democracy.

28. For analyses of the 1993 parliamentary elections and the constitutional referendum, see: Urban, "December 1993"; Richard Sakwa, "The Russian Elections of December 1993," *Europe-Asia Studies* 47, no. 2 (March 1995): 195–227; *Elections and Political Order in Russia. The Implications of the 1993 Elections to the Federal Assembly,* ed. Peter Lentini (Budapest: Central European University Press, 1995); *Growing Pains*; *Elections in Russia, 1993–1996.*

29. For the accusations of authorities being involved in large-scale fraud in both the 1993 elections and referendum, see Aleksandr Sobyanin and Vladislav Sukhovol'skii, *Demokratiya, ogranichennaya fal'sifikatsiyami* (Moscow: Proektnaya gruppa po pravam cheloveka, 1995). Some experts disregarded these accusations as statistically groundless. See Mikhail Filippov, "Voobrazhaya fal'sifikatsii: Spory o voleiz"yavlenii 1993 goda," *Neprikosnovennyi zapas* 5 (October 2008), http://magazines.russ.ru/nz/2008/5/fi7.html. However, due to the impossibility of obtaining proof from hard data, speculations on the genuineness of the 1993 voting results are doomed to be endless.

30. See Timothy Frye, "A Politics of Institutional Choice: Post-Communist Presidencies," *Comparative Political Studies* 30, no. 5 (October 1997): 523–52; M. Steven Fish, *Democracy Derailed in Russia: The Failure of Open Politics* (Cambridge: Cam-

bridge University Press, 2005), chapter 7; Vladimir Gel'man, "Out of the Frying Pan, Into the Fire? Post-Soviet Regime Changes in Comparative Perspective," *International Political Science Review* 29, no. 2 (March 2008): 157–80.

31. Przeworski, *Democracy and the Market*, 86.

32. On authoritarian regime strategies in Belarus, see Lucan Way, "Authoritarian State Building and the Sources of Regime Competitiveness in the Fourth Wave: The Cases of Belarus, Moldova, Russia, and Ukraine," *World Politics* 57, no. 2 (January 2005): 231–61; Vitali Silitski, "Preempting Democracy: The Case of Belarus," *Journal of Democracy* 16, no. 4 (October 2005): 83–97; Gel'man, "Out of the Frying Pan," 167–69.

33. See Maurice Duverger, "A New Political System Model: Semi-Presidential Government," *European Journal of Political Research* 8, no. 2 (April 1980): 165–87; for an extension of this argument to the analysis of Russian presidentialism in the 1990s, see Eugene Huskey, *Presidential Power in Russia* (Armonk, NY: M. E. Sharpe, 1999).

34. See Daniel Treisman, *After the Deluge: Regional Crises and Political Consolidation in Russia* (Ann Arbor, MI: University of Michigan Press, 1999); Steven L. Solnick, "Is the Center Too Weak or Too Strong in the Russian Federation?" in *Building the Russian State: Institutional Crisis and the Quest for Democratic Governance*, ed. Valerie Sperling (Boulder, CO: Westview, 2000), 137–56; Kathryn Stoner-Weiss, *Resisting the State: Reform and Retrenchment in Post-Soviet Russia* (Cambridge: Cambridge University Press, 2006).

35. See Russell Bova, "Democratization and the Crisis of the Russian State," in *State-Building in Russia: Yeltsin's Legacy and the Challenge of the Future*, ed. Graham Smith (Armonk, NY: M. E. Sharpe, 1999), 17–40; Vadim Volkov, *Violent Entrepreneurs: The Role of Force in the Making of Russian Capitalism* (Ithaca, NY: Cornell University Press, 2002).

36. See Remington, *The Russian Parliament*; Steven S. Smith and Thomas F. Remington, *The Politics of Institutional Choice: The Formation of the Russian State Duma* (Princeton, NJ: Princeton University Press, 2001); Paul Chaisty, *Legislative Politics and Economic Power in Russia* (London and New York: Palgrave Macmillan, 2006).

37. For a detailed analysis, see Treisman, *After the Deluge*.

38. On the Chechen war of 1994–1996 and its impact on Russia's development, see Anatol Lieven, *Chechnya: The Tombstone of Russian Power* (New Haven, CT: Yale University Press, 1999); Carlotta Gall and Thomas De Waal, *Chechnya: Calamity in the Caucasus* (New York: New York University Press, 1999).

39. See Thomas F. Remington, Steven S. Smith, and Moshe Haspel, "Decrees, Laws, and Inter-Branch Relations in the Russian Federation," *Post-Soviet Affairs* 14, no. 4 (October–December 1998): 287–322.

40. For critical analyses of loans-for-shares deals, see Chrystia Freeland, *Sale of the Century: Russia's Wild Rule from Communism to Capitalism* (New York: Crown Publishers, 2000); David Hoffmann, *Oligarchs: The Wealth and Power in the New Russia* (New York: Public Affairs Books, 2002); for a more positive assessment see Daniel Treisman, "Loans for Shares Revisited," *Post-Soviet Affairs* 26, no. 3 (July–September 2010): 207–27; Thane Gustafson, *Wheel of Fortune: The Battle for Oil and Power in Russia* (Cambridge, MA: Harvard University Press, 2012).

41. On the rise of public discontent and on the logic of the "resigned acceptance" of Russian citizens vis-à-vis an unpopular status quo regime, see Richard Rose, Neil Munro, and William Mishler, "Resigned Acceptance of an Incomplete Democracy: Russia's Political Equilibrium," *Post-Soviet Affairs* 20, no. 3 (July–September 2004): 195–218; Richard Rose, William Mishler, and Neil Munro, *Popular Support for an Undemocratic Regime: The Changing Views of Russians* (Cambridge: Cambridge University Press, 2011).

42. See Daniel Treisman, "Why Yeltsin Won," *Foreign Affairs* 74, no. 5 (October 1996): 64–75; Daniel Treisman and Vladimir Gimpelson, "Political Business Cycles and Russian Elections, or The Manipulations of 'Chudar,'" *British Journal of Political Science* 31, no. 2 (April 2001): 225–46.

43. See Graeme Robertson, *The Politics of Protest in Hybrid Regimes: Managing Dissent in Post-Communist Russia* (Cambridge: Cambridge University Press, 2011).

44. See Vladimir Gel'man, "Political Opposition in Russia: A Dying Species?" *Post-Soviet Affairs* 21, no. 3 (July–September 2005): 226–46.

45. See, for example, Sergei Guriev and Andrei Rachinsky, "The Role of Oligarchs in Russian Capitalism," *Journal of Economic Perspectives* 19, no. 1 (2005): 131–50; Treisman, "Loans for Shares Revisited"; Vladimir Gel'man, "The Logic of Crony Capitalism: Big Oil, Big Politics, and Big Business in Russia," in *Resource Curse and Post-Soviet Eurasia*, eds. Vladimir Gel'man and Otar Marganiya (Lanham, MD: Lexington Books, 2010), 97–122; Gustafson, *Wheel of Fortune.*

46. See Mancur Olson, *Power and Prosperity: Outgrowing Communist and Capitalist Dictatorships* (New York: Basic Books, 2000).

47. On these elections, see Laura Belin, Robert W. Orttung, Ralph S. Clem, and Peter R. Craumer, *The Russian Parliamentary Elections of 1995: The Battle for the Duma* (Armonk, NY: M. E. Sharpe, 1997); M. Steven Fish, "The Predicament of Russian Liberalism: Evidence from the December 1995 Parliamentary Elections," *Europe-Asia Studies* 49, no. 2 (March 1997): 191–220; *Elections in Russia, 1993–1996.*

48. See Remington, Smith, and Haspel, "Decrees, Laws, and Inter-Branch Relations."

49. See Boris Doktorov, Aleksandr Oslon, and Elena Petrenko, *Epokha El'tsina: Mneniya rossiyan. Sotsiologicheskie ocherki* (Moscow: Institut fonda "Obshchestvennoe mnenie," 2002), 195.

50. See Juan Jose Linz, "The Perils of Presidentialism," *Journal of Democracy* 1, no. 1 (January 1990): 51–69; for an alternative approach, see Jose Antonio Cheibub, *Presidentialism, Parliamentarism, and Democracy* (Cambridge: Cambridge University Press, 2007).

51. See McFaul, *Russia's Unfinished Revolution*, 300–304.

52. See the memoirs of some participants of these behind-the-scenes preparations: Yurii Baturin, Aleksandr Il'yin, Vladimir Kadatskii, Vyacheslav Kostikov, Mikhail Krasnov, Alesksandr Livshits, Konstantin Nikiforov, Lyudmila Pikhoya, Georgii Satarov, *Epokha El'tsina: Ocherki politicheskoi istorii Rossii* (Moscow: Vagrius, 2001); Anatoly Kulikov, *Tyazhelye zvezdy* (Moscow: Voina i mir Books, 2002).

53. On the role of political finance in Russia's electoral politics of the 1990s, see

Daniel Treisman, "Dollars and Democratization: The Role and Power of Money in Russia's Transitional Elections," *Comparative Politics* 31, no. 1 (October 1998): 1–21; Vladimir Gel'man, "The Iceberg of Russian Political Finance," in *Funding Democratization*, eds. Peter Burnell and Alan Ware (Manchester: Manchester University Press, 1998), 158–79.

54. According to the account provided by the European Institute for the Media, the TV news coverage of the three major national channels during the 1996 campaign period demonstrated the balance of positive and negative assessments of Yeltsin and Zyuganov as +492 and –313 respectively. See Stephen White, Richard Rose, and Ian McAllister, *How Russia Votes* (Chatham, NJ: Chatham House Publishers, 1997), 252.

55. See McFaul, *Russia's Unfinished Revolution*, 289–304.

56. On the role of the "semi-opposition," see Juan Jose Linz, "Opposition In and Under an Authoritarian Regime: the Case of Spain," in *Regimes and Oppositions*, ed. Robert A. Dahl (New Haven, CT: Yale University Press, 1973), 171–259; on the extension of this argument to post-Soviet Russia, see Gel'man, "Political Opposition in Russia."

57. For analyses of the campaign, see Michael McFaul, *Russia's 1996 Presidential Election: The End of Polarized Politics* (Stanford, CA: Hoover Institution Press, 1997); Yitzhak Brudny, "In Pursuit of the Russian Presidency: Why and How Yeltsin Won the 1996 Presidential Election," *Communist and Post-Communist Studies* 30, no. 3 (September 1997): 255–75; *Elections in Russia, 1993–1996*; Shevtsova, *Yeltsin's Russia*, chapter 9; McFaul, *Russia's Unfinished Revolution*, 292–316; Colton, *Yeltsin: A Life*, chapter 12.

58. Timothy J. Colton, *Yeltsin: A Life*; Leon Aron, *Yeltsin: A Revolutionary Life* (New York: St. Martin's Press, 2000).

59. See Hellman, "Winners Take All"; Shleifer and Treisman, *Without a Map*. For an alternative approach, see Timothy Frye, "Capture or Exchange? Business Lobbying in Russia," *Europe-Asia Studies* 54, no. 7 (November 2002): 1017–36.

60. See Shevtsova, *Yeltsin's Russia*; Shleifer and Treisman, *Without a Map*; Freeland, *Sale of the Century*; Hoffman, *Oligarchs*.

61. See, for example, Steven L. Solnick, "Russia's Transition: Is Democracy Delayed Democracy Denied?" *Social Research* 66, no. 3 (Fall 1999): 789–824; Hans-Henning Schroeder, "El'tsin and the Oligarchs: the Role of Financial Groups in Russian Politics Between 1993 and July 1998," *Europe-Asia Studies* 51, no. 6 (September 1999): 957–88.

62. See Martin Gilman, *No Precedent, No Plan: Inside Russia's 1998 Default* (Cambridge, MA: MIT Press, 2010).

63. See Shevtsova, *Yeltsin's Russia*, chapter 12.

64. See Yakov Pappe, *Oligarkhi: Ekonomicheskaya Khronika 1992–2000* (Moscow: State University—Higher School of Economics, 2000).

65. The concept of a "cartel of anxiety" was coined by Ralf Dahrendorf with regard to the West German elite after the Second World War, but it is also relevant in the context of elite behavior in post-Soviet Russia. See Ralf Dahrendorf, *Society and Democracy in Germany* (New York: Doubleday, 1967), 256.

66. See Vladimir Gel'man, "Leviathan's Return: The Policy of Recentralization in Contemporary Russia," in *Federalism and Local Politics in Russia*, eds. Cameron Ross and Adrian Campbell (London and New York: Routledge, 2009), 1–24.

67. See Evgenia Popova, "Programmnye strategii i modeli elektoral'nogo sorevnovaniya na dumskikh i prezidentskikh vyborakh 1995–2004 godov," in *Tretii elektoral'nyi tsikl v Rossii, 2003–2004*, ed. Vladimir Gel'man (St. Petersburg: European University at St. Petersburg Press, 2007), 156–95.

68. On this issue, see Philip Roeder, "Varieties of Post-Soviet Authoritarian Regimes," *Post-Soviet Affairs* 10, no. 1 (January–March 1994): 61–101.

69. See Boris Makarenko, "Otechestvo—vsya Rossiya," in *Rossiya v izbiratel'nom tsikle 1999–2000 godov*, eds. Michael McFaul, Nikolay Petrov, and Andrei Ryabov (Moscow: Gandalf, 2000), 156–58.

70. Putin even claimed in an interview that he would "murder [terrorists] in the toilet" (*mochit' v sortire*) if necessary.

71. Makarenko, "Otechestvo—vsya Rossiya," 158.

72. See Timothy J. Colton and Michael McFaul, "Reinventing Russia's Party of Power: Unity and the 1999 Duma Election," *Post-Soviet Affairs* 16, no. 3 (July–September 2000): 201–23.

73. See Olga Shvetsova, "Resolving the Problem of Preelection Coordination: The 1999 Parliamentary Elections as an Elite Presidential 'Primary,'" in *The 1999–2000 Elections in Russia: Their Impact and Legacy*, eds. Vicki L. Hesli and Willam M. Reisinger (Cambridge: Cambridge University Press, 2003), 213–31; Henry Hale, *Why Not Parties in Russia? Federalism, Democracy, and the State* (Cambridge: Cambridge University Press, 2006).

74. See Ruben Enikolopov, Maria Petrova, and Ekaterina Zhuravskaya, "Media and Political Persuasion: Evidence from Russia," *American Economic Review* 101, no. 7 (2011): 3253–85.

75. See Luke March, *The Communist Party in Post-Soviet Russia* (Manchester: Manchester University Press, 2002), 232–44; Thomas F. Remington, "Putin, the Duma, and Political Parties," in *Putin's Russia: Past Imperfect, Future Uncertain*, ed. Dale Hespring (Lanham, MD: Rowman and Littlefield, 2003), 39–59.

76. Colton, *Yeltsin: A Life*, chapters 15–16.

77. For this argument, see Henry Hale, "Regime Cycles: Democracy, Autocracy, and Revolution in Post-Soviet Eurasia," *World Politics* 58, no. 1 (October 2005): 133–65; Henry Hale, "Democracy or Autocracy on the March? The Colored Revolutions as Normal Dynamics of Patronal Presidentialism," *Communist and Post-Communist Studies* 39, no. 3 (September 2006): 305–29.

78. On various aspects of the 1999–2000 elections in Russia, see Michael McFaul, "One Step Forward, Two Steps Back," *Journal of Democracy* 11, no. 3 (July 2000): 19–33; *Rossiya v izbiratel'nom tsikle 1999–2000 godov*; Timothy J. Colton and Michael McFaul, *Popular Choice and Managed Democracy: The Russian Elections of 1999 and 2000* (Washington, DC: Brookings Institution Press, 2003); *The 1999–2000 National Elections in Russia: Analyses, Documents, and Data*, eds. Vladimir Gel'man, Grigorii V Golosov, and Elena Meleshkina (Berlin: edition sigma, 2005).

79. See Yevgenia Borisova, "And the Winner Is?" *Moscow Times*, 2000, 9 September.

80. For discussion of the mixed assessments of Russia's record of political regime changes in the 1990s, see, for example: Andrei Melville, "Russia in the 1990s: Democratization, Postcommunism, or Something Else?" *Demokratizatsiya: The Journal of Post-Soviet Democratization* 7, no. 2 (1999): 165–87; Archie Brown, "Russia and Democratization," *Problems of Post-Communism* 46, no. 5 (October 1999): 3–13; *Russian Politics: Challenges of Democratization*, eds. Zoltan Barany and Robert G. Moser (Cambridge: Cambridge University Press, 2001); McFaul, *Russia's Unfinished Revolution*; Lilia Shevtsova, "Russia's Hybrid Regime," *Journal of Democracy* 12, no. 4 (October 2001): 65–70; M. Steven Fish, "Putin's Path," *Journal of Democracy* 12, no. 4 (October 2001): 71–78.

81. For detailed analyses, see Grigorii V. Golosov, *Political Parties in the Regions of Russia: Democracy Unclaimed* (Boulder, CO: Lynne Rienner, 2004); Hale, *Why Not Parties in Russia?*

82. See Gel'man, "Leviathan's Return."

83. See Volkov, *Violent Entrepeneurship*; Stoner-Weiss, *Resisting the State*.

84. For some details, see *The Dynamics of Russian Politics: Putin's Reform of Federal-Regional Relations*, vols. 1–2, eds. Peter Reddaway and Robert W. Orttung (Lanham, MD: Rowman and Littlefield, 2004–2005).

85. On the role of the regional elites in Russia's economic and political development in the 1990s, see, for example: Yakov Pappe, "Treugol'nik sobstvennikov v regional'noi promyshlennosti," in *Politika i ekonomika v regional'nom izmerenii*, eds. Vladimir Klimanov and Natalia Zubarevich (Moscow and St. Petersburg: Letnii sad, 2000), 109–20; Vladimir Gel'man, Sergei Ryzhenkov, and Michael Brie, *Making and Breaking Democratic Transitions: The Comparative Politics of Russia's Regions* (Lanham, MD: Rowman and Littlefield, 2003); Stoner-Weiss, *Resisting the State*; Gulnaz Sharafutdinova, *Political Consequences of Crony Capitalism inside Russia* (South Bend, IN: University of Notre Dame Press, 2011).

86. See Remington, Smith, and Haspel, "Decrees, Laws, and Inter-Branch Relations."

87. See Shleifer and Treisman, *Without a Map*; Gilman, *No Precedent, No Plan*.

CHAPTER 4. THE (IN)FAMOUS 2000s

1. See, for example: Timothy J. Colton and Henry Hale, "The Putin Vote: Presidential Electorates in a Hybrid Regime," *Slavic Review* 68, no. 3 (Fall 2009): 473–503; Daniel Treisman, "Presidential Popularity in a Hybrid Regime: Russia under Yeltsin and Putin," *American Journal of Political Science* 55, no. 3 (August 2011): 590–609; Richard Rose, William Mishler, and Neil Munro, *Popular Support for an Undemocratic Regime: The Changing Views of Russians* (Cambridge: Cambridge University Press, 2011).

2. See Andrei Shleifer and Daniel Treisman, "A Normal Country," *Foreign Affairs* 83, no. 2 (April 2004): 20–38; Andrei Shleifer, *A Normal Country: Russia after Communism* (Cambridge, MA: Harvard University Press, 2005).

3. The label BRIC (Brazil, Russia, India, China) was coined by Goldman Sachs in

the early 2000s and served as an acronym for the fast-growing hopefuls of the global economy who claimed to be the new international leaders for the twenty-first century. In the 2010s, with addition of South Africa, it was renamed BRICS.

4. See, for example, a typical book title: Tom Bjorkman, *Russia's Road to Deeper Democracy* (Washington, DC: Brookings Institution Press, 2003). Many analysts of Russia in the early 2000s preferred to use descriptive adjectives with an emphasis on the incompleteness of Russia's democratic transition and/or the poor quality of Russia's democracy, along the lines of widespread critical assessments of so-called "new democracies." See David Collier and Steven Levitsky, "Democracy with Adjectives: Conceptual Innovation in Comparative Research," *World Politics* 49, no. 3 (April 1997): 430–51. However, by the end of the 2000s, almost nobody employed the discourse of democracy regarding Russia, and even the most positive assessments cautiously used the residual term "hybrid regime." Incidentally, the coauthor of the article on "democracy with adjectives" later advocated the label of "competitive authoritarianism" for Russia and other nondemocratic regimes. See Steven Levitsky and Lucan Way, *Competitive Authoritarianism: Hybrid Regimes after the Cold War* (Cambridge: Cambridge University Press, 2010).

5. This statement was actually abridged by journalists. Originally, after becoming chair of the State Duma in December 2003, Boris Gryzlov mentioned: "I believe that the Parliament should not be a ground for political battles, for fighting for political slogans and ideologies. This is a place where [MPs] should be engaged in constructive, effective legislative activity," http://www.gryzlov.ru/index.php?page=bio. In fact, the meaning of his statement was nearly the same.

6. See Vladimir Gel'man, "Party Politics in Russia: From Competition to Hierarchy," *Europe-Asia Studies* 60, no. 6 (August 2008): 913–30.

7. See Andrei Yakovlev, "The Evolution of State-Business Interactions in Russia: From State Capture to Business Capture?" *Europe-Asia Studies* 58, no. 7 (November 2006): 1033–56.

8. See Elena Belokurova, "NGOs and Politics in Russian Regions," in *The Politics of Sub-National Authoritarianism in Russia*, eds. Vladimir Gel'man and Cameron Ross (Burlington, VT: Ashgate, 2010), 107–22.

9. See Bruce Bueno de Mesquita and Alastair Smith, *The Dictator's Handbook: Why Bad Behavior Is Almost Always Good Politics* (New York: Public Affairs Books, 2011), especially chapter 5.

10. See Boris Yeltsin, *Struggle for Russia* (New York: Times Books, 1994), 6.

11. For an overview of Russia's economic development in the 2000s, see, for example, *Russia After the Global Economic Crisis*, eds. Anders Aslund, Sergei Guriev, and Andrew Kuchins (Washington, DC: Peterson Institute for International Economics, 2010). For analyses of state building, see, for example, Gerald Easter, "The Russian State in the Time of Putin," *Post-Soviet Affairs* 24, no. 3 (July–September 2008): 199–230; Brian Taylor, *State Building in Putin's Russia: Policing and Coercion after Communism* (Cambridge: Cambridge University Press, 2011).

12. For a more detailed overview of "imposed consensus," see Vladimir Gel'man,

"Russian Elites in Search of Consensus: What Kind of Consolidation?" *Demokratizatsiya: The Journal of Post-Soviet Democratization* 10, no. 3 (Summer): 343–61.

13. Bueno de Mesquita and Smith, *The Dictator's Handbook*, 127.

14. On postrevolutionary stabilization, see Arthur Stinchkombe, "Ending Revolutions and Building New Governments," *Annual Review of Political Science* 2 (1999): 49–73. See also Vladimir Mau and Irina Starodubrovskaya, *The Challenge of Revolution: Contemporary Russia in Historical Perspective* (Oxford: Oxford University Press, 2001).

15. Philipp Chapkovski, "Sotsial'nye seti i administrativnoe rekrutirovanie v Rossii: Na primere federal'nogo pravitel'stva 2000–2008" (MA thesis, Department of Political Science and Sociology, European University at St. Petersburg, 2011).

16. See, for example, Nikolay Petrov, "Nomenklatura and the Elite," in *Russia in 2020: Scenarios for the Future*, eds. Maria Lipman and Nikolay Petrov (Washington, DC: Carnegie Endowment for International Peace, 2011), 499–530.

17. See Viktor Sheinis, "Tretii raund: k itogam parlamentskikh i prezidentskikh vyborov," *Mirovaya ekonomika i mezhdunarodnye otnosheniya* no. 9 (September 2000): 45–61; Michael McFaul, "One Step Forward, Two Steps Back," *Journal of Democracy* 11, no. 3 (July 2000): 19–33; Lilia Shevtsova, "Can Electoral Autocracy Survive?" *Journal of Democracy* 11, no. 3 (July 2000): 36–38.

18. See, for example, Daniel Treisman, "Russia Renewed?" *Foreign Affairs* 81, no. 6 (December 2002): 58–72; *Russia Rebounds*, eds. David Owen and David O. Robinson (Washington, DC: International Monetary Fund, 2003); *Russia after the Global Economic Crisis*.

19. See Rose, Mishler, and Munro, *Popular Support of an Undemocratic Regime*; Treisman, "Presidential Popularity in a Hybrid Regime."

20. On this parallel, see Vladimir Gel'man, "'Ukrotit' khishchnika: Pochemu sil'noe gosudarstvo ne reshaet problem strany," *slon.ru*, 2011, February 16, http://slon.ru/russia/ukrotit_hishhnika-533958.xhtml.

21. See, for example, Olga Kryshtanovskaya and Stephen White, "Putin's Militocracy," *Post-Soviet Affairs* 19, no. 4 (October–December 2003): 289–306. For criticism of this approach, see Bettina Renz, "Putin's Militocracy? An Alternative Interpretation of *Siloviki* in Contemporary Russian Politics," *Europe-Asia Studies* 58, no. 6 (September 2006): 903–24. See also: Daniel Treisman, "Putin's Silovarchs," *Orbis* 51 (Winter 2007): 141–53.

22. See Adam Przeworski, *Democracy and the Market: Political and Economic Reforms in Eastern Europe and Latin America* (Cambridge: Cambridge University Press, 1991), 86.

23. See Thomas F. Remington, *The Russian Parliament: Institutional Evolution in a Transitional Regime* (New Haven, CT: Yale University Press, 2001).

24. See, for example, Timothy J. Colton and Michael McFaul, *Popular Choice and Managed Democracy: The Russian Elections of 1999 and 2000* (Washington, DC: Brookings Institution Press, 2003); Henry Hale, *Why Not Parties in Russia? Federalism, Democracy, and the State* (Cambridge: Cambridge University Press, 2006).

25. See Steven S. Smith and Thomas Remington, *The Politics of Institutional Choice: The Formation of the Russian State Duma* (Princeton, NJ: Princeton University Press, 2001), 148–53; Thomas F. Remington, "Putin and the Duma," *Post-Soviet Affairs* 17, no. 4 (October–December 2001): 285–308.

26. See Luke March, *The Communist Party in Post-Soviet Russia* (Manchester: Manchester University Press, 2002), 240–44; Vladimir Gel'man, "Political Opposition in Russia: A Dying Species?" *Post-Soviet Affairs* 21, no. 3 (July–September 2005): 226–46.

27. See Thomas F. Remington, "Presidential Support in the Russian State Duma," *Legislative Studies Quarterly* 31, no. 1 (January 2006): 5–32.

28. For more detailed overviews, see *The Dynamics of Russian Politics: Putin's Reform of Federal-Regional Relations*, eds. Peter Reddaway and Robert W. Orttung, volumes 1 and 2 (Lanham, MD: Rowman and Littlefield, 2004–2005); Vladimir Gel'man, "Leviathan's Return? The Policy of Recentralization in Contemporary Russia," in *Federalism and Local Politics in Russia*, eds. Cameron Ross and Adrian Campbell (London: Routledge, 2009), 1–24; J. Paul Goode, *The Decline of Regionalism in Putin's Russia* (London: Routledge, 2011).

29. See Nikolay Petrov, "Sovet Federatsii i predstavitel'stvo interesov regionov v tsentre," in *Regiony Rossii v 1998 g.*, ed. Nikolay Petrov (Moscow: Gandalf, 1999), 180–222.

30. See Thomas F. Remington, "Majorities without Mandates: The Federation Council since 2000," *Europe-Asia Studies* 55, no. 5 (July 2003): 667–91.

31. For more details, see David Hoffman, *Oligarchs: Wealth and Power in the New Russia* (New York: Public Affairs Books, 2002). On Berezovsky's role in Russian politics and business in the 1990s, see also Paul Khlebnikov, *Godfather of the Kremlin: Boris Berezovsky and Looting of Russia* (New York: Harcourt, 2000).

32. For a more detailed overview, see Anna Kachkaeva, "Istoriya televideniya v Rossii: Mezhdu vlast'yu, svobodoi i sobstvennost'yu," in *Istoriya novoi Rossii. Ocherki, interview*, vol. 3, ed. Petr Filippov (St. Petersburg: Norma, 2011), 81–127. For a critical discussion of the decline of media freedom in Russia in the 2000s, see Maria Lipman and Michael McFaul, "Putin and the Media," in *Putin's Russia: Past Imperfect, Future Uncertain*, ed. Dale R. Hespring (Lanham, MD: Rowman and Littlefield, 2003), 63–84; for an alternative perspective of analysis, see Scott Gehlbach, "Reflections on Putin and the Media," *Post-Soviet Affairs* 26, no. 1 (January–March 2010): 77–87.

33. See Vadim Volkov, "Problema nedezhnykh garantii prav dobstvennosti i tossiiskii variant vertikal'noi politicheskoi integratsii," *Voprosy ekonomiki* no. 8 (August 2010): 4–27; Vladimir Gel'man, "The Logic of Crony Capitalism: Big Oil, Big Politics, and Big Business in Russia," in *Resource Curse and Post-Soviet Eurasia: Oil, Gas, and Modernization*, eds. Vladimir Gel'man and Otar Marganiya (Lanham, MD: Lexington Books, 2010), 97–122; Thane Gustafson, *Wheel of Fortune: The Battle for Oil and Power in Russia* (Cambridge, MA: Harvard University Press, 2012).

34. See Natalia Zubarevich, "State-Business Relations in Russia's Regions," in *The Politics of Sub-National Authoritarianism in Russia*, eds. Vladimir Gel'man and Cameron Ross (Burlington, VT: Ashgate, 2010), 211–26.

35. See Alexey Zudin, "Neokorporativizm v Rossii? Gosudarstvo i biznes pri Vladimire Putine," *Pro et Contra* 6, no. 4 (Fall 2001): 171–98.

36. See, for example, Robert Sharlet, "Putin and the Politics of Law in Russia," *Post-Soviet Affairs* 17, no. 3 (July–September 2001): 195–234; Jeffrey Kahn, *Federalism, Democratization, and the Rule of Law in Russia* (Oxford: Oxford University Press, 2002). See also Vladimir Gel'man, "The Dictatorship of Law in Russia: Neither Dictatorship Nor Rule of Law," *PONARS Policy Memos* no. 146 (October 2000), http://www.ponarseurasia.org/sites/default/files/policy-memos-pdf/pm_0146.pdf.

37. See Vadim Radaev, "Deformalizatsiya pravil i ukhod ot nalogov v rossiiskoi khozyaistvennoi deyatel'nosti," *Voprosy ekonomiki* no. 6 (June 2001): 60–79; Ella Paneyakh, "Neformal'nye instituty i ispol'zovanie formal'nykh pravil: zakon deistvuyushchii vs. zakon primenyaemyi," *Politicheskaia nauka* no. 1 (2003): 33–52; Alena V. Ledeneva, *Can Russia Modernise? Sistema, Power Networks, and Informal Governance* (Cambridge: Cambridge University Press, 2013).

38. See Vladimir Gel'man, "The Unrule of Law in the Making: The Politics of Informal Institution Building in Russia," *Europe-Asia Studies* 56, no. 7 (November 2004): 1021–40.

39. See Anna Likhtenchtein, "Parties of Power: The Electoral Strategies of Russia's Elites," in *The 1999–2000 National Elections in Russia: Analyses, Documents, and Data*, eds. Vladimir Gel'man, Grigorii V. Golosov, and Elena Meleshkina (Berlin: edition sigma, 2005), 59–75.

40. For more detailed analyses, see Timothy J. Colton and Michael McFaul, "Reinventing Russia's Party of Power: 'Unity' and the 1999 Duma Election," *Post-Soviet Affairs* 16, no. 3 (July–September 2000): 201–24; Henry E. Hale, "The Origins of United Russia and the Putin Presidency: The Role of Contingency in Party-System Development," *Demokratizatsiya: The Journal of Post-Soviet Democratization* vol. 12, no. 2 (Spring 2004): 169–94.

41. See Gel'man, "Party Politics in Russia."

42. See John Higley, Oksan Bayulgen, and Julie George, "Political Elite Integration and Differentiation in Russia," in *Elites and Democratic Development in Russia*, eds. Anton Steen and Vladimir Gel'man (London: Routledge, 2003), 11–28.

43. See Henry Hale, "Regime Cycles: Democracy, Autocracy, and Revolution in Post-Soviet Eurasia," *World Politics* 58, no. 1 (October 2005): 133–65.

44. See Olga Shvetsova, "Resolving the Problem of Pre-election Coordination: The 1999 Parliamentary Elections as an Elite Presidential 'Primary,'" in *The 1999–2000 Elections in Russia: Their Impact and Legacy*, eds. Vicky Hesli and William M. Reisinger (Cambridge: Cambridge University Press, 2003), 213–31; Hale, "The Origins of United Russia"; Likhtenchtein, "Parties of Power."

45. See Robert A. Dahl, *Polyarchy: Participation and Opposition* (New Haven, CT: Yale University Press, 1971), 15.

46. On varieties of repressive and non-repressive authoritarian regimes, see Ronald Wintrobe, *The Political Economy of Dictatorship* (Cambridge: Cambridge University Press, 1998).

47. On these functions of dominant parties, see Kenneth Greene, *Why Dominant*

Parties Lose: Mexico's Democratization in Comparative Perspective (Cambridge: Cambridge University Press, 2007).

48. See Stephen E. Hanson, "Instrumental Democracy: The End of Ideology and the Decline of Russian Political Parties," in *The 1999–2000 Elections in Russia: Their Impact and Legacy*, eds. Vicky Hesli and William M. Reisinger (Cambridge: Cambridge University Press, 2003), 163–85; Hale, *Why Not Parties in Russia?*

49. For a more detailed overview, see Vladimir Gel'man, "The Dynamics of Sub-National Authoritarianism: Russia in Comparative Perspective," in *The Politics of Sub-National Authoritarianism in Russia*, eds. Vladimir Gel'man and Cameron Ross (Burlington, VT: Ashgate, 2010), 1–18; for an alternative perspective of analysis, see Grigorii V. Golosov, "Machine Politics: The Concept and Its Implications for Post-Soviet Studies," *Demokratizatsiya: The Journal of Post-Soviet Democratization* 21, no. 4 (Fall 2013): 459–80.

50. On the role of economic statism in maintaining authoritarian regimes, see Levitsky and Way, *Competitive Authoritarianism*, especially chapter 2.

51. Regional chief executives in Russia bear different titles in various regions (and some of these titles change over time), but for the sake of simplicity I will use the term "governors" for all of them.

52. See Grigorii V. Golosov, "Elektoral'nyi avtoritarizm v Rossii," *Pro et Contra* 12, no. 1 (January–March 2008): 22–35.

53. See Andrew Konitzer, *Voting for Russia's Governors: Regional Elections and Accountability under Yeltsin and Putin* (Washington, DC: Woodrow Wilson Center Press, 2005); Bryon J. Moraski and William M. Reisigner, "Eroding Democracy: Federal Intervention in Russia's Gubernatorial Elections," *Democratization* 14, no. 4 (August 2007): 603–21; Gel'man, "Leviathan's Return."

54. See Gel'man, "The Unrule of Law in the Making."

55. For a detailed analysis, see Grigorii V. Golosov, *Political Parties in the Regions of Russia: Democracy Unclaimed* (Boulder, CO: Lynne Rienner, 2004).

56. See, for example, Grigorii V. Golosov, "What Went Wrong? Regional Electoral Politics and Impediments to State Centralization in Russia, 2003–2004," *PONARS Policy Memos* 337 (December 2004), http://www.csis.org/media/csis/pubs/pm_0337.pdf; Aleksandr Kynev, "Politicheskie partii v rossiskikh regionakh: Vzglyad skvoz' prizmu reformy izbiratel'noi sistemy," *Polis* no. 6 (2006): 145–60.

57. See Petr Panov, "Electoral Practices at the Sub-National Level in Contemporary Russia," in *The Politics of Sub-National Authoritarianism in Russia*, eds. Vladimir Gel'man and Cameron Ross (Burlington, VT: Ashgate, 2010), 151–69.

58. See Edward Gibson, "Boundary Control: Subnational Authoritarianism in Democratic Countries," *World Politics* 58, no. 1 (October 2005): 101–32.

59. See, for example, Vladimir Gel'man, Sergei Ryzhenkov, and Michael Brie, *Making and Breaking Democratic Transitions: The Comparative Politics of Russia's Regions* (Lanham, MD: Rowman and Littlefield, 2003); Golosov, *Political Parties in the Regions of Russia*; Gulnaz Sharafutdinova, *Political Consequences of Crony Capitalism Inside Russia* (South Bend, IN: University of Notre Dame Press, 2011).

60. See Nikolay Petrov, "Demokratichnost' Regionov Rossii," *Carnegie Moscow Center Briefing* 7, no. 9 (October 2005).

61. See J. Paul Goode, "The Puzzle of Putin's Gubernatorial Appointments," *Europe-Asia Studies* 59, no. 3 (May 2007): 365–99; Ora John Reuter, "The Politics of Dominant Party Formation: United Russia and Russia's Governors," *Europe-Asia Studies* 62, no. 2 (March 2010): 293–327.

62. See Regina Smyth, "Building State Capacity from Inside Out: Parties of Power and the Success of the President's Reform Agenda in Russia," *Politics and Society* 30, no. 4 (December 2002): 555–78; Remington, "Presidential Support in the Russian State Duma."

63. See Grigorii V. Golosov, "Sfabrikovannoe bol'shinstvo: Konversiya golosov v mesta na dumskikh vyborakh," in *Tretii elektoral'nyi tsikl v Rossii, 2003–2004,* ed. Vladimir Gel'man (St. Petersburg: European University at St. Petersburg Press, 2007), 39–58.

64. See Ora John Reuter and Thomas F. Remington, "Dominant Party Regimes and the Commitment Problem: the Case of United Russia," *Comparative Political Studies* 42, no. 4 (April 2009): 501–26; Reuter, "The Politics of Dominant Party Formation."

65. For empirical analyses, see Ora John Reuter and Graeme Robertson, "Subnational Appointments in Authoritarian Regimes: Evidence from Russia's Gubernatorial Appointments," *Journal of Politics* 74, no. 4 (October 2012): 1023–37; William M. Reisinger and Bryon Moraski, "Deference or Governance? A Survival Analysis of Russia's Governors under Presidential Control," in *Russia's Regions and Comparative Subnational Politics,* ed. William M. Reisinger (London and New York: Routledge, 2013), 40–62.

66. Golosov, "Elektoral'nyi avtoritarizm v Rossii," 30.

67. See Kenneth Wilson, "Party-System Development under Putin," *Post-Soviet Affairs* 22, no. 4 (October–December 2006): 314–39.

68. See Regina Smyth, Anna Lowry, and Brandon Wilkening, "Engineering Victory: Institutional Reform, Informal Institutions and the Formation of a Hegemonic Party Regime in the Russian Federation," *Post-Soviet Affairs* 23, no. 2 (April–June 2007): 118–37.

69. See Hale, *Why Not Parties in Russia?*

70. See Gel'man, "Party Politics in Russia"; Reuter and Remington, "Dominant Party Regimes."

71. For a comparative analysis, see Stephen E. Hanson, *Post-Imperial Democracies: Ideology and Party Formation in Third Republic France, Weimar Germany, and Post-Soviet Russia* (Cambridge: Cambridge University Press, 2010).

72. See Gel'man, "Political Opposition in Russia."

73. See Greene, *Why Dominant Parties Lose.*

74. See Kynev, "Politicheskie partii v rossiskikh regionakh."

75. For detailed analyses, see Eugene Huskey, *Presidential Power in Russia* (Armonk, NY: M. E. Sharpe, 1999); Iulia Shevchenko, *The Central Government of Russia:*

From Gorbachev to Putin (Burlington, VT: Ashgate, 2004); M. Steven Fish, *Democracy Derailed in Russia: The Failure of Open Politics* (Cambridge: Cambridge University Press, 2005), chapter 7; Petra Schleiter, "Democracy, Authoritarianism, and Ministerial Selection in Russia: How Presidential Preferences Shape Technocratic Cabinets," *Post-Soviet Affairs* 29, no. 1 (2013): 31–55.

76. See Hale, *Why Not Parties in Russia?*; Gel'man, "Party Politics in Russia."

77. See Andrew Wilson, *Virtual Politics: Faking Democracy in the Post-Soviet World* (New Haven, CT: Yale University Press, 2005).

78. See Aleksey Titkov, *Partiya No. 4: 'Rodina' i okrestnosti* (Moscow: Panorama, 2006), http://www.orodine.ru/kniga/party4.html.

79. See Wilson, *Virtual Politics*, 129–50.

80. On Mexico's satellite parties under the PRI, see, for example, Bo Anderson and James Cockroft, "Cooptation and Control in Mexican Politics," *International Journal of Comparative Sociology* 7, no. 1 (March 1966): 11–28; Dan A. Cothran, *Political Stability and Democracy in Mexico: The "Perfect Dictatorship"?* (Westport, CT: Praeger, 1994).

81. See Greene, *Why Dominant Parties Lose*.

82. See Philip Hanson and Elizabeth Teague, "Big Business and the State in Russia," *Europe-Asia Studies* 57 no. 5 (2005): 657–80; William Tompson, "Putin and the 'Oligarchs': A Two-Sided Commitment Problem," in *Leading Russia: Putin in Perspective,* ed. Alex Pravda (Oxford: Oxford University Press, 2005), 179–203.

83. Philip Hanson, "Observations on the Costs of the Yukos Affair to Russia," *Eurasian Geography and Economics* 46, no. 7 (2005): 481–94.

84. Fish, *Democracy Derailed in Russia*, chapter 6.

85. See Yakovlev, "The Evolution of State-Business Interactions."

86. See Irina Denisova, Markus Eller, Timothy Frye, and Ekaterina Zhuravskaya, "Who Wants to Revise Privatization? The Complementarity of Market Skills and Institutions," *American Political Science Review* 103, no. 2 (May 2009): 284–304.

87. See William Tompson, "Putting Yukos in Perspective," *Post-Soviet Affairs* 21, no. 2 (April–June 2005): 159–81; Gustafson, *Wheel of Fortune*.

88. See Anders Aslund, "Comparative Oligarchy: Russia, Ukraine, and the United States," *CASE Network Studies and Analyses* no. 296 (2005), http://papers.ssrn.com/sol3/papers.cfm?abstract_id=1441910; Vadim Volkov, "Standard Oil and Yukos in the Context of Early Capitalism in the United States and Russia," *Demokratizatsiya: The Journal of Post-Soviet Democratization* 16, no. 3 (2008): 240–64.

89. See Yakovlev, "The Evolution of State-Business Interactions"; on comparative analysis of models of state-business relationships, see David Kang, *Crony Capitalism: Corruption and Development in South Korea and the Philippines* (Cambridge: Cambridge University Press, 2002). The term "predatory state" was coined by North in his analysis of economic history. See Douglass North, *Structure and Change in Economic History* (New York: W. W. Norton, 1981).

90. See Leonid Polishchuk, "Biznesmeny i filantropy," *Pro et Contra* 10, no. 1 (January–February 2006): 59–73. Timothy Frye, however, argued that large-scale corporate philanthropy in Russia may be also perceived as a side payment by business

people for their "original sin" of privatization of enterprises. See Timothy Frye, "Original Sin, Good Works, and Property Rights in Russia," *World Politics* 58, no. 4 (July 2006): 479–504.

91. See Treisman, "Putin's Silovarchs."

92. See Gel'man, "Political Opposition in Russia."

93. See, for example, Graeme Robertson, "Managing Society: Protests, Civil Society, and Regime in Putin's Russia," *Slavic Review* 68, no. 3 (Fall 2009): 528–47; Samuel A. Greene, "Citizenship and the Social Contract in Post-Soviet Russia," *Demokratizatsiya: The Journal of Post-Soviet Democratization* 20, no. 2 (Spring 2012): 133–40.

94. See Vladimir Gel'man and Tomila Lankina, "Authoritarian versus Democratic Diffusions: Explaining Institutional Choices in Russia's Local Government," *Post-Soviet Affairs* 24, no. 1 (January–March 2008): 40–62; Robert Orttung, "Center-Periphery Relations," in *Russia in 2020: Scenarios for the Future*, eds. Maria Lipman and Nikolay Petrov (Washington, DC: Carnegie Endowment for International Peace, 2011), 329–47.

95. See Nikolay Petrov, "Corporatism vs. Regionalism," *Pro et Contra* 11, no. 4–5 (September–October 2007): 75–89. On late-Soviet corporatist relationships in subnational politics, see Peter Rutland, *The Politics of Economic Stagnation in the Soviet Union: The Role of Local Party Organs in Economic Management* (Cambridge: Cambridge University Press, 1993).

96. For the concept of regional Communist party leaders as "Soviet prefects," see Jerry F. Hough, *The Soviet Prefects: The Local Party Organs in Industrial Decision-Making* (Cambridge, MA: Harvard University Press, 1969).

97. See Olga Kryshtanovskaya and Stephen White, "The Sovietization of Russian Politics," *Post-Soviet Affairs* 25, no. 4 (October–December 2009): 283–309.

98. See *Elections without Choice*, eds. Guy Hermet, Richard Rose, and Alain Rouquie (London: Macmillan, 1978).

99. Wilson, *Virtual Politics*, 41.

100. On the distinction between "hard" and "soft" coercion of electoral competition, see Fish, *Democracy Derailed in Russia*, 54–61.

101. See, for example, Mikhail Myagkov, Peter C. Ordeshook, and Dmitry Shakin, *The Forensics of Electoral Fraud: With Applications to Russia and Ukraine* (Cambridge: Cambridge University Press, 2009); Walter Mebane and Kirill Kalinin, "Electoral Fraud in Russia: Vote Count Analysis Using Second-Digit Mean Tests." Paper for the Annual Meeting of the Midwest Political Science Association (Chicago, April 2010).

102. See Andreas Schedler, "The Menu of Manipulations," *Journal of Democracy* 13, no. 2 (April 2002): 36–50.

103. See Grigorii V. Golosov, *Demokratiya v Rossii: Instruktsiya po Sborke* (St. Petersburg: BHV-Peterburg, 2012).

104. The Soviet 1977 Constitution granted the Communist Party of the Soviet Union the official status of the "core of the political system of the USSR"; in a similar vein, one can also speak of an institutional core of the current political regime in Russia.

105. See Douglass North, *Institutions, Institutional Changes, and Economic Performance* (Cambridge: Cambridge University Press, 1990), 16.

106. The 2008 survey of the Russian elite conducted by Mikhail Afanas'ev indicated that a large share of the Russian ruling class supported democratization, free elections, party competition, and checks and balances on presidential powers, although a significant number of those with a background in the coercive apparatus unequivocally opposed any democratic changes. See Mikhail Afanas'ev, *Rossiiskie elity razvitiya: Zapros na novyi kurs* (Moscow: "Liberal'naya missiya" Foundation, 2009).

107. See *Obshchestvo i vlast' v usloviyakh politicheskogo krizisa: Doklad ekspertov Tsentra strategicheskikh razrabotok,* http://www.echo.msk.ru/doc/891815-echo.html.

108. See Victor Polterovich, "Institutional Trap," in *New Palgrave Dictionary of Economics Online* (New York: Palgrave Macmillan, 2008), http://dictionaryof economics.com/article?id=pde2008_I000262. See also Vladimir Gel'man, "Institution Building and Institutional Traps in Russian Politics," in *Russia 2020: Scenarios for the Future,* eds. Maria Lipman and Nikolay Petrov (Washington, DC: Carnegie Endowment for International Peace, 2011), 215–32.

109. See, for example, Dmitrii Travin, *Ocherki noveishei istorii Rossii, kniga 1: 1985–1999* (St. Petersburg: Norma, 2010).

CHAPTER 5. THE UNPREDICTABLE 2010s

1. For overviews, see Serhiy Kudelia, "The House That Yanukovych Built," *Journal of Democracy* 25, no. 3 (July 2014): 19–34; Lucan Way, "Civil Society and Democratization," *Journal of Democracy* 25, no. 3 (July 2014): 35–43.

2. For overviews, see Andrew Wilson, *Ukraine's Orange Revolution* (New Haven, CT: Yale University Press, 2005); *Revolution in Orange: The Origins of Ukraine's Democratic Breakthrough,* eds. Anders Aslund and Michael McFaul (Washington, DC: Carnegie Endowment for International Peace, 2006).

3. See Robert Horvath, "Putin's Preventive Counter-Revolution: Post-Soviet Authoritarianism and the Spectre of Velvet Revolution," *Europe-Asia Studies* 63, no. 1 (January 2011): 1–25.

4. For an overview of Russia's encroachment into Ukrainian domestic politics after the overthrow of Yanukovych, and especially military actions in Donbass, see Nikolay Mitrokhin, "Grubye lyudi," *Grani.ru,* 2014, August 27, http://grani.ru/opin ion/mitrokhin/m.232396.html.

5. According to the nationwide survey of Russians conducted by WCIOM in September 2013, 56 percent of respondents considered Crimea to be a Russian territory, while the number of those who identified Dagestan and Chechnya as parts of Russia were 41 percent and 39 percent respectively. See *Sovremennaya rossiiskaya identichnost': Izmereniya, voprosy, otvety* (Moscow: Valdai Club, 2013), 7, http://vid-1.rian.ru/ig/valdai/Russian_Identity_2013_rus.pdf.

6. See Sam Greene and Graeme Robertson, "Explaining Putin's Popularity: Rally

Around the Russian Flag," *Washington Post* 2014, September 9, http://www.washing-tonpost.com/blogs/monkey-cage/wp/2014/09/09/explaining-putins-popularity-rally ing-round-the-russian-flag/.

7. See Konstantin Gaaze, "Poker dlya odnogo: Kto i kak v Rossii prinimaet resh-eniya," *New Times* 2014, September 1, http://www.newtimes.ru/articles/detail/86540.

8. See, especially, *Russia 2025: Scenarios for the Russian Future*, eds. Maria Lip-man and Nikolay Petrov (New York: Palgrave, 2013); *Osnovnye tendentsii politichesk-ogo razvitiya Rossii v 2011–2013 godakh: Krizis i transformatsiya rossiiskogo avtorita-rizma*, ed. Kirill Rogov (Moscow: Liberal'naya missiya, 2014), http://www.liberal.ru/upload/files/Osnovnie%20tendentsii%20politicheskogo%20razvitiya.pdf.

9. See Milan Svolik, *The Politics of Authoritarian Rule* (Cambridge: Cambridge University Press, 2012).

10. See Beatriz Magaloni, "The Game of Electoral Fraud and the Ousting of Au-thoritarian Rule," *American Journal of Political Science* 54, no. 3 (August 2010): 751–65.

11. See *Democratization by Elections: A New Mode of Transition*, ed. Staffan I. Lindberg (Baltimore, MD: Johns Hopkins University Press, 2009); Joshua Tucker, "Enough! Electoral Fraud, Collective Action Problems, and Post-Communist Colored Revolutions," *Perspectives on Politics* 5, no. 3 (September 2007): 535–51.

12. See Adam Przeworski, *Democracy and the Market: Political and Economic Re-forms in Latin America and Eastern Europe* (Cambridge: Cambridge University Press, 1991), 58–59.

13. For overviews, see Christian Davenport, "State Repression and Political Or-der," *Annual Review of Political Science* 10 (2007): 1–23; Jennifer Earl, "Political Re-pressions: Iron First, Velvet Gloves, and Diffuse Control," *Annual Review of Sociology* 37 (2011): 261–84.

14. See Johannes Gereshewski, "The Three Pillars of Stability: Legitimation, Repression, and Co-Optation in Authoritarian Regimes," *Democratization* 20, no. 1 (2013): 13–38.

15. See Sergei Guriev and Ekaterina Zhuravskaya, "Why Russia Is Not South Ko-rea," *Journal of International Affairs* 63, no. 2 (Spring–Summer 2010): 125–30.

16. Most of the possible scenarios of Russia's political development in the 2010s proposed by American, European, and Russian experts were based upon a projection of inertia and considered preservation of the status quo as a baseline. See *Russia in 2020: Scenarios for the Future*, eds. Maria Lipman and Nikolay Petrov (Washington, DC: Carnegie Endowment for International Peace, 2011).

17. After his inauguration in May 2012, Putin released a number of decrees that announced tremendous rises in salaries of public sector employees, especially in public health and education sectors. The regional authorities, which had to cover these ex-penditures from subnational budgets, had no financial resources with which to fulfill these promises.

18. For a detailed analysis of economic policy under Putin, see Sergei Aleksashen-ko, "Rossiiskaya ekonomika k nachalu epokhi 'posle Putina,'" *Pro et Contra* 18, no. 3–4 (2014): 104–17.

19. See Guillermo O'Donnell and Philippe Schmitter, *Transitions from Author-*

itarian Rule: Tentative Conclusions about Uncertain Democracies (Baltimore, MD: Johns Hopkins University Press, 1986), 3.

20. See Jason Brownlee, "Hereditary Succession in Modern Autocracies," *World Politics* 59, no. 4 (July 2007): 595–628.

21. See Henry Hale, "Regime Cycles: Democracy, Autocracy, and Revolution in Post-Soviet Eurasia," *World Politics* 58, no. 1 (October 2005): 133–65; Henry Hale, "Democracy or Autocracy on the March? Colored Revolutions as Normal Dynamics of Patronal Presidentialism," *Communist and Post-Communist Studies* 39, no. 3 (September 2006): 305–29.

22. See Rudra Sil and Cheng Chen, "State Legitimacy and the (In)Significance of Democracy in Post-Communist Russia," *Europe-Asia Studies* 56, no. 3 (May 2004): 347–68; Henry Hale, "The Myth of Mass Russian Support for Autocracy: The Public Opinion Foundations of a Hybrid Regime," *Europe-Asia Studies* 63, no. 8 (October 2011): 1357–75.

23. According to a survey by the Levada Center conducted in April 2007, 51 percent of respondents agreed to abandoning the presidential term limit for Putin. Moreover, 35 percent of respondents even agreed to his lifetime presidency (although 54 percent objected to this solution). At the same time, 65 percent of respondents were ready to vote for a presidential candidate nominated by Putin. See "Issledovanie Levada-tsentra: Tret' rossiyan khoteli by videt' Vladimira Putina pozhiznennym pravitelem Rossii," *gtmarket.ru*, May 7, 2007, http://gtmarket.ru/news/state/2007/05/07/899.

24. See Mebane and Kalinin, *Electoral Fraud in Russia*.

25. See Richard Rose and William Mishler, "How Do Electors Respond to an 'Unfair' Election? The Experience of Russians," *Post-Soviet Affairs* 25, no. 2 (April–June 2009): 118–36.

26. See Kenneth Wilson, "How Russians View Electoral Fairness: A Qualitative Analysis," *Europe-Asia Studies* 64, no. 1 (January 2012): 152.

27. See Lipman and Petrov, eds., *Russia in 2020: Scenarios for the Future.*

28. See, for example, Vladimir Gel'man, "Party Politics in Russia: From Competition to Hierarchy," *Europe-Asia Studies* 60, no. 6 (August 2008): 913–30; Ora John Reuter, "The Politics of Dominant Party Formation: United Russia and Russia's Governors," *Europe-Asia Studies* 62, no. 2 (March 2010): 293–327.

29. See Vladimir Gel'man and Tomila Lankina, "Authoritarian versus Democratic Diffusions: Explaining Institutional Choices in Russia's Local Government," *Post-Soviet Affairs* 24, no. 1 (January–March 2008): 40–62.

30. On these developments see, for example, Vladimir Gel'man and Sergei Ryzhenkov, "Local Regimes, Sub-National Governance, and the 'Power Vertical' in Contemporary Russia," *Europe-Asia Studies* 63, no. 3 (May 2011): 449–65; Ora John Reuter and Graeme Robertson, "Subnational Appointments in Authoritarian Regimes: Evidence from Russia's Gubernatorial Appointments," *Journal of Politics* 74, no. 4 (October 2012): 1023–37; Thomas F. Remington, Irina Soboleva, Anton Sobolev, and Mark Urnov, "Economic and Social Policy Trade-Offs in the Russian Regions: Evidence from Four Case Studies," *Europe-Asia Studies* 65, no. 10 (December 2013): 1855–76.

31. Among the voluminous literature on modernization, the linkage between socioeconomic and political changes is discussed, among others, in: Samuel P. Huntington, *Political Order in Changing Societies* (New Haven, CT: Yale University Press, 1968); Mancur Olson, "Democracy, Dictatorship, and Development," *American Political Science Review* 87, no. 3 (September 1993): 567–76; Adam Przeworski, Michael E. Alvarez, Jose Antonio Cheibub, and Fernando Limongi, *Democracy and Development: Political Institutions and Well-being in the World, 1950–1990* (Cambridge: Cambridge University Press, 200); Daron Acemoglu and James Robinson, *Why Nations Fail: The Origins of Property, Prosperity, and Poverty* (New York: Crown Business, 2012). On the role of cultural changes, see, for example, Lawrence E. Harrison, *Who Prospers: How Cultural Values Shape Economic and Political Success* (New York: Basic Books, 1992); Ronald Inglehart and Christian Welzel, *Modernization, Cultural Change and Democracy: The Human Development Sequence* (Cambridge: Cambridge University Press, 2005); Douglass North, John Wallis, and Barry Weingast, *Violence and Social Orders: A Conceptual Framework for Interpreting Recorded Human History* (Cambridge: Cambridge University Press, 2009).

32. For a manifestation of this approach proposed by Medvedev's own think-tank, INSOR, see *Demokratiya: Razvitie rossiiskoi modeli*, ed. Igor Yurgens (Moscow: Institute for Contemporary Development, 2008), http://www.insor-russia.ru/files/LowRes Democracy_Books_final.pdf. INSOR (Institut sovremennogo razvitiya) was at that time considered the major proponent of cautious and gradual regime liberalization without challenging the existing political order in Russia.

33. This was openly stated in Medvedev's programmatic statement: Dmitry Medvedev, *Rossiya, vpered!*, http://www.gazeta.ru/comments/2009/09/10_a_3258568.shtml.

34. See, for example, Richard Sakwa, *The Crisis of Russian Democracy: The Dual State, Factionalism, and Medvedev Succession* (Cambridge: Cambridge University Press, 2011).

35. See, for example, Vladimir Milov, *Stop, Rossiya!*, http://www.gazeta.ru/col umn/milov/3260272.shtml, as well as numerous other statements.

36. See Mikhail Afanas'ev, *Rossiiskie elity razvitiya: Zapros na novyi kurs* (Moscow: Liberal'naya missiya, 2009).

37. On the political constraints of authoritarian modernization, see Barbara Geddes, *Politician's Dilemma: Building State Capacity in Latin America* (Berkeley, CA: University of California Press, 1994).

38. See Sakwa, *The Crisis of Russian Democracy*.

39. See Afanas'ev, *Rossiiskie elity razvitiya*.

40. See Geddes, *Politician's Dilemma*; Stephan Haggard and Robert R. Kaufman, *The Political Economy of Democratic Transitions* (Princeton, NJ: Princeton University Press, 1995).

41. See Bruce Bueno de Mesquita, Alastair Smith, Randolph M. Siverson, and James D. Morrow, *The Logic of Political Survival* (Cambridge, MA: MIT Press, 2003).

42. See Barbara Geddes, *Paradigms and Sand Castles; Theory Building and Re-*

search Design in Comparative Politics (Ann Arbor, MI: University of Michigan Press, 2003), 47–88.

43. See Dani Rodrik, "The Myth of Authoritarian Growth," *Project Syndicate* 2010, August 9 http://www.project-syndicate.org/commentary/the-myth-of-authoritarian-growth.

44. See, for example, Robert J. Brym and Vladimir Gimpelson, "The Size, Composition, and Dynamics of the Russian State Bureaucracy in the 1990s," *Slavic Review* 63, no. 1 (Spring 2004): 90–112.

45. The practice of appointment and dismissal of Russia's regional governors after the abolishment of popular elections is clear evidence for this. See Nikolay Petrov, "The Excessive Role of a Weak Russian State," in *Russia in 2020: Scenarios for the Future*, eds. Maria Lipman and Nikolay Petrov (Washington, DC: Carnegie Endowment for International Peace, 2011), 303–27; Reuter and Remington, "Subnational Appointments."

46. Although in 2008 Dmitry Medvedev loudly announced the establishment of presidential lists of "cadre reserves," it had little impact on actual decision making in Russia, including major appointments.

47. See, for example: "Zhestkim kursom . . . analiticheskaya zapiska Leningradskoi assotsiatsii sotsial'no-ekonomicheskikh nauk," *Vek XX i mir* no. 6 (June 1990): 15–19.

48. "Coercive apparatus" is here considered to be an umbrella term that includes military, police, and security services, despite important differences between these agencies.

49. The interbranch struggle of various agencies during the anticorruption campaign initiated by Yuri Andropov in the 1980s was a typical instance of this rivalry. See Luc Duhamel, *The KGB Campaign Against Corruption in Moscow, 1982–1987* (Pittsburgh, PA: University of Pittsburgh Press, 2010).

50. See Brian Taylor, "Russia's Passive Army: Rethinking Military Coups," *Comparative Political Studies* 34, no. 8 (October 2001): 924–52. See also Aleksandr Golts, "The Armed Forces in 2020: Modern or Soviet?" in *Russia 2020: Scenarios for the Future*, eds. Maria Lipman and Nikolay Petrov (Washington, DC: Carnegie Endowment for International Peace, 2011), 371–94.

51. For a detailed analysis, see Vadim Volkov, *Violent Entrepreneurs: The Role of Force in the Making of Russian Capitalism* (Ithaca, NY: Cornell University Press, 2002).

52. See, for example, Olga Kryshtanovskaya and Stephen White, "Putin's Militocracy," *Post-Soviet Affairs* 19, no. 4 (October–December 2003): 289–306.

53. For an open objection to the commercialization of the coercive apparatus of the Russian state, see Viktor Cherkesov, "Nel'zya dopustit,' chtoby voiny prevrashchalis' v torgovtsev," *Kommersant* October 9, 2007, http://www.kommersant.ru/doc.aspx?DocsID=812840.

54. See Afanas'ev, *Rossiiskie elity razvitiya*.

55. For a detailed and in-depth state-of-the-art analysis of law enforcement agencies in Russia and a proposal for their comprehensive reform, see Vadim Volkov, Ivan Grigor'ev, Arina Dmitrieva, Ekaterina Moiseeva, Ella Paneyakh, Kirill Titaev, Irina Chetverikova, and Maria Shklyaruk, *Kontseptsiya kompleksnoi organizatsionno-upravlencheskoi reformy pravookhranitel'nykh organov v RF* (St. Petersburg: Institute

for the Rule of Law of the European University at St. Petersburg, 2013), http://www
.enforce.spb.ru/images/Issledovanya/IRL_KGI_Reform_final_11.13.pdf.

56. On Mexico under the PRI, see, for example, Wayne A. Cornelius, "Nation Building, Participation, and Distribution: The Politics of Social Reform under Cardenas," in *Crisis, Choice, and Change: Historical Studies of Political Development*, eds. Gabriel A. Almond, Scott C. Flanagan, and Robert R. Mundt (Boston, MA: Little, Brown, 1973), 392–498; Susan Kaufman Purcell, "Decision-Making in Authoritarian Regime: Theoretical Implications from a Mexican Case Study," *World Politics* 26, no. 1 (October 1973): 28–54; Dale Story, *The Mexican Ruling Party: Stability and Authority* (New York: Praeger, 1986).

57. See Gel'man, "Party Politics in Russia"; Reuter and Remington, "Subnational Appointments."

58. On the role of organizational autonomy for the politics of modernization, see Huntington, *Political Order in Changing Societies*, 20–32.

59. On the overcoming of the global economic crisis of 2008–2009 in Russia, see, for example, Neil Robinson, "Russia's Response to Crisis: The Paradox of Success," *Europe-Asia Studies* 65, no. 3 (May 2013): 450–72.

60. See Kirill Rogov, "The 'Third Cycle': Is Russia Headed Back to the Future?" in *Russia 2020: Scenarios for the Future*, eds. Maria Lipman and Nikolay Petrov (Washington, DC: Carnegie Endowment for International Peace, 2011), 125–48. See also Paul Chaisty and Stephen Whitefield, "The Effects of the Global Financial Crisis on Russian Political Attitudes," *Post-Soviet Affairs* 28, no. 2 (April–July 2012): 187–208.

61. *Thaw (Ottepel)* is the title of a novel by Ilya Ehrenburg published in 1954 on the eve of major political liberalization; later on, this term was used as a label for the entire period of Khrushchev's reforms and as a symbol of the half-hearted liberalization of an authoritarian regime.

62. These constitutional changes came into force after the presidential elections of 2012 and the parliamentary elections of 2011, respectively.

63. See, for example, Ivan Krastev and Stephen Holmes, "An Autopsy of Managed Democracy," *Journal of Democracy* 23, no. 3 (July 2012): 33–45. See also Vladimir Gel'man, "Cracks in the Wall: Challenges for Electoral Authoritarianism in Russia," *Problems of Post-Communism* 60, no. 2 (April 2013): 3–10.

64. See Tatyana Vorozheikina, "Samozashchita kak pervyi shag k solidarnosti," *Pro et Contra* 12, no. 2–3 (April–May 2008): 6–23; Graeme Robertson, "Managing Society: Protests, Civil Society, and Regime in Putin's Russia," *Slavic Review* 68, no. 3 (Fall 2009): 528–47.

65. See Markku Lonkila, "Driving at Democracy in Russia: Protest Activities of St. Petersburg Car Drivers' Associations," *Europe-Asia Studies* 63, no. 2 (March 2011): 291–309; Samuel A. Greene, "Russia: Society, Politics, and the Search for Community," in *Russia 2020: Scenarios for the Future*, eds. Maria Lipman and Nikolay Petrov (Washington, DC: Carnegie Endowment for International Peace, 2011), 459–75; Carine Clement, *Gorodskie dvizheniya v Rossii v 2009–2012 godakh: Na puti k politicheskomu* (Moscow: Novoe literaturnoe obozrenie, 2013).

66. To a certain degree, these developments repeated the experience of Gor-

bachev's perestroika, when at the initial stage of political liberalization, environmental and cultural movements (which were not coerced by authorities) served as an umbrella for political groups that played an active role in undermining the regime at the latter stages of electoral campaigns in 1989–1990. See Fish, *Democracy from Scratch*; Urban, Igrunov, and Mitrokhin, *The Rebirth of Politics in Russia*.

67. For a more detailed analysis of the impact of the generation shift on economic and political changes in late-Soviet and post-Soviet Russia, see Vladimir Gel'man, Otar Marganiya, and Dmitry Travin, *Reexamining Economic and Political Reforms in Russia, 1985–200: Generations, Ideas, and Changes* (Lanham, MD: Lexington Books, 2014).

68. On Navalny's political background, see, for example, Grigori Golosov, "Navalny Steps into the Ring," *OD Russia,* July 19, 2013, http://www.opendemocracy.net/od-russia/grigorii-golosov/navalny-steps-into-ring.

69. One should take into account that the Russian authorities in the post-Soviet period did not practice mass violence in domestic politics beyond Chechnya.

70. See Samuel P. Huntington, *The Third Wave: Democratization in the Late Twentieth Century* (Norman, OK: University of Oklahoma Press, 1991), 174–80.

71. On the 1989 elections in the Soviet Union and their political consequences, see, for example, *Vesna 89: Geografiya i anatomiya parlamentskikh vyborov,* eds. Vladimir Kolosov, Nikolay Petrov, and Leonid Smirnyagin (Moscow: Progress, 1990); Archie Brown, *The Gorbachev Factor* (Oxford: Oxford University Press, 1996), chapter 5; M. Steven Fish, *Democracy from Scratch: Opposition and Regime in the New Russian Revolution* (Princeton, NJ: Princeton University Press, 1995); Urban, Igrunov, and Mitrokhin, *The Rebirth of Politics in Russia*; Hough, *Democratization and Revolution in the USSR*; Michael McFaul, *Russia's Unfinished Revolution: Political Changes from Gorbachev to Putin* (Ithaca, NY: Cornell University Press, 2001), chapter 2.

72. See Adam Przeworski, Michael E. Alvarez, Jose Antonio Cheibub, and Fernando Limongi, *Democracy and Development: Political Institutions and Well-being in the World, 1950–1990* (Cambridge: Cambridge University Press, 2000).

73. See W. Lance Bennett and Alexandra Segerberg, "The Logic of Connective Action," *Information, Communication, and Society* 15, no. 5 (June 2012): 739–68.

74. On the impact of economic factors on public opinion and political support in Russia, see, for example, Rudra Sil and Cheng Chen, "State Legitimacy and the (In)Significance of Democracy in Post-Communist Russia," *Europe-Asia Studies* 56, no. 3 (May 2004): 347–68; Daniel Treisman, "Presidential Popularity in a Hybrid Regime: Russia under Yeltsin and Putin," *American Journal of Political Science* 55, no. 3 (August 2011): 590–609; Richard Rose, William Mishler, and Neil Munro, *Popular Support for an Undemocratic Regime: The Changing Views of Russians* (Cambridge: Cambridge University Press, 2011).

75. On the falsification of preferences in nondemocracies, see Timur Kuran, "Now out of Never: The Element of Surprise in East European Revolution of 1989," *World Politics* 44, no. 1 (October 1991): 7–48.

76. See Tucker, "Enough!"; Mark R. Beissinger, "Structure and Example in Mod-

ular Political Phenomena: The Diffusion of Bulldozer / Rose / Orange / Tulip Revolutions," *Perspectives on Politics* 5, no. 2 (June 2007): 259–76; Valerie J. Bunce and Sharon L. Wolchik, "Defeating Dictators: Electoral Change and Stability in Competitive Authoritarian Regimes," *World Politics* 62, no. 1 (January 2010): 43–86; Valerie J. Bunce and Sharon L. Wolchik, *Defeating Authoritarian Leaders in Postcommunist Countries* (Cambridge: Cambridge University Press, 2011).

77. See Steven Levitsky and Lucan Way, *Competitive Authoritarianism: Hybrid Regimes after the Cold War* (Cambridge: Cambridge University Press, 2010).

78. For a detailed analysis, see Timothy Frye, Ora John Reuter, and David Szakonyi, "Political Machines at Work: Voter Mobilization and Electoral Subversion in Russia," *World Politics* 66, no. 2 (April 2014): 195–228.

79. On spatial divisions of Russian society along the axes of political, social, and economic modernization, see Natalia Zubarevich, "Four Russias: Human Potential and Social Differentiation of Russian Regions and Cities," in *Russia 2025: Scenarios for the Russian Future*, eds. Maria Lipman and Nikolay Petrov (New York: Palgrave Macmillan, 2013), 67–85.

80. For a highly critical assessment, see, for example, Lilia Shevtsova, "Pritvornaya Modernizatsiya," *gazeta.ru*, 2012, May 3, http://www.gazeta.ru/comments/2012/05/03 _x_4570813.shtml.

81. See Bennett and Segerberg, "The Logic of Connective Action."

82. *Navalny ili Fedorov: Za Kem Pravda?*, http://www.youtube.com/watch?v=cc E-zCR1ej4, 2011, 21 February.

83. On the role of "niche parties" in authoritarian regimes, see Kenneth Greene, *Why Dominant Parties Lose: Mexico's Democratization in Comparative Perspective* (Cambridge: Cambridge University Press, 2007).

84. See Gel'man, "Cracks in the Wall."

85. Although the data of exit polls were soon erased from the official FOM website www.fom.ru, this information as well as initial results were widely distributed by and discussed among Internet users, thus expanding the accusation of large-scale electoral fraud on the part of the authorities.

86. See Enikolopov, Korovkin, Petrova, Sonin, and Zakharov, "Field Experiment Estimate of Fraud."

87. On the role of these factors in the collapse of authoritarian regimes, see Kuran, "Now out of Never."

88. See Przeworski, *Democracy and the Market*, 58–59.

89. For more detailed analyses, see Graeme Robertson, "Protesting Putinism: The Election Protests of 2011–2012 in Broader Perspective," *Problems of Post-Communism* 60, no. 2 (April 2013): 11–23; Samuel A. Greene, "Beyond Bolotnaya: Bridging Old and New in Russia's Election Protest Movement," *Problems of Post-Communism* 60, no. 2 (April 2013): 40–52.

90. Among the voluminous literature on the role of mass social movements in protest political mobilization, see, for example, Charles Tilly, *From Mobilization to Revolution* (Reading, MA: Addison-Wesley, 1978); Sidney Tarrow, *Power in Movement:*

Collective Action, Social Movements, and Politics (Cambridge: Cambridge University Press, 1994); Doug McAdam, Sidney Tarrow, and Charles Tilly, *Dynamics of Contention* (Cambridge: Cambridge University Press, 2001).

91. For an early discussion of the conditions of elite pacts/settlements and their role in democratization, see Guillermo O'Donnell and Philippe Schmitter, *Transitions from Authoritarian Rule,* 37–41; Michael Burton, Richard Gunther, and John Higley, "Introduction: Elite Transformations and Democratic Regimes," in *Elites and Democratic Consolidation in Latin America and Southern Europe,* eds. John Higley and Richard Gunther (Cambridge: Cambridge University Press, 1992), 1–37. On the role of intraelite agreements for democratization in Eastern Europe, see *Roundtable Talks and the Breakdown of Communism,* ed. Jon Elster (Chicago, IL: University of Chicago Press, 1996). For criticism of this approach, see William Case, "Can the 'Halfway House' Stand? Semidemocracy and Elite Theory in Three Southeast Asian Countries," *Comparative Politics* 28, no. 4 (July 1996): 437–64; Vladimir Gel'man, "Post-Soviet Transitions and Democratization: Toward a Theory-Building," *Democratization* 10, no. 2 (June 2003): 87–104.

92. See Przeworski, *Democracy and the Market,* 83–88.

93. See *Negotiating Radical Change: Understanding and Extending the Lessons of the Polish Round Table Talks,* eds. Michael D. Kennedy and Brian Porter (Ann Arbor, MI: University of Michigan, 2000), http://webapps.lsa.umich.edu/ii/PolishRoundTable/pdf/negotiatingradicalchange.pdf; Grzegorz Ekiert and Jan Kubik, *Rebellious Civil Society: Popular Protest and Democratic Consolidation in Poland, 1989–1993* (Ann Arbor, MI: University of Michigan Press, 2001).

94. See Regina Smyth, Irina Soboleva, and Anton Sobolev, "A Well-Organized Play: Symbolic Politics and the Effects of Pro-Putin Rallies," *Problems of Post-Communism* 60, no. 2 (April 2013): 24–39.

95. Alexei Navalny, "Borba s korruptsiei i est moia ekonomicheskaia programma," *Vedomosti,* March 1, 2012, www.vedomosti.ru/opinion/news/1519747/ne_vrat_i_ne_vorovat.

96. See Greene, *Why Dominant Parties Lose.*

97. See Tucker, "Enough!"; Bunce and Wolchik, "Defeating Dictators."

98. On the effects of "weak ties," see Mark Granovetter, "The Strength of Weak Ties," *American Journal of Sociology* 78, no. 6 (May 1973): 1360–80; on the role of social media in 2011 postelection protests in Russia, see Markku Lonkila, "Russian Protest On- and Offline: The Role of Social Media in Moscow Opposition Demonstrations in December 2011," *Finnish Institute of International Affairs Briefing Papers* no. 98 (February 2012), http://www.fiia.fi/en/publication/244/russian_protest_on-_and_offline/.

99. See Bennett and Segerberg, "The Logic of Connective Action."

100. Although some visible figures from the Communist Party of the Russian Federation, as well as from Just Russia, joined the protests, these organizations as a whole had little incentive to subvert the status quo regime; in the case of hypothetical democratization, their chances for political survival were rather dubious.

101. On the reaction of some opposition activists, see, for example, Vladimir Mi-

lov, "Kak Putin oppozistiyu perekhitril," *Gazeta.ru*, 2012, March 5, http://www.gazeta.ru/column/milov/4026641.shtml.

102. See Grigorii V. Golosov, "The 2012 Political Reform in Russia: The Interplay of Liberalizing Concessions and Authoritarian Corrections," *Problems of Post-Communism* 59, no. 6 (November–December 2012): 3–14; for an alternative perspective, see J. Paul Goode, "The Unintended Consequences of Russia's Gubernatorial Elections," *PONARS Eurasia Policy Memos* no. 283 (September 2013), http://www.ponarseurasia.org/sites/default/files/policy-memos-pdf/Pepm_283_Goode_Sept2013.pdf.

103. These criminal charges were abolished under Medvedev's presidency in 2011 in the wake of the "virtual thaw."

104. See "The Stalinization of Putinism: A Doomed Effort," in *Russia 2025: Scenarios for the Russian Future*, eds. Maria Lipman and Nikolay Petrov (London and New York: Palgrave Macmillan, 2013), 268–83.

105. See Daniel Treisman, "Can Putin Keep His Grip on Power?" *Current History* 112, no. 756 (October 2013): 251–58.

106. On political repressions and the role of threat perception, see Christian Davenport, "Multi-Dimensional Threat Perception and State Repressions: An Inquiry into Why States Apply Negative Sanctions," *American Journal of Political Science* 38, no. 3 (August 1993): 683–713. See also Davenport, "State Repressions and Political Order."

107. For the best-known analysis of the Russian dissident movement, which provides compelling evidence for this argument, see Lyudmila Alexeyeva, *Soviet Dissent: Contemporary Movements for National, Religious, and Human Rights* (Middletown, CT: Wesleyan University Press, 1984). The peak of open public dissent in the Soviet Union after Stalin occurred in the second half of 1960, after which a gradual decline continued until the early 1980s. At the time of Gorbachev's reforms, Soviet dissidents played a relatively negligible role in the prodemocratic movement despite the fact that some of the members of the dissident movement (first and foremost, Andrei Sakharov) served as iconic figures for the new democrats. One might suggest that this decline was a byproduct of the Soviet state's repressive policy, although it coincided with other factors, such as the impact of generation changes and changing attitudes among Soviet citizens. See, for example, Vladislav Zubok, *Zhivago's Children: The Last Russian Intelligentsiya* (Cambridge, MA: Harvard University Press, 2009), especially chapter 9.

108. See Golosov, "The 2012 Political Reform"; Regina Smyth, "Beyond United Russia: The Kremlin's Efforts to Engineer Ruling Majorities," *PONARS Eurasia Policy Memos* no. 302 (September 2013), http://www.ponarseurasia.org/sites/default/files/policy-memos-pdf/Pepm_302_Smyth_Sept2013.pdf.

109. For a detailed overview, see Aleksandr Kynev, Arkadii Lyubarev, and Andrei Maksimov, 8/09/2013: *Rozhdenie novoi paradigmy vyborov: Doklad No. 4 po monitoringu izbiratel'noi kampanii 8 sentyabrya 2013* (Moscow: Committee for Civil Initiatives, 2013), http://komitetgi.ru/upload/iblock/602/602bc8619d848d1b76661cd8f938ec3e.doc.

110. See Daniel Treisman, "Presidential Popularity in a Hybrid Regime: Russia under Yeltsin and Putin," *American Journal of Political Science* 55, no. 3 (2011): P.590–

609; for an alternative perspective, see Kirill Rogov, "Forty Years in the Desert: The Political Cycles of Post-Soviet Transition," in *Russia 2025: Scenarios for the Russian Future*, eds. Maria Lipman and Nikolay Petrov (London and New York: Palgrave Macmillan, 2013), 18–45.

111. According to the Levada Center's weekly nationwide surveys of Russians, Putin's approval rating (the difference between the number of positive and negative assessments of him) fell from 38 percent in August 2011 to 27 percent in December 2011 but returned to 37 percent in September 2012. However, by November 2013 it fell again to 24 percent (www.levada.ru/indeksy). The Public Opinion Foundation (FOM), the other major polling agency, reported a major decline of popular trust in Putin from 59 percent in the first quarter of 2011 to 45 percent in December 2011, while the number of respondents who expressed their distrust of Putin increased from 15 percent to 24 percent in this period. In 2011–2013, according to the FOM, these indicators revolved around the same numbers—in November 2013, they showed 43 percent and 22 percent of respondents, respectively (http://bd.fom.ru/map/dominant).

112. See Richard Rose, William Mishler, and Neil Munro, *Popular Support for an Undemocratic Regime: The Changing Views of Russians* (Cambridge: Cambridge University Press, 2011).

113. For an overview of the data of a number of surveys and focus groups, see Sergei Belanovsky, Mikhail Dmitriev, Svetlana Misikhina, and Tatyana Omelchuk, *Socio-Economic Change and Political Transformation in Russia* (Moscow: Center for Strategic Research, 2011).

114. For evidence from survey results, see Paul Chaisty and Stephen Whitefield, "Forward to Democracy or Back to Authoritarianism: The Attitudinal Bases of Mass Support for the Russian Election Protests of 2011–2012," *Post-Soviet Affairs* 29, no. 5 (September–October 2013): 387–403.

115. For these arguments, see Henry E. Hale, "The Myth of Mass Russian Support for Autocracy: The Public Opinion Foundations of a Hybrid Regime," *Europe-Asia Studies* vol. 63, no. 8 (October 2011): 1357–75.

116. For survey data, see, for example: "Moskva pered vyborami: Elektoral'nyi rasklad," *FOM*, July 30, 2013, http://fom.ru/Politika/11011; "Prognoz itogov golosovaniya po vyboram mera Moskvy," *FOM* September 2, 2013, http://fom.ru/Politika/11063; see also "Moskva nakanune vyborov mera: Polnoe issledovanie," *Levada-Center* July 17, 2013, http://www.levada.ru/17–07–2013/moskva-nakanune-vyborov-mera-polnoe-issledovanie.

117. On the distinction between hegemonic and electoral (competitive) authoritarian regimes, see Mark Morje Howard and Philip G. Roessler, "Liberalizing Electoral Outcomes in Competitive Authoritarian Regimes," *American Journal of Political Science* 50, no. 2 (April 2006): 365–81; for the use of these categories with regard to subnational elections in Russia, see Petr Panov and Cameron Ross, "Patterns of Electoral Competition in Russian Regional Assemblies: Between 'Hegemonic' and 'Competitive' Authoritarianism," *Demokratizatsiya: The Journal of Post-Soviet Democratization* 21, no. 3 (Summer 2013): 369–99.

118. According to the Levada Center's weekly nationwide surveys of Russians, Putin's approval rating varied between 62 percent and 73 percent in March–August 2014, and the percentage of positive assessments of him at that time reached 80 percent to 86 percent (www.levada.ru/indeksy).

119. See Vladimir Gel'man and Andrey Starodubtsev, "Vozmozhnosti i ogranicheniya avtoritarnoi modernizatsii: Rossiiskie reformy 2000-kh godov," *Politeia* no. 4 (2014): 6–30.

120. See Gaaze, "Poker dlya odnogo."

121. See Bruce Bueno de Mesquita and Alastair Smith, *The Dictator's Handbook: Why Bad Behavior Is Almost Always Good Politics* (New York: Public Affairs, 2011).

CHAPTER 6. THE AGENDA FOR TOMORROW

1. See Hélène Carrère d'Encausse, *L'Empire éclate* (Paris: Flammarion, 1978).

2. For an overview, see Alexander Dallin, "Causes of the Collapse of the USSR," *Post-Soviet Affairs* 8, no. 4 (October–December 1992): 279–302; for a further discussion, see the symposium in *Slavic Review* 63, no. 3 (Fall 2004): 459–554 (with contributions by Stephen F. Cohen, Archie Brown, Mark Kramer, Karen Dawisha, Stephen E. Hanson, and Georgi Derguluian).

3. For different forecasts of Russia's political development, see *Russia 2020: Scenarios for the Future*, eds. Maria Lipman and Nikolay Petrov (Washington, DC: Carnegie Endowment for International Peace, 2011), and the follow-up volume *Russia 2025: Scenarios for the Russian Future*, eds. Maria Lipman and Nikolay Petrov (New York: Palgrave, 2013). For a critical analysis of political and economic forecasting in Russia, see Edwin Bacon, "Writing Russia's Future: Paradigms, Drivers, and Scenarios," *Europe-Asia Studies* 64, no. 7 (September 2012): 1165–89.

4. See Daniel Treisman, "Russia's Political Economy: The Next Decade," in *Russia 2020: Scenarios for the Future*, eds. Maria Lipman and Nikolay Petrov (Washington, DC: Carnegie Endowment for International Peace, 2011), 150.

5. See Treisman, "Russia's Political Economy."

6. For advocacy of this argument in a cross-national comparative perspective, see Adam Przeworski, Michael E. Alvarez, Jose Antonio Cheibub, and Fernando Limongi, *Democracy and Development: Political Institutions and Well-being in the World, 1950–1990* (Cambridge: Cambridge University Press, 2000). For an extension of its implications to politics in Russia's regions, see, for example, Maria Gaidar and Maria Snegovaya, "Dremlet pritikhshii severnyi gorod," *Vedomosti* 2012, 3 February.

7. See Henry Hale, *Why Not Parties in Russia: Democracy, Federalism, and the State* (Cambridge: Cambridge University Press, 2006); Grigorii V. Golosov, "Sfabrikovannoe bol'shinstvo: Konversiya golosov v mesta na dumskikh vyborakh," in *Tretii elektoral'nyi tsikl v Rossii, 2003–2004*, ed. Vladimir Gel'man (St. Petersburg: European University at St. Petersburg Press, 2007), 39–58.

8. See Grigorii V. Golosov, "The 2012 Political Reform in Russia: The Interplay of Liberalizing Concessions and Authoritarian Corrections," *Problems of Post-Communism* 59, no. 6 (November–December 2012): 3–14.

9. See Albert O. Hirschman, *Exit, Voice, and Loyalty: Response to Decline in Firms, Organizations, and States* (Cambridge, MA: Harvard University Press, 1970).

10. On political repressions and the role of threat perception, see Christian Davenport, "Multi-Dimensional Threat Perception and State Repressions: An Inquiry into Why States Apply Negative Sanctions," *American Journal of Political Science* 38, no. 3 (August 1993): 683–713. See also Christian Davenport, "State Repressions and Political Order," *Annual Review of Political Science* 10 (2007): 1–23.

11. For this argument, see Vladimir Gel'man, "Regime Changes Despite Legitimacy Crises: Exit, Voice, and Loyalty in Post-Communist Russia," *Journal of Eurasian Studies* 1, no. 1 (January 2010): 54–63.

12. For a detailed and in-depth analysis, see Vadim Volkov, Ivan Grigoriev, Arina Dmitrieva, Ekaterina Moiseeva, Ella Paneyakh, Mikhail Pozdnyakov, Kirill Titaev, Irina Chetverikova, and Mariya Shklyaruk, *Kontseptsiya organizatsionno-upravlencheskoi reformy pravookhranitel'nykh organov v RF* (St. Petersburg: Institute for the Rule of Law at the European University at St. Petersburg, 2013), http://www.enforce.spb.ru/images/Issledovanya/IRL_KGI_Reform_final_11.13.pdf.

13. According to the official figures from Eurostat, more than half a million Russian citizens became holders of residence permits in various member states of the European Union by March 2013. See http://epp.eurostat.ec.europa.eu/statistics_explained/index.php/Migration_and_migrant_population_statistics.

14. For a classical analysis of revolutionary situations and revolutionary outcomes, see Charles Tilly, *From Mobilization to Revolution* (Reading, MA: Addison-Wesley, 1978).

15. See Mancur Olson, "Dictatorship, Democracy, and Development," *American Political Science Review* 87, no. 3 (September 1993): 573.

16. See Adam Przeworski, *Democracy and the Market: Political and Economic Reforms in Eastern Europe and Latin America* (Cambridge: Cambridge University Press, 1991), 69–72.

17. Przeworski, *Democracy and the Market*, 54–66.

18. See *Korea's Democratization*, ed. Samuel S. Kim (Cambridge: Cambridge University Press, 2003).

19. See Greene, *Why Dominant Parties Lose*.

20. See Steven Levitsky and Lucan Way, *Competitive Authoritarianism: Hybrid Regimes after the Cold War* (Cambridge: Cambridge University Press, 2010), chapter 2.

21. See Greene, *Why Dominant Parties Lose*; Jennifer Gandhi, *Political Institutions under Dictatorship* (Cambridge: Cambridge University Press, 2008); Beatriz Magaloni, "Credible Power Sharing and the Longvelity of Authoritarian Rule," *Comparative Political Studies* 41, no. 4–5 (May 2008): 715–41.

22. See Nikolay Marinov, "Do Economic Sanctions Destabilize Country Leaders?" *American Journal of Political Science* 49, no. 3 (August 2005): 564–76; Gary Clyde Hulfbauer, Jeffrey J. Scott, and Kimerly Ann Elliott, *Economic Sanctions Reconsidered*, 3rd ed. (Washington, DC: Peterson Institute for International Economics, 2007).

23. See Vladimir Gel'man, "The Troubled Rebirth of Political Opposition in Rus-

sia," *PONARS Policy Memos* no. 341 (September 2014), http://www.ponarseurasia.org/sites/default/files/policy-memos-pdf/Pepm341_Gelman_September2014.pdf .

24. See, for example, Joshua Tucker, "Enough! Electoral Fraud, Collective Action Problems, and Post-Communist Colored Revolutions," *Perspectives on Politics* 5, no. 3 (September 2007): 535–51; Valerie Bunce and Sharon Wolchik, "Defeating Dictators: Electoral Change and Stability in Competitive Authoritarian Regimes," *World Politics* 62, no. 1 (January 2010): 43–86.

25. See Alfred Stepan, "On the Tasks of a Democratic Opposition," *Journal of Democracy* 1, no. 2 (April 1990): 41–49.

26. For a discussion of the Russian opposition after the 2011–2012 protests, see also David White, "Taking It to the Streets: Raising the Costs of Electoral Authoritarianism in Russia," *Perspectives on European Politics and Society* 14, no. 4 (2013): 582–98.

27. See Samuel Huntington, *The Third Wave: Democratization in the Late Twentieth Century* (Norman, OK: University of Oklahoma Press, 1991), 174–80.

28. For a detailed overview, see Olexiy Haran, "From Viktor to Viktor: Democracy and Authoritarianism in Ukraine," *Demokratizatsiya: The Journal of Post-Soviet Democratization* 19, no. 2 (Spring 2011): 93–110.

29. For these arguments, see Henry Hale, "Formal Constitutions in Informal Polities: Institutions and Democratization in Post-Soviet Eurasia," *World Politics* 63, no. 4 (October 2011): 581–617.

30. See Serhiy Kudelia, "The House That Yanukovych Built," *Journal of Democracy* 25, no. 3 (July 2014): 19–34.

31. For outlines of proposals on institutional changes, see Grigorii V. Golosov, *Demokratiya v Rossii: Instruktsiya po Sborke* (St. Petersburg: BHV-Peterburg, 2012).

32. See Volkov et al., *Kontseptsiya organizatsionno-upravlencheskoi reformy pravookhranitel'nykh organov v RF* and a number of other policy papers by the Institute for the Rule of Law, http://www.enforce.spb.ru.

33. See, for example, *Russia 2025: Scenarios for the Russian Future*; *Osnovnye tendentsii politicheskogo razvitiya Rossii: Krizis i transformatsiya rossiiskogo avtoritarizma*, ed. Kirill Rogov (Moscow: Liberal'naya missiya, 2014), http://www.liberal.ru/upload/files/Osnovnie%20tendentsii%20politicheskogo%20razvitiya.pdf.

34. See Timur Kuran, "Now Out of Never: The Element of Surprise in East European Revolution of 1989," *World Politics* 44 (October 1991): 7–48.

35. See Kirill Kalinin, "Unifying the Concepts of Electoral Fraud and Preference Falsification: The Case of Russia." Paper for the Annual Meeting of the American Political Science Association (Chicago, IL, August 2013).

36. For some evidence on the late-Soviet opposition, see, for example, M. Steven Fish, *Democracy from Scratch: Opposition and Regime in the New Russian Revolution* (Princeton, NJ: Princeton University Press, 1995).

37. See the OSCE Office for Democratic Institutions and Human Rights, *Preliminary Findings on the Events on Andijan, Uzbekistan, 13 May 2005* (Warsaw, June 20, 2005), http://www.osce.org/odihr/15653.

38. I am grateful to Daniel Treisman for drawing my attention to this issue.

39. See Yegor Gaidar, *Collapse of an Empire: Lessons for Modern Russia* (Washington, DC: Brookings Institution Press, 2007), 91.

40. For an account of these developments, see Doug McAdam, Sidney Tarrow, and Charles Tilly, *Dynamics of Contention* (Cambridge: Cambridge University Press, 2001), 307–22. For an extension of this argument in a broader comparative perspective, see also Steven Levitsky and Lucan Way, "The Durability of Revolutionary Regimes," *Journal of Democracy* 24, no. 3 (July 2013): 5–17.

41. For a detailed critical account, see John B. Dunlop, *The 2002 Dubroka and 2004 Beslan Hostage Crises: A Critique of Russian Counter-Terrorism* (Stuttgart: Ibidem-Verlag, 2006). See also Fiona Hill and Clifford C. Gaddy, *Mr. Putin: Operative in the Kremlin* (Washington, DC: Brookings Institution Press, 2013).

42. Przeworski, *Democracy and the Market*, 64.

43. See Gulnaz Sharafutdinova, "Subnational Governance in Russia: How Putin Changed the Contract with His Agents," *Publius* 40, no. 4 (Fall 2010): 672–96; Ora John Reuter and Graeme Robertson, "Subnational Appointments in Authoritarian Regimes: Evidence from Russia's Gubernatorial Appointments," *Journal of Politics* 74, no. 4 (October 2012): 1023–37.

44. See Konstantin Gaaze, "Poker dlya odnogo: Kto i kak v Rossii prinimaet resheniya," *New Times* 2014, September 1, http://www.newtimes.ru/articles/detail/86540.

45. See Milan Svolik, *The Politics of Authoritarian Rule* (Cambridge: Cambridge University Press, 2012).

46. For some accounts of these developments, see Fish, *Democracy from Scratch*; Archie Brown, *The Gorbachev Factor* (Oxford: Oxford University Press, 1996); Michael Urban, with Vyacheslav Igrunov and Sergei Mitrokhin, *The Rebirth of Politics in Russia* (Cambridge: Cambridge University Press, 1997); Jerry F. Hough, *Democratization and Revolution in the USSR, 1985–1991* (Washington, DC: Brookings Institution Press, 1997); Michael McFaul, *Russia's Unfinished Revolution: Political Change from Gorbachev to Putin* (Ithaca, NY: Cornell University Press, 2001), chapter 2; and numerous other works.

47. See Urban, *The Rebirth of Politics in Russia*; Hough, *Democratization and Revolution in the USSR*; Mark Beissinger, *Nationalist Mobilization and the Collapse of the Soviet State* (Cambridge: Cambridge University Press, 2002).

48. See Levitsky and Way, *Competitive Authoritarianism*, especially chapter 5.

49. For further elaboration of this argument, see Vladimir Gel'man, Otar Marganiya, and Dmitry Travin, *Reexamining Economic and Political Reforms in Russia, 1985–2000: Generations, Ideas, and Changes* (Lanham, MD: Lexington Books, 2014).

50. Among the voluminous literature on the subject, see especially Andrei Shleifer and Daniel Treisman, *Without a Map: Political Tactics and Economic Reforms in Russia* (Cambridge, MA: MIT Press, 2000); *The New Russia: Transition Gone Awry*, eds. Lawrence R. Klein and Mark Pomer (Stanford, CA: Stanford University Press, 2001); Peter Reddaway and Dmitri Glinski, *The Tragedy of Russian Reforms: Market Bolshevism Against Democracy* (Washington, DC: United States Institute of Peace, 2001); *Russia's Post-Communist Economy*, eds. Brigitte Granville and Peter Oppen-

heimer (Oxford: Oxford University Press, 2002); Anders Aslund, *Russia's Capitalist Revolution: Why Market Reforms Succeeded and Democracy Failed* (Washington, DC: Peterson Institute for International Economics, 2007).

51. On path-contingency in post-Soviet political and economic developments, see Juliet Jonson, "Path Contingency in Postcommunist Transformations," *Comparative Politics* 33, no. 3 (April 2001): 253–74; Vladimir Gel'man, Sergei Ryzhenkov, and Michael Brie, *Making and Breaking Democratic Transitions: The Comparative Politics of Russia's Regions* (Lanham, MD: Rowman and Littlefield, 2003).

52. See, for example, some discussions on the authoritarian model of market reforms: Sergei Vasil'ev and Boris Lvin, "Sotsial'nye mekhanizmy ekonomicheskoi reformy i kharakhter perekhodnogo protsessa," in *Postizhenie*, ed. Fridrikh Borodkin (Moscow: Progress, 1989), 409–21; "Zhestkim kursom . . . analiticheskaya zapiska Leningradskoi assotsiatsii sotsial'no-ekonomicheskikh nauk," *Vek XX i Mir* no. 6 (June 1990): 15–19. On the reasons for rejection of the democratization agenda in Russia in 1991, see also Yegor Gaidar, *Days of Defeat and Victory* (Seattle, WA: University of Washington Press, 1999), 265.

53. For some comparative analyses, see M. Steven Fish, "The Determinants of Economic Reforms in the Post-Communist World," *East European Politics and Societies* 12, no. 1 (Winter 1998): 31–78; Michael McFaul, "The Fourth Wave of Democracy and Dictatorship: Non-Cooperative Transitions in the Post-Communist World," *World Politics* 54, no. 2 (January 2002): 212–44; Timothy Frye, *Building States and Markets after Communism: The Perils of Polarized Democracy* (Cambridge: Cambridge University Press, 2010).

54. For some critical assessments of these developments in the 2000s, see Philip Hanson and Elizabeth Teague, "Big Business and the State in Russia," *Europe-Asia Studies* 57, no. 5 (July 2005): 667–80; Andrei Yakovlev, "The Evolution of Business-State Interaction in Russia: From State Capture to Business Capture," *Europe-Asia Studies* 58, no. 7 (November 2006): 1033–56; Aslund, *Russia's Capitalist Revolution*; Gulnaz Sharafutdinova, *Political Consequences of Crony Capitalism Inside Russia* (South Bend, IN: University of Notre Dame Press, 2011).

55. For a summary of recent discussions on historical trajectories, see John Gerring, Philip Bond, William T. Barndt, and Carola Moreno, "Democracy and Economic Growth: A Historical Perspective," *World Politics* 57, no. 3 (April 2005): 325–64; for a strong argument for the key role of democracy in economic progress, see Daron Acemoglu and James A. Robinson, *Why Nations Fail: The Origins of Power, Prosperity, and Poverty* (New York: Crown Business, 2012).

56. See Daniel Treisman and Vladimir Gimpelson, "Political Business Cycles and Russian Elections, or the Manipulations of 'Chudar,'" *British Journal of Political Science* 31, no. 2 (April 2001): 225–46.

57. See Anton Shirickov, *Anatomiya bezdeistviya: Politicheskie instituty i byudzhetnye konflikty v regionakh Rossii* (St. Petersburg: European University at St. Petersburg Press, 2010).

58. See Ella Paneyakh, "Faking Performances Together: Systems of Performance

Evaluation in Russian Enforcement Agencies and Production of Bias and Privilege," *Post-Soviet Affairs* 30, no. 2–3 (2014): 115–36; Andrei Yakovlev, Anton Sobolev, and Anton Kazun, "Means of Production versus Means of Coercion: Can Russian Business Limit the Violence of a Predatory State?" *Post-Soviet Affairs* 30, no. 2–3 (2014): 171–94.

59. For a detailed analysis of the role of patronage in post-Soviet politics, see Henry E. Hale, *Patronal Politics: Eurasian Regime Dynamics in Comparative Perspective* (Cambridge: Cambridge University Press, 2014).

60. For an overview and case studies, see *Historical Legacies of Communism in Russia and Eastern Europe*, eds. Mark Beissinger and Stephen Kotkin (Cambridge: Cambridge University Press, 2014).

61. For conflicting assessments of economic reforms in the 1990s see, for example, *The New Russia: Transition Gone Awry; Russia's Post-Communist Economy*, Clifford C. Gaddy and Barry W. Ickes, *Russia's Virtual Economy* (Washington, DC: Brookings Institution Press, 2002); see also several chapters in the most recent compendium: *The Oxford Handbook of Russian Economy*, eds. Mikhail Alexeev and Shlomo Weber (Oxford: Oxford University Press, 2013).

62. See Brian D. Taylor, "From Police State to Police State? Legacies and Law Enforcement in Russia," in *Historical Legacies of Communism in Russia and Eastern Europe*, 128–51.

63. See Sharafutdinova, "Subnational Governance in Russia"; Vladimir Gel'man and Sergei Ryzhenkov, "Local Regimes, Sub-National Governance, and the 'Power Vertical' in Contemporary Russia," *Europe-Asia Studies*, 63, no. 3 (May 2011): 449–65.

64. For some critical assessments, see Anders Aslund, *Building Capitalism: The Transformation of the Former Soviet Bloc* (Cambridge: Cambridge University Press, 2003), 406; Martin Gilman, *No Precedent, No Plan: Inside Russia's 1998 Default* (Cambridge, MA: MIT Press, 2010), 35. On the impact of disillusionment in Western assistance to Russia in the 1990s on the attitudes of the Russian elite, see Gel'man, Margainiya, and Travin, *Reexamining Economic and Political Reforms in Russia*, chapter 5.

65. See Levitsky and Way, *Competitive Authoritarianism*, especially chapter 3; on the role of Western influence in overcoming of some legacies of the past, see Hale, *Patronal Politics; Historical Legacies of Communism in Russia and Eastern Europe*.

66. For revealing evidence presented by an advisor of Bill Clinton, see Strobe Talbott, *The Russia Hand: A Memoir of Presidential Diplomacy* (New York: Random House, 2003). Even small-scale programs of democracy assistance to Russia had a rather controversial impact on the recipients of Western funds. See Lisa Mcintosh Sundstrom, *Funding Civil Society: Foreign Assistance and NGO Development in Russia* (Stanford, CA: Stanford University Press, 2006).

67. See, especially, Graeme Robertson, "Strikes and Labor Organizations in Hybrid Regimes," *American Political Science Review* 101, no. 4 (November 2007): 781–98.

68. See Andrew Wilson, *Virtual Politics: Faking Democracy in the Post-Soviet World* (New Haven, CT: Yale University Press, 2005).

69. See Hale, *Patronal Politics*.

70. See Boris Gladarev and Markku Lonkila, "Justifying Civil Activism in Rus-

sia and in Finland," *Journal of Civil Society* 9, no. 4 (2013): 375–90; Carine Clement, *Gorodskie dvizheniya v Rossii v 2009–2012 godakh: Na puti k politicheskomu* (Moscow: Novoe literaturnoe obozrenie, 2013); for an alternative perspective, see Samuel Greene, *Moscow in Movement: Power and Opposition in Putin's Russia* (Stanford, CA: Stanford University Press, 2014).

71. For a detailed analysis, see Richard Rose, William Mishler, and Neil Munro, *Popular Support for an Undemocratic Regime: The Changing Views of Russians* (Cambridge: Cambridge University Press, 2011).

72. "Since any order is better than disorder, any order is established." Przeworski, *Democracy and the Market*, 86.

73. See Egor Lazarev, Anton Sobolev, Irina V. Soboleva, and Boris Sokolov, "Trial by Fire: A Natural Disaster's Impact on Support for the Authorities in Rural Russia," *World Politics* 66, no. 4 (October 2014): 641–68.

74. Samuel Greene, "Society, Politics, and the Search for Community in Russia," in *Russia 2020: Scenarios for the Future*, 459.

75. See Przeworski et al., *Democracy and Development*.

76. See Daniel Treisman, "Presidential Popularity in a Hybrid Regime: Russia under Yeltsin and Putin," *American Journal of Political Science* 55, no. 3 (August 2011): 590–609; Kirill Rogov, "Forty Years in the Desert: The Political Cycles of Post-Soviet Transition," in *Russia 2025: Scenarios for the Russian Future*, 18–45.

77. See Stephen Holmes, "What Russia Teaches Us Now: How Weak States Threaten Freedom," *The American Prospect* 33 (July–August 1997): 30–39; Synthia Roberts and Thomas Sherlock, "Bringing the Russian State Back in: Explanations of Derailed Transition to Market Democracy," *Comparative Politics* 31, no. 4 (July 1999): 477–98; Russell Bova, "Democratization and the Crisis of the Russian State," in *State-Building in Russia: The Yeltsin Legacy and the Challenge of the Future*, ed. Graham Smith (Armonk, NY: M. E. Sharpe, 1999), 17–40.

78. See Michael McFaul, "Lessons of Russia's Protracted Transition from Communist Rule," *Political Science Quarterly* 114, no. 1 (March 1999): 103–30.

79. See Lucan Way, "Authoritarian State Building and Sources of Regime Competitiveness in the Fourth Wave: The Cases of Belarus, Moldova, Russia, and Ukraine," *World Politics* 57, no. 2 (January 2005): 231–61.

80. On varieties of presidential rule, see Juan J. Linz, "The Perils of Presidentialism," *Journal of Democracy* 1, no. 1 (January 1990): 51–69; Matthew Soberg Shugart and John M. Carey, *Presidents and Assemblies: Constitutional Design and Electoral Dynamics* (Cambridge: Cambridge University Press, 1992); Jose Antonio Cheibub, *Presidentialism, Parliamentarianism, and Democracy* (Cambridge: Cambridge University Press, 2007); on electoral systems, see Joseph Colomer, *Political Institutions: Democracy and Social Choice* (Oxford: Oxford University Press, 2001); Michael Gallagher and Paul Mitchell, *The Politics of Electoral Systems* (Oxford: Oxford University Press, 2005).

81. On post-Soviet presidentialism, see Timothy Frye, "A Politics of Institutional Choice: Post-Communist Presidencies," *Comparative Political Studies* 30, no. 5 (October 1997): 523–52; M. Steven Fish, *Democracy Derailed in Russia: The Failure of Open*

Politics (Cambridge: Cambridge University Press, 2005), chapter 7; Timothy J. Colton and Cindy Skach, "The Russian Predicament," *Journal of Democracy* 16, no. 3 (July 2005): 113–26.

82. On the use of formal rules under authoritarian regimes, see Bruce Bueno de Mesquita and Alastair Smith, *The Dictator's Handbook: Why Bad Behavior Is Almost Always Good Politics* (New York: Public Affairs, 2011); for an extension of this argument with regard to authoritarian party systems, see Grigorii V. Golosov, "Authoritarian Party Systems: Patterns of Emergence, Stability, and Survival," *Comparative Sociology* 12, no. 5 (September–October 2013): 617–44.

83. See Gandhi, *Political Institutions under Dictatorship.* .

84. See Alena Ledeneva, *Can Russia Modernise? Sistema, Power Networks, and Informal Governance* (Cambridge: Cambridge University Press, 2013); Hale, *Patronal Politics.*

85. See Hans-Joachim Lauth, "Informal Institutions and Democracy," *Democratization* 7, no. 4 (Winter 2000): 21–50; Vladimir Gel'man, "The Unrule of Law in the Making: The Politics of Informal Institution Building in Russia," *Europe-Asia Studies* 56, no. 7 (November 2004): 1021–40.

86. See Huntington, *The Third Wave.*

87. For some cross-regional analyses and generalizations, see Przeworski, *Democracy and the Market*; Juan J. Linz and Alfred Stepan, *Problems of Democratic Transition and Consolidation: Southern Europe, South America, and Post-Communist Europe* (Baltimore, MD: Johns Hopkins University Press, 1996); Valerie Bunce, "Comparative Democratization: Big and Bounded Generalizations," *Comparative Political Studies* 33, no. 6–7 (August 2000): 703–34.

88. For an overview, see Yonatan L. Morse, "The Era of Electoral Authoritarianism," *World Politics* 64, no. 1 (January 2012): 161–98.

89. For an in-depth historical analysis, see Daniel Ziblatt, "How Did Europe Democratize?" *World Politics* 58, no. 2 (January 2006): 311–38.

90. See, for example, Dmitrii Travin, *Ocherki noveishei istorii Rossii, Kniga 1: 1985–1999* (St. Petersburg: Norma, 2010).

91. See Vladimir Gel'man, "Mediocrity Syndrome in Russia: Domestic and International Perspectives," *PONARS Eurasia Policy Memo Series* no. 258 (June 2013), http://www.ponarseurasia.org/sites/default/files/policy-memos-pdf/Pepm_258_Gelman_June_2013.pdf.

92. See Rogov, "Forty Years in the Desert."

93. See Paul Chaisty and Stephen Whitefield, "Forward to Democracy or Back to Authoritarianism: The Attitudinal Bases of Mass Support for the Russian Election Protests of 2011–2012," *Post-Soviet Affairs* 29, no. 5 (September–October 2013): 387–403.

94. See Albert O. Hirschman, *A Bias for Hope: Essays on Development and Latin America* (New Haven, CT: Yale University Press, 1971).

95. One might expect that these costs may be very high, especially given the risks of increasing political violence, sparked by the Kremlin. These risks became visible February 27, 2015, when Boris Nemtsov, one of the leaders of the Russian opposition, was shot dead in the center of Moscow.

INDEX

accountability, 6, 65, 69, 110
All-Russia People's Front, 115
antimodernism, 20
Arab Spring (2011), 7, 27, 137
Argentina, 153
Armenia, 43
arrests, intimidation through, 54, 79–80, 92–93
Aslund, Anders, 92
assets. *See* resources
authoritarianism, 2; challenges to, 116–17; classical, 37, 94; classical *vs.* electoral, 7, 60, 105; collapse of Communist regimes, 8; collapse of regime in possible alternatives for change, 132, 137; consolidation of, 40–42, 133, 151; constraints on, 10–11, 27; cost of transitioning from electoral authoritarianism to classical, 60, 105; critical junctures and, 13–15, 116, 147; democracy not default after, 137–38, 140–41, 152; democratic façade for, 35, 37, 135; difficulty maintaining equilibrium in, 6, 12–13, 15–16, 37; effects of, 22, 116; elections' ambiguity in, 18, 95, 140; importance of understanding, 3, 15, 130; institutions of, 96; international influence in promotion of, 30–31; longevity of, 128; methods of overcoming, 22, 26–27, 109, 120–21; modernization under, 109–11; pillars of equilibrium for, 102, 128; political actors' strategic choices toward, 49–50; problem of leadership succession in, 104–7 (*see also* "war of Yeltsin succession"); public preferences and, 21, 116; Russia's descent into, 3, 15; Russia's *vs.* neighbors,' 81–82; tactics of, 12, 29–30, 37, 91, 119, 135; tendency toward, 7, 10–12, 152; threats to, 15–16, 95, 101; transitions of, 104; transition to classical in possible alternatives for regime change, 130, 132, 135; types of, 81–82. *See also* electoral authoritarianism
authoritarian modernization, 127
"Autumn of Nations" (1989), 27

bankers, benefiting from loans-for-shares deals, 58–59

"barbeque deal," between Putin and business, 80, 91–92
Belarus, 43, 56, 83, 104, 136, 138
Berezovsky, Boris, 62, 79–80
Berlusconi, Silvio, 25
Beslan, North Ossetia, 10, 86, 144
brainwashing, 13
Brezhnev, Leonid, 97
BRIC, Russia in, 71–72, 173n3
Bueno de Mesquita, Bruce, 17, 74
bureaucracy, 37, 38, 109–10
Burton, Michael, 4, 29
business, 64, 72, 100, 180n90; agreement to status quo, 97, 123; benefiting from loans-for-shares deals, 58–59; coercive apparatus involved in, 111; effects of lack of rule of law on, 45, 57; Putin's "barbeque deal" with, 79–80, 91–92; state-controlled, 62, 80; support for Putin, 68, 80

campaigns: effects of 2011–2012, 119, 123–24; media in, 55, 60, 67; Navalny's mayoral, 126; opposition's, 54–55, 118–20, 123–24; for parliamentary elections, 65; Putin's presidential, 121; unequal resources in, 55, 60; Yeltsin's presidential, 60
Carrère d'Encausse, Hélène, 128
center-regional relations, 23–24, 33, 57, 87, 133; devolution in, 69–70; effects of economic growth on, 23–24
Chapkovski, Philipp, 75
Chechnya, 58, 66, 182n15; effects of military success in, 40, 76–77; elections and, 56; war in, 59, 60
Chernobyl disaster, effects of, 145
Chernomyrdin, Viktor, 53, 59, 61–63
Chile, 31–32, 110–11
China, 30–31, 144
Chinese Communist Party, reforms under, 111
Chubais, Anatoly, 61–62, 67, 75
Churov, Vladimir, 104
civic initiatives, state resistance to, 114
class struggle, in democratization, 28–29

clientelism, Russia as case of, 145
coalitions. *See* winning coalitions
coercion: citizens less susceptible to, 115; costs/
dangers of, 83, 95; difficulty switching to, 38, 143;
increased use of, 103, 124, 135; protests growing
beyond control of, 119, 144; settlement pacts oc-
curring after failures of, 120–21; state's capacity
for, 57, 58, 73, 91, 116–17; through institutions, 81
coercive apparatus, 12, 37, 66, 182n106, 186n48;
expanded power for, 135, 139; incapable of
governance, 136; increasing dependence on, 101,
103, 127, 135; as instrument of reform, 109–11; involved in business, 111; loyalty/disloyalty of, 136,
144; public pride in, 100; Putin revitalizing state
capacity through, 76–77; regional or criminal
control over, 70; use as Soviet legacy, 148–49; in
Yeltsin *vs.* parliament fight, 52–53
Cold War, ideological biases of, 22
color revolutions, 99, 115, 121; against personalist
authoritarian regimes, 81–82, 84; protests and,
7, 115
Communism: celebrating end of, 1; collapse of, 23,
36, 137–38; constraints present at fall of, 146;
Gorbachev's efforts to reform, 32
Communist Party of the Russian Federation
(KPRF), 17, 54–55, 59, 67, 190n100
Communist Party of the Soviet Union, 1, 4, 50, 112
Communists: loss of power in parliament, 67, 77–78,
90; Unity bloc and, 77; Yeltsin *vs.*, 60, 64
competitive authoritarianism, 174n4
constitution, 4, 104; in fight of Yeltsin *vs.* parliament, 51–54; Lukashenko imposing, 56; in
possible alternatives for regime change, 47, 135;
referendum on, 53, 55–56; Yeltsin imposing, 10,
13, 39, 47–48, 54, 56, 69, 73
constitutional amendments, to extend term limits,
14, 41, 113
constraints, political, 27, 70, 81; lack of, 144, 146,
152; on Medvedev, 109, 112; on opposition and
regime, 123–24; on political actors, 11; present at
fall of Communism, 146; on presidential power,
39, 53–57, 73; on regime change, 130–31; weakness of, 10, 73
cooption, 84, 120; cheaper than coercion, 58, 68;
difficulty switching to coercion from, 38, 102; of
elites into winning coalitions, 6, 10, 37; failures of,
29, 135; of opposition, 39, 91; uses of, 82, 103, 134
corporatism, state-led, 23
corruption, 2, 38, 74, 110; efforts against, 114, 122;
growing dissatisfaction with, 108; influence of,
96, 145–46; likely increase of, 133, 136; pervasive-
ness of, 53, 62, 72, 118; Russia as case of, 145
coup, by conservative Communists, 1, 11, 50, 54
courts, biased, 2. *See also* legal system
Crimea: annexation of, 14, 99–100, 127–28; effects of
annexation of, 12, 42, 100–101, 130, 135; seen as
Russian territory, 182n15
criminal entrepreneurs, 23–24
criminal violence, 44, 57

critical junctures, for Russian authoritarianism,
13–15, 116, 137, 143, 145, 147
crony capitalism, 40, 75, 80, 148
culture, Russian, 19–22, 32
"culture war," 124, 125
currency, devaluation of Russian, 48, 63

Dagestan, 66, 182n15
Dahl, Robert, 4, 83
democracy: adjective applied to Russia as, 174n4;
causes of, 18; definitions of, 5, 25; façade of, 35, 37,
135; failures of, 8–9, 43, 146; historical trajectories
of, 153; lack of incentives for, 49–50; predictors of,
28; prerequisites for, 32, 38, 69; public preference
for, 126; rhetoric abandoned, 127; Russia lacking
background of, 20–21; spread of, 27; Western, 31
democratization: authoritarianism as stage in, 19–20,
22–24; class struggle in, 28–29; creeping, in possible
alternatives for regime change, 132, 138–42; critical
junctures for Russian, 13–15; as default after authoritarianism, 140–41, 152; demand for, 126, 131;
difficulty predicting, 27; in "dilemma of simultaneity," 44–50, 69; economic growth's relation to, 131,
147, 151; elite support for, 182n106; expectation of,
50–51, 108; factors belying, 72; factors promoting,
21, 24, 28–37, 32, 36; failures of, 8, 37, 141, 146,
147–50, 153; ideology in, 31–32, 36; international
influence in, 30–31, 149; lack of incentives for,
38, 147; need for total overhaul of institutions in,
141–42; obstacles to, 44, 150; in possible alternatives for regime change, 130, 138; postponed, 47, 50;
in post-Soviet countries, 43; prerequisites for, 11,
122; Russia's possibilities for, 9–10; signs of progress
toward, 71; successes of, 139, 153
A Dictator's Handbook (Bueno de Mesquita and
Smith), 26
dictatorships, as label for nondemocracy, 6
"dilemma of simultaneity," 44–50, 47, 69, 147–48
disillusionment, 2, 69, 118, 146
dissent: suppression of, 12–13, 100, 135. *See also*
opposition
dissident movement, 125, 191n107. *See also* opposition
dominant actors, 75, 152; coercing loyalty to, 73–74,
81; Luzhkov as, 65; Putin recognized as, 67–68
dominant party: as instrument of reform, 109, 111–12;
Kremlin controlling alternatives to, 90–91; lack of
ideology of, 83, 89; in tools of authoritarianism, 37,
116–17; United Russia as, 38, 82, 87–88
Duverger, Maurice, 57
East Europe, 8, 21, 29, 31, 35, 45, 48–49, 148
East Germany, 91, 143–44
economic crises: authoritarian regimes' responses to,
131, 136; democratization and, 49–51; effects of, 59,
63, 101, 134; extent of Russia's, 38, 46; 2008 global,
112–13; recovery from, 64, 117
economic development: democratization's relation to,
28, 32, 151; Medvedev's modernization limited to,
107–8; strengthening Putin's control, 73–74
economic growth, 102; benefiting Putin, 12, 40, 68, 73,

★

76; democratization and, 24, 147; in "dilemma of simultaneity," 69; effects of, 11, 23, 40, 68, 83, 131; expectation of continued, 106; obstacles to, 127, 148; Russia as BRIC nation, 71–72, 173n3

economic policy, 103, 148; irresponsible, 13, 103, 183n17

economic recession: effects of, 33, 44–45, 51, 57, 131; elite conflict in, 38–39; market reform and, 45, 47–48

economic reform, 76; in "dilemma of simultaneity," 44–50, 69; influences on, 51, 63; relation to democratization, 147–48; Yeltsin's attempt at, 61–62

economy, 48–49, 102; effects of Ukrainian crisis on, 103, 127; sanctions against Russia, 100; state control of, 23, 139; state use of power of, 2, 72

Egypt, 104

election fraud, 72; in authoritarianism, 2; cover-up of, 189n85; effectiveness of, 42, 56, 60–61, 105, 119, 123, 126; *Golos* documenting, 159n1; levels of, 95; protests of, 14; public and, 17, 143

elections, 6, 32; 1989, leading to Communist collapse, 116; ambiguity in authoritarianism, 140; competitive, 38, 45, 57, 69; declarations of invalidity of, 25–26; democracy as parties losing, 5, 25, 28; elimination, in possible alternatives for regime change, 135; founding, 13, 47; further restrictions on, in possible alternatives for regime change, 135; legitimacy from, 57, 94, 96, 116; methods of controlling, 25, 55, 60–61, 95–96, 120, 171n54; monitoring of, 122, 159n1; moratorium on new, 49–50; opposition excluded from, 17, 54, 79; opposition monitoring, 122; protests after, 14, 42, 115–23; public belief in fairness of, 17–18, 105; public support for, 105; regime's control of, 7, 84, 94; role of regional political machines in, 86; Russian regime retaining, 12; Soviets' noncompetitive, 94; successful transfer of power through, 62, 68, 71; unfair, 2, 13, 39–40, 55, 72, 102, 159n1; uses in authoritarianism, 7, 12, 18; winning coalition's fear of losing, 50, 59–60. *See also* campaigns

elections, mayoral, 126

elections, of governors: elimination of, 10, 14, 86–87; reinstatement of, 120, 125, 133

elections, parliamentary, 40, 65, 119; 1995, 59; 2011, 106, 117–18; competitive, 69; held with constitutional referendum, 53, 55–56; results of, 67–68

elections, presidential, 105; legitimating already-made decisions, 68; parliamentary elections as primary for, 59, 65; Putin's 1996, 60, 69, 76; Putin's 2000, 76; Putin's 2012, 121, 123; in "war of Yeltsin's succession," 39–40, 53

elections, subnational, 127

electoral authoritarianism, 130; classical *vs.*, 7, 60, 105; in decline, 104; democratic façade for, 35, 37, 135; elections in, 94–96; following failed democracies, 146; international influence insufficient to end, 139; irresolvable problems of, 102; longevity of, 7–8; methods of restraining competition in, 95–96; preference falsification effect in, 142–43; Russia as case study of, 145–46. *See also* authoritarianism

electoral commissions, 25–26, 55–56

electoral reforms: prohibition of regional parties in, 85; proposals for, 141–42

electoral system, 69; federal reforms of regional, 85–86; regime manipulation of, 25, 117, 151; slight liberalization of, 42

elites, 7, 64, 95, 105, 111; cartel-like deals among, 29–30, 34, 69; class struggle pressuring toward democratization, 28–29; conflicts among, 34, 38, 39, 51, 75, 131; conflicts among as constraint on political actors, 11, 146; conflicts among as obstacle to democratization, 11, 29–30, 44; desire for change, 97, 108, 113, 182n106; dissatisfactions of, 97, 107, 108; fragmentation of, 70, 73, 82; loyalty of, 6, 82, 83; market reform as top priority for, 48; preferences of, 59, 65, 143; Putin coercing loyalty of, 40, 68, 73–74, 81; Putin's control over, 41, 67–68, 75–76; Putin's deals with, 40, 73; settlements/pacts among, 30, 33–34, 36, 120–21, 139; taboo on electoral competition among, 96, 152; "war of Yeltsin's succession" as conflict among, 40, 49, 54, 62, 67; Yeltsin's deals with, 39, 57–59. *See also* winning coalitions

emigration, 194n13; allowing regime continuity, 134, 136; of Guriev, 124

England, 30

equilibrium, political, 11–12, 136; authoritarianism's difficulty maintaining, 6, 37, 123–24, 133–34; definitions of, 5, 156n15; inefficiency of, 58, 70, 133; opposition trying to shake regime's, 123–24; pillars of authoritarianism's, 102, 128; stable but ineffective as "institutional trap," 97–98; threats to, 15–16, 42, 83, 96

ethnic conflicts, 38; in former Yugoslavia, 45; in Georgia and Moldova, 43; in North Caucasus, 44; rise of, 46, 147–48

ethnic republics, 49, 56–59, 57

Europe, democratization in, 28–29

European Union, 31, 99; post-Communist countries joining, 45; Russians' residence permits in, 194n13

exogenous shocks, 130–32, 150

Fatherland—All Russia (OVR) bloc, 65–68, 77–78

fear/intimidation, 102–3; decreasing effectiveness of, 119, 134–35; difficulty switching to violence after, 143; against opposition's recruits, 125; personalist authoritarianism depending on, 83; uses of, 42, 124–25, 133

fears, citizens,' 13, 121

federal reform, recentralization of state called, 78–79, 83–86

Federation Council, 40, 78–79

Fedorov, Yevgeniy, 118

forecasts, political: role of unknown variables on, 142–45; unreliability of, 129–30

foreign policy, Russian, 100; aggressive, 42, 127; public support for, 103, 127

France, 35–36, 57, 153

freedoms, 6, 37, 93; civic, 2, 21, 38; in constitution, 55, 135; individual, 21, 38; political, 2, 21, 38; reduction of civic and political, 42, 99, 103
Fukuyama, Francis, 1

Gaidar, Yegor, 48, 51–53, 55, 67
Gazprom, Putin reasserting control over, 80
generational shift, 114, 134; and call for change, 11–12, 42; effects of, 146–47
Georgia, 43, 81, 84, 95
Germany, 30, 149
Glaziev, Sergei, 90
globalization, in democratization, 24
Golos, documenting unfair elections, 159n1
Golosov, Grigorii V., 84
Gorbachev, Mikhail, 36, 50, 187n66; reforms by, 1, 32, 38, 97, 146
governance: demand for good, 125–26; quality of, 127, 133–34; security apparatus incapable of, 136
government, federal, 120; Congress accusing of corruption, 53; designed for subnational governing, 48–49; desiring "insulation" from public pressure, 49; president's power over, 54; Primakov's, 64; weakness of, 63, 128, 144–45; Yeltsin's attempt at reform of, 61–62
governors, 86; elimination of elections for, 10, 14, 86–87; incumbency of, 84–85; president's power to appoint and dismiss, 48, 54, 107; reinstatement of elections for, 120, 125, 133; United Russia and, 87, 119. *See also* regional leaders
Greene, Samuel, 150
Gryzlov, Boris, 174n5
Guriev, Sergei, 124
Gusinsky, Vladimir, 62, 79–80

Hale, Henry, 36
Hanson, Stephen, 35–36
Higley, John, 4, 29
Hobbes, Thomas, 4
homogeneity, 28, 32
Huntington, Samuel, 115–16

ideology, 111; in Cold War, 22; in democratization, 31–32; of opposition, 140; United Russia lacking, 83, 89, 112, 118; as weak constraint in Russia, 11, 35–36, 152
impeachment, Yeltsin's, 39, 53–54, 64
"imposed consensus," 41; methods of achieving, 74, 77; Putin's, 13–14, 81
India, 28
inequality, economic, 28, 32
information problems, 128, 144–45
information streams: challenges to authoritarianism and, 101–2; control over, 95, 116; effects of lacking, 31–32
institutional core, 101, 133, 135, 152, 181n104
institutional decay, Russia as case of, 145
institutional trap, 97–98, 102

institutions, 47, 96, 98; auxiliary, 128; changed to increase regime dominance, 12, 14, 75, 88; coercion through, as "dictatorship of law," 81; creation of biased, 25, 36, 56; democratic, 38, 43, 102, 127, 135; lack of incentives to change, 38, 98, 132–33; need for total overhaul of, 141–42; poisoning of, 39, 41–42, 73; political as rules of the game, 4; role of, 10, 38, 48–49, 151–52; semblance of democratic, 12, 69; Soviet collapse and, 23, 48–49; "subversive," 20
interest groups, 62, 96
international influence: as constraint on political actors, 11, 137; in democratization, 24, 30–31; effectiveness of, 95, 127, 139; in promotion of authoritarianism, 30–31; Russia's, 102, 108, 139, 146; weak effects on Russia, 11, 34–36, 152
Internet, 17, 118–19, 122
intimidation. *See* fear/intimidation
Iraq, 30

Japan, 30
A Just Russia, 90–91, 190n100

Karimov, Islam, 105
Kazakhstan, 104
Khodorkovsky, Mikhail, 41, 92
Kirienko, Sergei, 62–63
Kliementiev, Andrei, 26
Kuchma, Leonid, 91
Kyrgyzstan, 81–82, 84, 95

labor movement, in democratization, 28–29
Latin America, 6, 28–29, 32, 49, 140, 152, 167n16
law enforcement, 70, 119, 135; selective use against opposition, 124, 126; Soviet legacy in, 148–49; weakness of, 57, 111. *See also* coercive apparatus
laws, in center-regional conflict, 69–70
Lebed, Aleksandr, 60
Lee Kwan Yew, 109
legal system: criminal violence *vs.,* 57; intimidation through, 41, 79–80
legitimacy, 37, 52; from elections, 7, 12, 57, 76, 94, 96, 105, 116; nondemocracies seeking, 6–7; regimes losing, 102–3, 105, 115; sources of, 83, 94
Lenin, Vladimir, 17
liberalization, 146, 185n32; in creeping democratization, 138–39; danger for politicians initiating, 97–98, 187n66; discursive, 113–15, 118; Medvedev's rhetoric about, 106–8, 112–14; of registration of political parties, 125, 133; small concessions in, 120, 187n61
lies: decreasing effectiveness of, 119, 134; from lower links of power vertical upward, 144–45; used to maintain authoritarianism equilibrium, 13, 102
living standards, Western *vs.* Russian, 34–35
loans-for-shares deals, 58–59
Lukashenko, Alexander, 105, 136, 138
Luzhkov, Yuri, 62, 65–66

macroeconomic populism, 49, 51
Malaysian Airlines plane, shot down over Ukraine, 100
market reform. *See* economic reform
mayors, 107, 119, 126
media, 56, 72; campaign against West in, 100–101; independent, 124, 127, 135; repression of, 2, 40; state control of, 55, 62, 79, 93; unequal access to in campaigns, 53, 55, 60, 67, 95, 114, 121, 171n54; used against opposition, 60, 114, 124
Medvedev, Dmitry, 41, 118; liberalization and, 114, 185n32; problems of power-share with Putin, 106–7, 109; Putin choosing as successor, 14, 71, 105; Putin's job swap with, 41, 102, 105–7; rhetoric about liberalization and modernization, 106–8, 112–14
metallurgy industry, 58–59
Mexico, 7, 91
middle class, 29, 131
military, 37, 100, 111; not used to shoot citizens, 143–44; Putin revitalizing state capacity through, 76–77; success in Chechnya by, 40, 66; in Ukrainian crisis, 100, 127; in Yeltsin *vs.* parliament fight, 52–53. *See also* coercive apparatus
military dictatorships, 6, 81, 110–11
Milov, Vladimir, 17, 24
Mitrokhin, Sergei, 17, 24
mobilization, 121, 124; through Internet, 116, 122. *See also* protests
modernization, 21; authoritarian, 109–11, 127; democratization and, 8; Medvedev's rhetoric about, 102, 106–8, 107–8, 112
Moldova, 43, 149
monarchies, 6, 30, 137–38
Moncloa Pact, in Spain, 30, 120–21
Moscow, 17, 66, 126, 144
Motherland ("Rodina") coalition, 90
Mubarak, Hosni, 104

Napoleon III, Putin compared to, 153
nation-state, development of, 44–50. *See also* state building
Navalny, Alexei, 114, 122, 124, 126; on strategy for 2011 elections, 117–18
Nazarbayev, Nursultan, 104
negative consensus, 89, 140; but lack of alternative to status quo, 121–22; formation of, 64, 119, 121; against status quo, 50, 58, 65, 117–18
Nemtsov, Boris, 61–62
neo-traditionalism, 20
NGOs, 68, 72, 80, 124, 135
Nizhny Novgorod, 26
nondemocracies, 38, 86; causes of, 19–22; seeking legitimacy, 6–7; as stage in democratization, 19–20, 22–24; types of, 6, 109–12. *See also specific types*
North, Douglass, 30
North Caucasus, ethnic conflict in, 32, 44
North Ossetia. *See* Beslan, North Ossetia
Novocherkassk massacre, 143–44

Offe, Claus, 44–45, 47
oil industry, 41, 58–59
oil prices, 40, 63, 91, 106, 113
oligarchs, 65, 70, 92, 93
oligarchy, 62–63
Olson, Mancur, 138
one-party regimes, as type of nondemocracy, 6
opportunism, of political actors, 20, 24–25, 35–36
opposition, 191n107; adjusting strategies, 123–24, 138–42; campaigning by, 118–19, 121; in creeping democratization, 138–42, 139; decline of support for regime not necessarily empowering, 139–40; discrediting of, 103, 115, 121, 124, 125; elections as opportunity for, 117, 126; factors influencing success of, 116–17; failures of, 40, 59, 77, 122–23, 127; fragmentation of, 58, 117, 127, 140; ideology of, 140; involvement in political process, 120, 139; Kremlin avoiding coordination of, 82, 84; lack of alternatives offered by, 121–22, 125; moderate left, 54–55; monitoring elections, 122; nonsystemic, 114; in parliament *vs.* Yeltsin, 54, 56, 77; radical, 54; regime coopting, 37, 39, 58; regime's refusal to negotiate with, 120–21, 122; regime's tactics against, 25, 54, 90–91, 95, 103, 115, 133; regime trying to contain, not eliminate, 124–25; squelching, 93, 100; systemic, 97, 123, 190n100; weaknesses of, 106, 121–22, 125, 139–40; weak state unable to eliminate, 39. *See also* coercion; repression
Orange Revolution, 141
Our Home is Russia, 59

Panov, Petr, 86
parliament, Russian, 34; appointments in conflict with Yeltsin, 52–53, 54, 62–63, 64; attempt to impeach Yeltsin by, 54, 64; Communists losing power in, 77–78; conflict with Yeltsin over constitution, 51–52, 53–54; defeating coup by conservative Communists, 1; designed for subnational governing, 46, 48–49; intraelite conflict in, 11, 38–39; perceptions of, 51, 54; power of, 59, 78, 128; as rubber stamp for Putin, 12, 40, 77–78; supporting Yeltsin's constitution, 47–48; terms limits for, 14, 41, 113; United Russia in, 40, 42, 71, 87, 105; Yeltsin's constitution reducing power of, 47–48, 55; Yeltsin *vs.*, 10, 13, 34, 47, 51–54, 56. *See also* elections, parliamentary
party-based authoritarianism, 81–83
party politics, 36, 90; development of, 69, 84, 91
path-dependency, 102, 124; in development of authoritarianism, 20, 147; institutions in, 151–52
perestroika, 36, 146, 187n66
performance, of regime, 37–38, 82, 106; in case of emergencies and natural disasters, 144–45; growing demand for good governance, 113; inefficiency of, 40, 44, 57, 144–45; influences on, 40, 74, 113; obstacles to improvement of, 110; public perceptions of, 57, 113

reforms, 70; demand for, 131; economic and political, 48–49; electoral, 85, 141–42; instruments of, 109–12; lack of incentive for, 109; prerequisites for, 109. *See also* economic reform

regime change, 8–9; authoritarianism tendency in, 10–11, 12; based on perception, *vs.* actual, threats, 135–36; collapse in possible alternatives for, 130, 137–38; constraints on, 97, 130–31; critical junctures for Russia, 13–14, 116; increased repression in possible alternatives for, 130, 132, 134–37; possible alternatives for, 130–32, 138–42; role of exogenous shocks in, 130–32, 151; role of institutions in, 151–52; time horizons of, 46–47, 75, 138; unexpected, 143

regional leaders, 55, 67, 183n17; coalitions among, 40, 65; deals with Yeltsin, 39, 58–59, 60; elections, of governors, 120, 125, 133; elections of, 10, 50, 86–87; Putin and, 68, 78–79; replaced on Federation Council, 40; resources and, 39–40, 57–59, 63, 70; sanctions *vs.* bargains for, 85. *See also* governors; oligarchs

rent-seeking behavior: by coercive apparatus, 111, 144; competition in, 96, 108; limits on, 75, 134; predatory state allowing, 84, 92

repression, 6, 21, 42, 124; costs/dangers of, 83, 137; effects on equilibrium, 133, 136; increasing use in possible alternatives for regime change, 130, 132, 134–37; increasing use of, 124, 135–37; of media, 2, 40; Putin "tightening the screws" as, 12, 135; regimes' willingness to use, 143–44; Russia's low levels of, 38, 130; selective use of, 38, 125, 191n107

resources, 111; election campaigns' unequal, 52–53, 55; from loans-for-shares deals, 58–59; regional leaders and, 39–40, 57–59, 63, 70; state control of, 41, 83–84, 92–93; winning coalition too large to share, 51; Yeltsin's, 52–53, 57–58, 60, 64

revolutionary situation, lacking in Russia, 137–38

rights. *See* freedoms

riots, by supporters of parliament, 54

Robertson, Graeme, 33

Rogozin, Dmitri, 90

Rosneft, gaining Yukos assets, 41, 92–93

roundtable talks, in Poland, 120–21

rule of law, 113, 148; dictatorship of law *vs.*, 81, 85; effects of lack of, 45

rules of the game, 29, 46, 65, 125; changing to consolidate power, 40–41, 54; lack of incentives to change, 49, 132–33; need for total overhaul of, 141; political institutions as, 4; used in authoritarianism, 18, 35–36

Russia's Choice, 55

Rutskoi, Alexander, 51, 54, 79

Sakharov, Andrei, 191n107

Schumpeter, Joseph, 5

Scott, James, 21

security apparatus. *See* coercive apparatus; law enforcement; military

separatism, 48; threat of, 38, 46, 49

Serbia, 8, 31, 95

Shoigu, Sergei, 66

Singapore, modernization of, 109

Skocpol, Theda, 24

Slovakia, 31

Smith, Alastair, 17, 74

Sobchak, Anatoly, xi–xiii, 12, 25, 38, 50, 167n27

Sobyanin, Sergei, 126

society at large: as constraint on political actors, 11; providing weak constraints on political actors, 10. *See* public

Solidarity movement, in Poland, 17, 120–21

South Korea, 135

Soviet Union, 32, 145; collapse of, 38, 46, 50, 128, 152; effects of collapse of, 23, 39, 43–44, 46; elections in, 94, 96; fear of return to policies of, 148; tactics against opposition, 125, 143

Spain, Moncloa Pact in, 30, 120–21

state, capacity of, 24; coercive, 40, 57; diminished, 47–48, 57; Putin increasing, 40, 73, 151; Putin's commitment to revitalizing, 76–77; weakness as constraint, 39, 70, 73

state, Russian, 38, 63, 114; business capture by, 40–41, 62, 92–93; designed for subnational governing, 46; ethnofederal structure of, 48; recentralization of, 65, 78–80, 83–86, 110; resources in Yeltsin's presidential campaign, 60; use of economic power of, 72, 117

state building, 111; avoiding territorial breakdown, 48–49; in "dilemma of simultaneity," 47, 69

state capture, 23, 70

State Duma. *See* parliament

statist economic policy, move toward, 91–92

status quo: acceptance of, 11, 58, 123, 125; disincentives to changing, 97, 120, 122, 150, 190n100; forecasts of preservation of, 102, 105–6, 183n16; growing dissatisfaction with, 65, 97, 113–14, 132–34; inertia of, 97–98, 102, 131–32, 183n16; lack of alternatives to, 11–12, 41, 97, 106, 121–22, 125, 139–40; maintaining as goal of regime, 38, 58–59, 105, 108, 132–34; preservation in center-regional relations, 87; public rejection of, 50, 119–20; resigned acceptance of, 11; support for, 11, 42, 71, 117, 120, 122; support for decreasing, 11, 12; territorial, 47

Stepashin, Sergei, 64

strikes, causes of, 33

"stunning elections," 116, 119, 140

subelite: sympathizing with opposition, 124

suffrage, universal, 28–29

Supreme Soviet. *See* parliament

Surkov, Vladislav, 91

surveys, 182n106; preference falsification effect in, 142–43; Putin approval ratings in, 127, 192n111; on Putin's term, 184n23; on Russian territory, 182n15; showing dissatisfaction with status quo, 11, 97